NEW ZEALAND

Brett Atkinson, Roxanne de Bruyn,
Craig McLachlan, Nicole Mudgway, Elen Turner

Hike through alpine valleys and around volcanic lakes. Be refreshed with craft beer made with local hops. Enjoy a relaxed long lunch at an island vineyard restaurant. Negotiate quieter coastal roads to remote beaches. Experience the spectacle and energy of a Māori *haka*. Feast on seasonal produce at a farmers market. Fly high above mountains and glaciers. Kayak to forest-clad coves. Challenge yourself on the end of a bungy cord. Explore protected bird and wildlife sanctuaries.

This is New Zealand.

TURN THE PAGE AND START PLANNING
YOUR NEXT BEST TRIP →

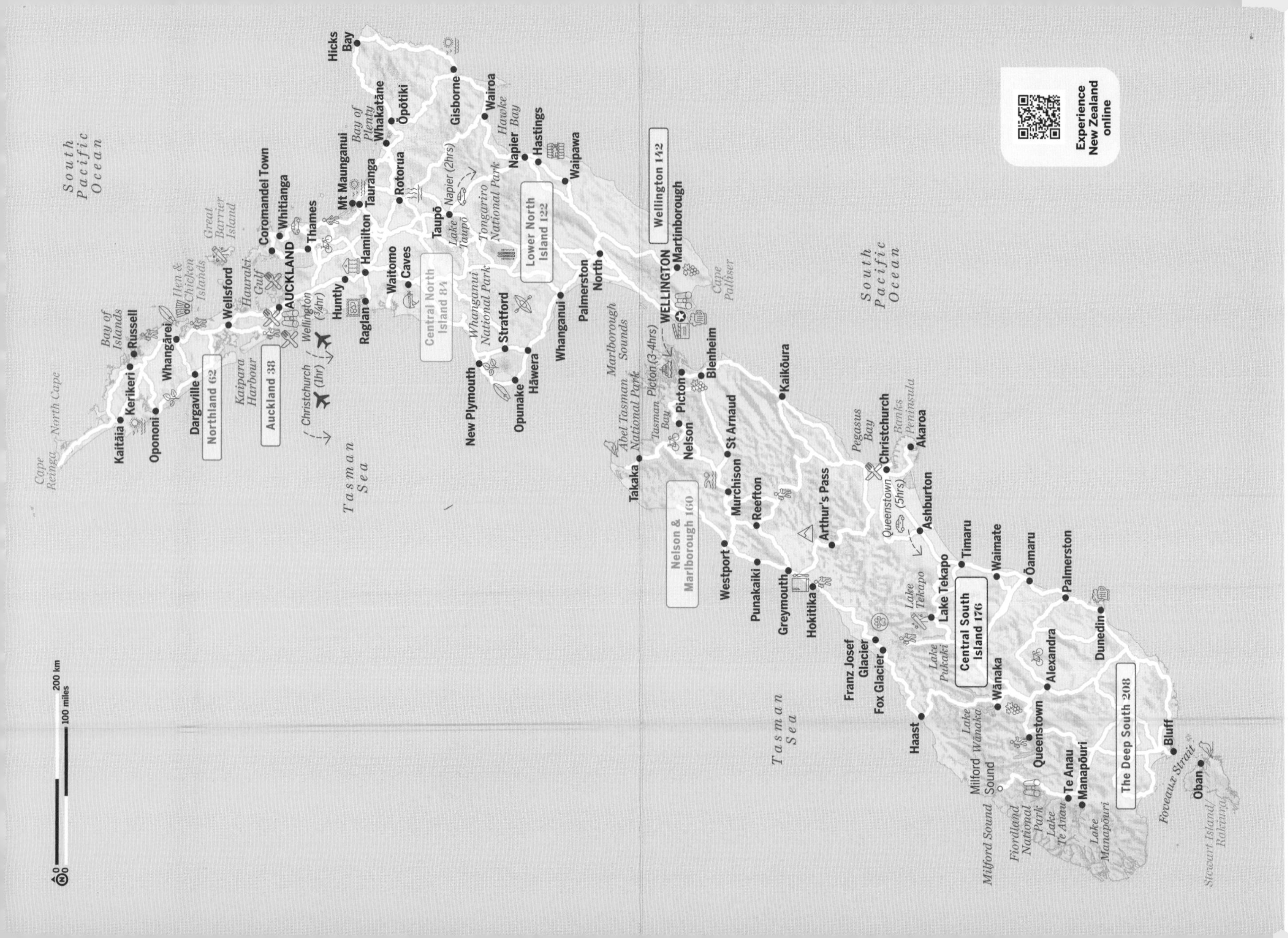

Experience New Zealand online
South Pacific Ocean
Tasman Sea
Cape Reinga
North Cape
Kaitāia
Kerikeri
Bay of Islands
Russell
Opononi
Whangārei
Dargaville
Northland 62
Kaipara Harbour
Wellsford
Hen & Chicken Islands
Hauraki Gulf
Great Barrier Island
AUCKLAND
Auckland 38
Christchurch (1hr)
Wellington (3/4hr)
Coromandel Town
Whitianga
Thames
Huntly
Raglan
Hamilton
Waitomo Caves
Mt Maunganui
Tauranga
Bay of Plenty
Whakatāne
Ōpōtiki
Rotorua
Hicks Bay
Gisborne
Wairoa
Hawke Bay
Napier
Hastings
Waipawa
Taupō
Lake Taupō
Napier (2hrs)
Tongariro National Park
Central North Island 84
Whanganui National Park
Lower North Island 122
New Plymouth
Stratford
Opunake
Hāwera
Whanganui
Palmerston North
Wellington 142
Martinborough
WELLINGTON
Cape Palliser
Marlborough Sounds
Picton (3-4hrs)
Picton
Blenheim
Abel Tasman National Park
Tasman Bay
Nelson
Takaka
St Arnaud
Murchison
Reefton
Nelson & Marlborough 160
Kaikōura
Pegasus Bay
Christchurch
Banks Peninsula
Akaroa
Queenstown (5hrs)
Arthur's Pass
Ashburton
Westport
Punakaiki
Greymouth
Hokitika
Timaru
Waimate
Ōamaru
Palmerston
Lake Tekapo
Central South Island 176
Lake Pukaki
Franz Josef Glacier
Fox Glacier
Haast
Lake Wānaka
Wānaka
Alexandra
Dunedin
Queenstown
The Deep South 208
Milford Sound
Fiordland National Park
Lake Te Anau
Te Anau
Manapōuri
Lake Manapōuri
Bluff
Foveaux Strait
Oban
Stewart Island/Rakiura
200 km
100 miles

Meet our writers

Brett Atkinson

@travelwriternz

Based in Auckland as a full-time travel, food and beer writer, Brett has been exploring Aotearoa New Zealand and many other countries around the world for Lonely Planet since 2005. He's researched and written guidebooks to 15 nations for the world's biggest travel publisher, and is often most happy exploring a destination's craft beer, street food and emerging dining scenes.

Roxanne de Bruyn

@faraway_worlds

Originally from South Africa, Roxanne has lived in New Zealand for over 20 years. She has travelled extensively through Europe, the Middle East and the South Pacific. As Roxanne is based in a relatively remote country, she tends to travel for longer periods of time and enjoys travelling slowly whenever possible. Sampling the local food and wine is also a priority for any trip!

Craig McLachlan

@yuricraig

Queenstowner Craig loves nothing more than opening the bedroom curtains each morning for views out over Lake Whakatipu and the Remarkables. A rebel at heart, he created his own job description of 'freelance anything'.

Nicole Mudgway

@travelwithsmudge

Nicole loves to cycle the Bridge Pa vineyards (p141) in summer. She enjoys not just the wine but the live music, platters and exercise too. The flat roads and well-spaced wineries means each stop feels especially deserved!

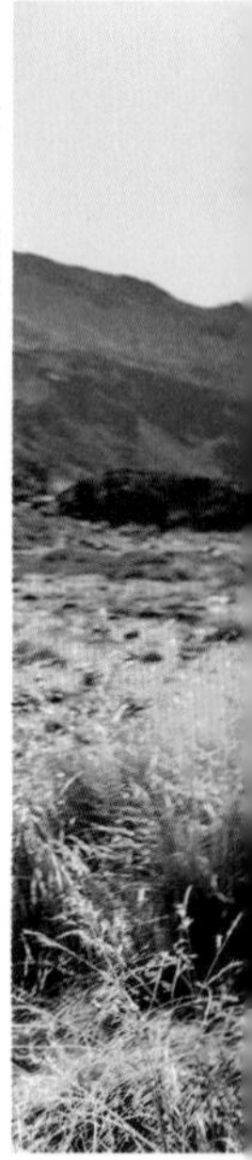

MARIDAV/SHUTTERSTOCK ©

Hiking, Tongariro National Park (p112)

Elen Turner

@ *@eleninthewilderness*

Elen is a writer and editor who grew up in Bream Bay, Northland. Her favourite local travel experience is following unsealed back roads through the Marlborough Sounds and seeing where they lead – usually a deserted, dazzling hidden bay.

Contents

TRABANTOS/SHUTTERSTOCK ©

Cable car (p158), Wellington

VISUAL GUIDE

ESSAYS

NZ'S MĀORI POPULATION

In 2021, NZ's Māori population was estimated at 875,000, representing 17% of the country's population.

Regions with the highest percentage of Māori include Tairāwhiti Gisborne (51%), Northland (34%) and the Bay of Plenty (28%).

EXPERIENCING
MĀORI CULTURE

Informing the increasingly confident heart of New Zealand art, music, sport and government, New Zealand's indigenous Māori culture is both accessible and engaging throughout the country. Watch a performance of *waiata* (traditional songs), enjoy the energetic *haka* (war challenge) or celebrate with a *hāngi* (food cooked underground). Big-city and regional museums and galleries showcase historical and cultural *taonga* (treasures), but this is also a vibrant and contemporary living culture.

→ THE THRILL OF THE ALL BLACKS' HAKA

New Zealand's national rugby team alternates between performing the traditional Ka Mate *haka* and its own Kapa o Pango.

CHRIS HYDE/GETTY IMAGES ©

Left Māori warriors commemorate Waitangi Day
Right All Blacks perform the *haka*
Below Nanaia Mahuta wears a *moko kauae*

LEARNING TE REO MĀORI

Scotty Morrison's bestselling book series *Māori Made Easy* provides an entertaining way to learn the basics of the Māori language (maorilanguage.net).

RIGHT: HAGEN HOPKINS/GETTY IMAGES ©
LEFT: UMOMOS/SHUTTERSTOCK ©

↑ TĀ MOKO (MĀORI TATTOO)

High-profile wearers of the *moko kauae* (women's chin tattoo) include New Zealand's Foreign Affairs Minister, Nanaia Mahuta.

Best Māori Cultural Experiences

▶ **Explore Auckland's Māori history atop its *maunga* (ancestral mountains).** (p49)

▶ **Discover contemporary Māori art at Whangārei's Wairau Māori Art Gallery.** (p72)

▶ **Learn about Aotearoa's shared Māori and colonial history in Waitangi.** (p68)

▶ **Feast on indigenous Māori foods in the Bay of Plenty.** (p108)

▶ **Rise before dawn for a spiritual experience atop the sacred summit of Mt Hikurangi.** (p133)

EXCELLENCE IN
FOOD & WINE

▬▬▬ Eating and drinking well is an undoubted highlight of travelling in New Zealand, and chefs, winemakers and artisan producers throughout the country all harness excellent local and seasonal ingredients. *Kai moana* (seafood) befits New Zealand's southern Pacific status as an island nation, vineyards often team with superb on-site restaurants, and local farmers markets make it easy for travellers to self-cater and maximise their on-the-road budget.

→ **THINK LOCAL, EAT SEASONAL**

Seek out Central Otago stone fruit and cherries from December to March, and Northland mandarins and oranges from May to September.

Left Vineyard cheese platter
Right Fresh apricots from Central Otago
Below White wine, Marlborough region (p166)

SAVING MONEY WHEN DINING OUT

Based in Queenstown, but operating globally, First Table (firsttable.co.nz) offers discounts of 50% for restaurant meals all around New Zealand.

↑ **ICONIC NEW ZEALAND WINES**

Deserved icons of NZ's winemaking scene include Kumeu River's Maté's Vineyard Chardonnay and the Ned Pinot Noir from Marlborough's Marisco Vineyards.

Best Food & Wine Experiences

▶ **Journey to Waiheke Island to experience Auckland's relaxed vineyard restaurants.** (p44)

▶ **Stock up on summer surprises and seasonal market bounty in Hawke's Bay.** (p126)

▶ **Negotiate two wheels to foodie surprises along Nelson-Tasman's flavour-packed Great Taste Trail.** (p170)

▶ **Discover there's more to the Marlborough region than world-beating sauvignon blanc.** (p166)

▶ **Explore the culinary renewal of post-earthquake Christchurch.** (p190)

ACTIVE
ADVENTURES

The southern hemisphere's adventure sports capital of Queenstown is a fine place to start – bungy jumping was invented here after all – but it's also easy to get an action sports buzz on in Auckland, Taupō and Rotorua.

Beyond the extreme rush of jetboating, skydiving and canyon swings, kayaking, white-water rafting and canoeing are all (usually...) more gentle alternatives to teaming Aotearoa's distinct scenery with action and adventure.

→ NZ'S BUNGY PIONEERS

Opened in 1998, and still going strong, Queenstown's Kawarau Bridge is the site of the world's first commercial bungy operation.

Left Jetboating, Queenstown (p214)
Right Bungy-jumping from Kawarau Bridge (p234)
Below Sea kayaks, Mission Bay (p61)

DOLLAR-SAVING THRILLS

When booking adventure activities, especially at Waitomo and Queenstown, check for online booking discounts or combo deals incorporating several different experiences.

Best Active Adventures

▶ **Tackle a zipline, abseil or negotiate subterranean rivers and waterfalls in the Waitomo Caves.** (p92)

▶ **Discover Auckland's urban thrills atop the Sky Tower and Harbour Bridge.** (p52)

▶ **Canoe down the Whanganui River on a journey combining history and remote scenery.** (p136)

▶ **Sea kayak amid the quieter bays of the northern part of Abel Tasman National Park.** (p168)

▶ **Boost your adrenaline levels by diving into Queenstown's exciting array of extreme adventures.** (p218)

↑ AN AUCKLAND ADVENTURE ALTERNATIVE

Te Ara Moana is a self-guided five-day sea kayak tour (aucklandseakayaks.co.nz) around the bays, cliffs and coves of Auckland's regional parks.

HIKING & BIKING

■ Many New Zealanders love to get active amid their country's stellar scenery, and well-defined hiking and biking trails also make it easy for travellers to experience the best of Aotearoa. Convenient trailhead transport, comprehensive online planning tools and a surprising range of accommodation all maximise the enjoyment of multiday trails, while shorter experiences mean you can be back in town for a great meal at the end of the day.

Ben Lomond
Stellar lake and mountain views
Completing the considerable challenge of walking up Ben Lomond (1748m) is compensated by superb 360-degree views of Lake Wakatipu. Once you've completed your descent, celebrate with a well-earned treat from the nearby Bespoke Kitchen cafe.
🕐 *1 day (11km)*
▶ p214

Routeburn Track
Just maybe NZ's greatest hike
A contender for the title of 'NZ's best multiday hike' (up there with the Milford Track), the Routeburn begins at Lake Wakatipu's northern end near a spot called Paradise, and continues through equally idyllic landscapes to Mt Aspiring National Park.
🕐 *3–4 days (33km)*
▶ p234

Tasman Sea

Greymouth ●

Hokitika ●

Franz Josef Glacier

Fox Glacier ● △ *Fox Glacier* ● *Aoraki/Mt Cook National Park*
△ *Aoraki/ Mt Cook*

○ Twizel

Milford Sound ○

Fiordland National Park

△ *Ben Lomond*

● Alexandra

● Te Anau

○ Middlemarch

Dunedin ●
Otago Peninsula

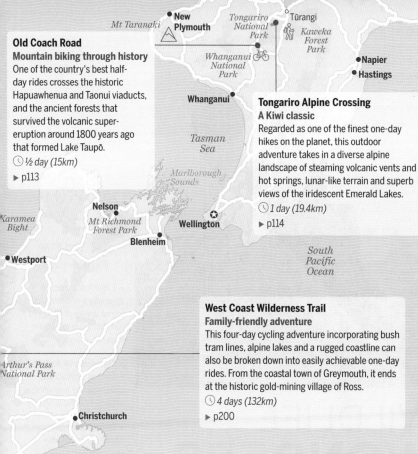

Mt Taranaki

● **New Plymouth**

Tongariro National Park

○ Tūrangi

Kaweka Forest Park

● **Napier**
● **Hastings**

Whanganui National Park

● **Whanganui**

Tasman Sea

Marlborough Sounds

Nelson

Mt Richmond Forest Park

⊛ **Wellington**

Karamea Bight

Blenheim

● **Westport**

South Pacific Ocean

Arthur's Pass National Park

● **Christchurch**

Canterbury Bight

Old Coach Road
Mountain biking through history
One of the country's best half-day rides crosses the historic Hapuawhenua and Taonui viaducts, and the ancient forests that survived the volcanic super-eruption around 1800 years ago that formed Lake Taupō.

🕐 ½ day (15km)
▶ p113

Tongariro Alpine Crossing
A Kiwi classic
Regarded as one of the finest one-day hikes on the planet, this outdoor adventure takes in a diverse alpine landscape of steaming volcanic vents and hot springs, lunar-like terrain and superb views of the iridescent Emerald Lakes.

🕐 1 day (19.4km)
▶ p114

West Coast Wilderness Trail
Family-friendly adventure
This four-day cycling adventure incorporating bush tram lines, alpine lakes and a rugged coastline can also be broken down into easily achievable one-day rides. From the coastal town of Greymouth, it ends at the historic gold-mining village of Ross.

🕐 4 days (132km)
▶ p200

Otago Central Rail Trail
History and scenery
Beautiful big-sky landscapes and the heritage streetscapes of former gold-mining towns combine on NZ's most popular and well-established cycle trail. En route there's the daily opportunity to enjoy a cold beer or a local pinot noir at historic pubs.

🕐 3–5 days (152km)
▶ p230

Ⓝ 0 ⌄ 200 km
0 ⌄ 100 miles

NATIVE BIRDS

Look out for these avian locals:

Kiwi NZ's flightless national icon

Kea The world's only alpine parrot (pictured)

Ruru Small nocturnal owl (also known as a morepork)

▶ Learn about the Birds of Aotearoa on p226

Best Wildlife Experiences

▶ Experience marine diversity while snorkelling or diving at the Poor Knights Islands Marine Reserve. (p80)

▶ Commune with giant cetacean visitors and other marine mammals around Kaikōura. (p198)

▶ Spend the night sharing the offshore eco-sanctuary of Kāpiti Island with 1200 little spotted kiwi. (p156)

▶ Say g'day to fur seals, sea lions, penguins and royal albatrosses around the Otago Peninsula. (p232)

▶ Explore the stellar bird life of Ulva Island's protected sanctuary. (p224)

CHRISTIAN KORNACKER/SHUTTERSTOCK ©

WILDLIFE
WONDERS

▬▬▬ It's a case of the big and the small when considering New Zealand wildlife. Sperm whales and humpbacks swing by the nutrient-rich waters of the Kaikōura Canyon from June to August (other whales are resident year-round), while delicate endemic bird life enlivens protected offshore island reserves. In-between, there are plenty of other marine mammals to check out, and larger birds including the spectacular ocean-going royal albatross.

CRAFT-BEER
COUNTRY

███████ Independent breweries all around New Zealand craft punchy pale ales, refreshing summer-friendly lagers, and interesting Kiwi takes on traditional American, Belgian and German beer styles. Definitely try beers harnessing Tasman's world-famous Riwaka, Nectaron and Nelson Sauvin hop varieties, often tinged with the distinctive flavours of citrus, cut grass or stone fruit.

Best Craft-Beer Experiences

▶ **Try beers from around NZ at the Auckland Beer Mile's bars and taprooms.** (p61)

▶ **Sample always innovative wild-fermented brews from Wellington's Garage Project.** (p151)

▶ **Team adventure sports with local craft beers around Queenstown and Wānaka.** (p218)

NEW ZEALAND BEST EXPERIENCES

BRETT ATKINSON/LONELY PLANET ©

↑ CLASSIC NZ BEERS

Popular beers reflecting the flavours of hops from the Tasman region include 8 Wired's Hopwired NZ IPA and Panhead's Port Road Pilsner.

★ **JUMP ABOARD A BEER TOUR**

Let someone else do the driving with Brewbus (brewbus.co.nz), Craft Beer Tours Wellington (craftbeertoursnz.co.nz) or Queenstown Beer Tours (queenstownbeertours. co.nz).

LAZINGBEE/GETTY IMAGES ©

Above Tasting flight, 8 Wired Brewing, Matakana (p61)
Left Hops used in craft-beer brewing

BEYOND
BEACHES

Up north, arcing beaches like the Karikari Peninsula's Maitai Bay contrast with the roiling surf of Ahipara, while on the South Island, the Marlborough Sounds' quiet coves and the sheltered bays of the Abel Tasman National Park attract summertime swimmers, kayakers and hikers. Freshwater lake and river destinations are also popular with travelling Kiwi families across warmer months.

Best Water Experiences

▶ Enjoy the sheltered beaches of Northland's east coast and also more rugged western alternatives. (p66)

▶ Relax in hot pools and cool lakes around Rotorua and Taupō. (p106)

▶ Join locals at swimming holes and river beaches around Nelson-Tasman. (p164)

STARGRASS/SHUTTERSTOCK ©

↑ HOT POOLS & THERMAL SPRINGS

Check out NZ Hot Pools (nzhotpools.co.nz) for maps and reviews of thermal springs and hot pools around the country.

ROD HILL/GETTY IMAGES ©

★ SWIMMING SAFELY

Water conditions around the Greater Auckland region, including storm-water overflows and surf reports, are monitored on Safeswim's (safeswim.org.nz) searchable online map.

Above Lake Tikitapu (p107)
Left River swimming, Rotorua

⬎ WORLD FAMOUS IN NZ

Highest mountain Aoraki/Mt Cook (pictured; 3724m). Dubbed 'cloud piercer' by Māori.

Longest glacier The 27km-long and 4km-wide leviathan of the Tasman Glacier.

Biggest lake Lake Taupō, formed by one of history's biggest eruptions.

Best Alpine Experiences

▶ Cross the mountainous spine of the South Island on the TranzAlpine train. (p196)

▶ Explore Aoraki/ Mt Cook National Park on the popular Tasman Glacier and Hooker Valley day walks. (p184)

▶ Splash out on a scenic flight high above the Fox and Franz Josef glaciers. (p186)

▶ Negotiate Milford Rd and Homer Tunnel to Milford Sound. (p220)

ALPINE
VIEWS

New Zealand is a country defined by spectacular alpine landscapes, which punctuate both North Island and South Island (with geothermal activity further enlivening the North Island's Central Plateau) away from the nation's coastline and rolling farmland. Volcanic peaks surge upwards on the North Island, while in the south, glaciers stretch to near the ocean, and Milford Sound/Piopiotahi rises steeply from the 300m depth of Milford Sound.

Demand for accommodation peaks after Christmas/New Year and continues throughout January. Book tours and activities in advance at lonelyplanet.com/new-zealand/activities.

Christmas Day, Boxing Day, New Year's Day and 2 January are public holidays. Cities are quiet and Kiwis head to the beach.

← Festival of Lights

New Plymouth's Pukekura Park is enlivened with music and family-friendly performances for six weeks from mid-December.
▶ New Plymouth, p130
▶ festivaloflights.nz

↖ Lupins Season

Wild lupins bloom around Central Otago and the Mackenzie Country, starting in December and continuing colourfully through to February.

DECEMBER

Average daytime max: 21°C
Days of rainfall: 9

JANUARY

New Zealand in
SUMMER

↘ Marlborough Wine & Food Festival

New Zealand's home of sauvignon blanc celebrates in mid-February with wine, craft beer and plenty of fine food.

▶ Blenheim, p166
▶ marlboroughwinefestival.com

→ Art Deco Festival

Napier's architectural style is celebrated with music, food, wine and heritage fashion across a February long weekend.

▶ Napier, p139
▶ artdecofestival.co.nz

January and February are peak months for Kiwis to enjoy hiking. Book Great Walks huts well ahead of travel (p24).

FEBRUARY

Average daytime max: 22°C
Days of rainfall: 8

Average daytime max: 23°C
Days of rainfall: 7

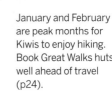

← Waitangi Day

Commemorating the 1840 signing of the Treaty of Waitangi, New Zealand's national day of 6 February is a public holiday.

NEW ZEALAND PLAN BY SEASON

🧳 Packing Notes

Wear a hat and apply sunscreen to protect against high summertime UV levels.

↓ Pasifika

Across a vibrant March weekend, Auckland's Pacific Island communities celebrate their shared Polynesian culture through food, music and dance.

▶ Auckland, p48

← Marchfest

The world-beating hops of the Tasman region are showcased at this popular Nelson craft-beer festival in late March.

▶ Nelson
▶ marchfest.com

↙ Wildfoods Festival

Head to Hokitika in mid-March for this foodie extravaganza, washing down challenging treats like insect larvae with wine and beer.

▶ Hokitika
▶ wildfoods.co.nz

MARCH

Average daytime max: 22°C
Days of rainfall: 7

APRIL

New Zealand in
AUTUMN

↓ Clyde Wine & Food Festival

It's pinot noir aplenty at this annual Easter Sunday celebration held in Clyde's historic 19th-century precinct.

▸ Clyde
▸ centralotagonz.com/explore/listing/clyde-wine-and-food-festival

→ Autumn Colours

Dappled autumn colours are at their best in Central Otago and the historic streets of Arrowtown around April.

▸ Arrowtown, p218

← New Zealand International Comedy Festival

Kiwi comedians combine with international performers to bring plenty of laughs to Auckland in May.

▸ Auckland
▸ comedyfestival.co.nz

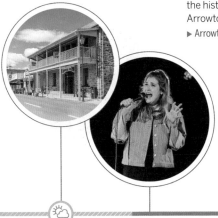

NEW ZEALAND PLAN BY SEASON

Average daytime max: 19°C
Days of rainfall: 8

MAY

Average daytime max: 17°C
Days of rainfall: 9

Settled weather and lower visitor numbers (excluding Easter) make March and April an ideal time to explore New Zealand.

← Bluff Oyster & Food Festival

Bivalves galore at this shuckingly good May festival at the southern tip of the South Island.

▸ Bluff
▸ bluffoysterfest.co.nz

 Packing Notes

Cooler weather makes dressing in layers important, especially when hiking in alpine regions.

Whale Watching

Migrating whales arrive to feed amid the nutrient-rich waters off Kaikōura from June to August.

▶ Kaikōura, p198

← Steampunk NZ Festival

Blending science fiction and Victoriana, Steampunk culture is celebrated in Ōamaru's historic precinct across June's Queen's Birthday weekend.

▶ Ōamaru, p228

▶ steampunk.org.nz

→ Queenstown Winter Festival

The June to September ski season is celebrated at this July festival held in NZ's adventure sports capital since 1975.

▶ Queenstown

▶ winterfestival.co.nz

JUNE

Average daytime max: 15°C
Days of rainfall: 10

JULY

New Zealand in
WINTER

← Matariki

Inaugurated as a public holiday in 2022, June or July's Māori New Year is celebrated nationwide with Māori art, music, culture and cosmology.

→ Wellington on a Plate

The country's best burgers and innovative fine dining also attract travelling foodies to the nation's capital in August.

▶ Wellington

▶ visawoap.com

→ Beervana

Kiwi craft-beer drinkers descend on Wellington in August for this annual hop-fuelled celebration at the city's Westpac Stadium.

▶ Wellington, p150

▶ beervana.co.nz

AUGUST

Average daytime max: 14°C
Days of rainfall: 11

Average daytime max: 14°C
Days of rainfall: 11

Book ahead for accommodation in popular snow sports locations including Queenstown, Wānaka and Ōhakune, especially during July's school holidays.

← Bay of Islands Jazz & Blues Festival

Warmer Northland winter weather is the relaxed background to this three-day mid-August festival.

▶ Russell, Paihia

▶ jazz-blues.co.nz

 Packing Notes

Weather can be very changeable. Be prepared for four seasons in one day.

DOC's Great Walks hiking season spans September to April. Book ahead for popular experiences including the Kepler, Milford and Routeburn Tracks.

▶ bookings.doc.govt.nz

↓ Nelson Arts Festival

Plenty of indoor distractions – including comedy, cabaret, music and dance – for two weeks in October.

▶ Nelson
▶ nelsonartsfestival.nz

↖ Winter Games

In early September, the world's best skiers and snowboarders arrive in Queenstown for a week of high-flying extreme action.

▶ Queenstown
▶ wintergamesnz.kiwi

SEPTEMBER

Average daytime max: 16°C
Days of rainfall: 10

OCTOBER

New Zealand in
SPRING

← Crayfest Kaikōura

Across two weeks in November, Kaikōura cafes and restaurants team New Zealand's favourite crustacean with local craft beer and wine.

▶ Kaikōura

▶ facebook.com/crayfestkaikoura

← Toast Martinborough

Wellington food and wine buffs cross the Remutaka Range for this one-day November celebration of pinot-noir-fuelled fun.

▶ Martinborough, p152

▶ toastmartinborough.co.nz

Spring lambs dot rolling pastures on the South Island. In Auckland, visitors can see them in centrally located Cornwall Park.

▶ Auckland region, p58

Average daytime max: 17°C
Days of rainfall: 9

NOVEMBER

Average daytime max: 19°C
Days of rainfall: 11

The first two weeks of October are usually school holidays in New Zealand. Book accommodation and activities in advance.

← Ōamaru Victorian Heritage Celebrations

Ōamaru's white-stone heritage precinct hosts November's week-long celebration of the Victorian era. Penny-farthing races are a highlight.

▶ Ōamaru

▶ vhc.co.nz

🧳 Packing Notes

A spring rain shower is never far away. Pack a lightweight waterproof jacket.

NORTHERN TOUR
Trip Builder

TAKE YOUR PICK OF MUST-SEES AND HIDDEN GEMS

▬▬▬ After big-city harbourside adventures around Auckland, head north to explore beaches and Māori and colonial history, or south to the caves and surf of the Waikato region. Gold-mining history and a spectacular coastline are highlights of the Coromandel Peninsula.

🗺 Trip Notes

Hub towns Auckland, Paihia, Hamilton

How long Allow around 2 weeks

Getting around Hire a car for off-the-beaten-track exploring at your own pace. Visiting Waiheke Island by passenger ferry and public bus is a recommended option for a short visit.

Tips During summer, leave your vehicle at the car park at the entrance to Hahei, and catch the shuttle bus to Cathedral Cove.

Hokianga Harbour
Browse heritage buildings in sleepy Rawene and stroll on forest boardwalks to Tāne Mahuta, a spiritually and culturally important kauri tree in the Waipoua Forest.
🚗 1hr from Paihia

Auckland
Experience the multicultural energy of this harbourside city, combine walking and wine tasting near West Coast surf beaches, and explore Auckland's volcanic *maunga* (ancestral mountains).

Waitomo Caves
Challenge yourself on a subterranean abseiling, ziplining or black-water rafting adventure, or ride a boat leisurely past glowworms on an underground river.
🚗 1hr from Hamilton

Bay of Islands
Explore Aotearoa's shared multicultural history at Waitangi, wander the quaint colonial streetscape of Russell, or tackle the challenging but spectacular Cape Brett Walkway.
 Russell: 30min from Paihia

Waiheke Island
Journey to Auckland's island of wine for relaxed vineyard restaurants or take in Hauraki Gulf views while ziplining or negotiating clifftop walking trails.
 45min from Auckland

Coromandel Town
Stroll through gold-mining history, ride the ziplines and bush railway at Driving Creek, and explore the remote isolation and beaches of Coromandel Peninsula's northern tip.
🚗 *2½hr from Auckland*

Hahei
Wander along the gently rolling coastal trail to Cathedral Cove, kayak the region's stellar coastline, and dig your own natural spa pool at Hot Water Beach.
🚗 *2½hr from Auckland*

Raglan
Combine local arts and crafts with good eating and drinking at New Zealand's favourite surf town. Savvy locals also recommend the area's kayaking and paddle boarding.
 🚗 *40min from Hamilton*

Cape Brett

Poor Knights Islands

South Pacific Ocean

• Whangārei

Hen & Chicken Islands

Wellsford •

Warkworth •

Great Barrier Island / Aotea Island

Hauraki Gulf

Woodhill Forest

Driving Creek

Whitianga •

Cathedral Cove

Hot Water Beach

Alderman Islands

Firth of Thames

Coromandel Forest Park

Ramarama •

Thames •

Coromandel Forest Park

Mayor Island / Tuhua

Tasman Sea

• Huntly   Te Aroha ○

Bay of Plenty

Hamilton •   Matamata ○

Cambridge ○

Kāwhia ○

Whakatāne •

• Ōpōtiki

 ○ Ōtorohanga

○ Te Kuiti

Ⓝ 0 ———— 100 km
0 ———— 50 miles

NORTH ISLAND EXPLORER
Trip Builder

TAKE YOUR PICK OF MUST-SEES AND HIDDEN GEMS

Mountain landscapes formed by a volcanic past, present and future provide the spectacular background for hiking, biking and canoeing. Explore Māori culture in Rotorua, navigate East Cape to sunny Gisborne and Hawke's Bay, or enjoy Wellington's culinary and cultural highlights.

🗺 Trip Notes

Hub towns Taupō, Napier, Gisborne, Wellington

How long Allow 2 to 3 weeks

Getting around Having a rental car or camper van is definitely needed for on-the-road flexibility. For winter travel to Mt Ruapehu's ski fields, tyre chains are essential.

Tips Shuttle operators in National Park village offer trailhead transport and vehicle relocation services for completing the Tongariro Alpine Crossing.

FROM LEFT: ED GOODACRE/SHUTTERSTOCK ©, JOSEF F. STUEFER/MOMENT MOBILE VIA GETTY IMAGES ©, RUDMER ZWERVER/SHUTTERSTOCK ©

Rotorua
Relax in hot pools warmed by geo-thermal activity, feast on a *hāngi*, and learn about traditional Māori arts and culture around Rotorua.
🚌 *1hr from Taupō*

● Ragla

Waitom Cave

Whanganui Journey
Embark on a classic New Zealand outdoor adventure by canoeing or kayaking down the scenic, and historically and culturally important, Whanganui River.
🚌 *2hr from Taupō*

Whanganui River

Whanganui ●

Wellington
Combine craft beer, exciting and spectacular coastal hikes, and learning about some of cinema's biggest movies in New Zealand's cool capital city.

Lak Wairarap

Cook Strait

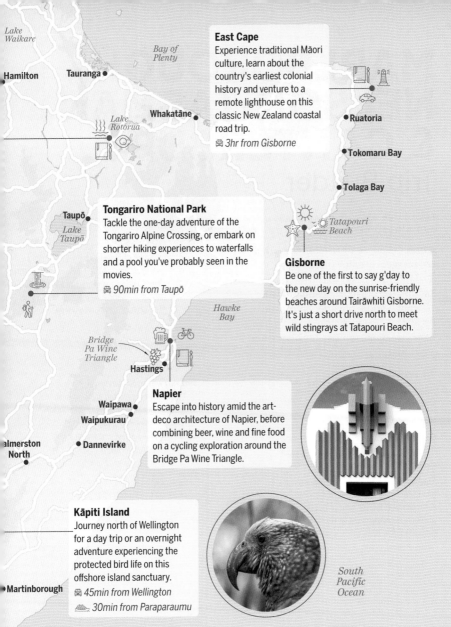

East Cape
Experience traditional Māori culture, learn about the country's earliest colonial history and venture to a remote lighthouse on this classic New Zealand coastal road trip.

🚗 *3hr from Gisborne*

Tongariro National Park
Tackle the one-day adventure of the Tongariro Alpine Crossing, or embark on shorter hiking experiences to waterfalls and a pool you've probably seen in the movies.

🚌 *90min from Taupō*

Gisborne
Be one of the first to say g'day to the new day on the sunrise-friendly beaches around Tairāwhiti Gisborne. It's just a short drive north to meet wild stingrays at Tatapouri Beach.

Napier
Escape into history amid the art-deco architecture of Napier, before combining beer, wine and fine food on a cycling exploration around the Bridge Pa Wine Triangle.

Kāpiti Island
Journey north of Wellington for a day trip or an overnight adventure experiencing the protected bird life on this offshore island sanctuary.

🚗 *45min from Wellington*
⛴ *30min from Paraparaumu*

Lake Waikare

Bay of Plenty

Hamilton • Tauranga •

Whakatāne •

Lake Rotorua

Taupō •
Lake Taupō

Hawke Bay

Bridge Pa Wine Triangle

Hastings •

Waipawa •
Waipukurau •

almerston North •

• Dannevirke

• Martinborough

• Ruatoria

• Tokomaru Bay

• Tolaga Bay

Tatapouri Beach

South Pacific Ocean

0 ——— 100 km
0 ——— 50 miles

MARLBOROUGH, NELSON-TASMAN & CANTERBURY
Trip Builder

TAKE YOUR PICK OF MUST-SEES AND HIDDEN GEMS

▰▰▰▰ Celebrate Christchurch's urban re-emergence, enjoy one of New Zealand's best food and wine regions, and discover diverse destinations for viewing wildlife big and small. And because you're in Aotearoa, of course there are opportunities for hiking and kayaking.

🗺 Trip Notes

Hub towns Blenheim, Christchurch, Nelson, Hokitika

How long Allow around 2 weeks

Getting around A good way to discover the Marlborough wine region is on a self-guided e-bike tour.

Tips Booking well ahead for the inter-island ferry linking Wellington to Picton is recommended for school holiday and public holiday periods. At other times, booking a few days prior is sufficient.

Hokitika
Check out New Zealand's feathered national icon at the National Kiwi Centre before admiring work from local glass and greenstone artisans or walking in the beautiful Hokitika Gorge.

Tasman Sea

Aoraki/Mt Cook National Park
Get adventurous around NZ's highest mountain. Bucket list activities include kayaking amid icebergs and flying above the Franz Josef and Fox glaciers.
🚌 *4hr from Christchurch*

Hokitika Gorge

Whataroa

Franz Josef Glacier
Franz Josef Glacier

Fox Glacier
Fox Glacier

Tasman Glacier
Aoraki/ Mt Cook
Mueller Glacier

Lake Tekapo

Abel Tasman National Park

Hike or kayak around the coves and bays of NZ's smallest national park. You'll also hear (and see) the diverse bird life making this region home.

🚌 *1hr from Nelson*

Takaka

Kahurangi National Park

Motueka

●**Karamea**

●**Nelson**
●**Richmond**

●**Picton**

0 —— 50 km
0 —— 25 miles

Mt Richmond Forest Park

Hope Saddle

Blenheim

Discover there's more to Marlborough than world-beating sauvignon blanc. Excellent restaurants abound, sometimes also offering family-friendly *pétanque* or croquet.

●**Westport**

Arthur's Pass

Journey through this alpine village on the TranzAlpine train or use it as a base for hiking and exploring the nearby natural spectacles of Castle Hill and Cave Stream.

🚌 *2hr from Christchurch* 🚆 *2½hr from Christchurch*

Nelson Lakes National Park

Lewis Pass

Hanmer Springs Forest Park

Lewis Pass Scenic Reserve

South Pacific Ocean

eymouth

Lake Brunner (Moana)

Lake Kaniere

Arthur's Pass National Park

Arthur's Pass

Craigieburn Forest Park

Lake Pearson

Castle Hill ○

Cave Stream

Kaikōura

Experience the natural grandeur of Kaikōura's marine mammal visitors, including leviathan humpback and sperm whales, before dining on local seafood such as ocean-fresh crayfish.

🚌 *90min from Blenheim*

Lake Tekapo

Combine hot-tub bathing with stargazing in the heart of the spectacular Mackenzie Country. An essential detour is coffee, cake and superb views at Mt John's Astro Cafe.

🚌 *3hr from Christchurch*

Pegasus Bay

●**Lyttelton**

Christchurch

Enjoy the Garden City's post-earthquake revival by eating and drinking at the Riverside Market, Little High Eatery and along New Regent St. Don't miss Dimitri's souvlaki.

Lake Ellesmere

Banks Peninsula

Akaroa ●

Canterbury Bight

SOUTHERN HIGHLIGHTS
Trip Builder

NEW ZEALAND BUILD YOUR TRIP

TAKE YOUR PICK OF MUST-SEES AND HIDDEN GEMS

▬▬▬ New Zealand's far south showcases the action sports thrills of Queenstown, heritage highlights around Ōamaru and Arrowtown, and Central Otago's brilliant food and wine scene. Outdoor adventures include NZ's favourite cycle trail and world-renowned Great Walks, while wildlife and bird-watching fans head to the Otago Peninsula and even further south.

🗺 Trip Notes

Hub towns Queenstown, Dunedin, Te Anau, Invercargill

How long Allow around 2 weeks

Getting around Exploring this diverse region is best accomplished with a rental car or camper van. The area contains some of New Zealand's most scenic Department of Conservation (DOC) campsites.

Tips DOC hut accommodation on the Milford, Routeburn and Kepler Tracks must be booked in advance during the Great Walks season from December to April.

Queenstown
Climb Ben Lomond before refuelling at the Bespoke Kitchen or enjoying a craft beer by the lake at Altitude Brewing. Exciting adrenaline-fuelled activities also abound around town.

Milford Sound/
Piopiotahi

Milfo
Sou

Homer
Tunnel

Ti
Divie

Lake Te
Anau

Fiordland
National
Park

Lake
Manapōuri

● Te Anau

● Manapōuri

Takitin
Fore

Really Great Walks
Book ahead for experiences on New Zealand's most popular Great Walks, including the Kepler Track (pictured). Both the Milford and Routeburn tracks showcase the rugged best of Te Waipounamu (the South Island).

🚌 *90min from Te Anau*

● Tuatapere

🧭 N

| 0 | | 50 km |
| 0 | | 25 miles |

Arrowtown

Wander the historic gold-rush-era streets of Arrowtown during the day before returning to some of the best bars and restaurants in the southern lakes region after dark.

🚗 30min from Queenstown

Waimate •

• Wānaka

Glenorchy •

Ben Lomond

Lake Wakatipu

• Cromwell

• Clyde

Alexandra •

Milford Road

Spend a day negotiating the road from Te Anau to Milford Sound/Piopiotahi, stopping for forest walks, before being dwarfed by the snow-framed entrance to the Homer Tunnel.

🚗 90min from Te Anau

Ōamaru

Experience quirky steampunk culture amid Ōamaru's 19th-century white-stone historic precinct before lining up to see the nightly arrival of the town's *kororā* (little blue penguins).

🚗 90min from Dunedin

Central Otago

Savour the best of Central Otago's world-beating wines, including excellent pinot noir from the rocky soils of Bannockburn. Visit during summer for fresh cherries and stone fruit around Cromwell.

🚗 45min from Queenstown

Dunedin

Hokonui Forest Park Gore •

• Winton

• Milton

• Balclutha

Otago Peninsula

Journey to the peninsula's northeastern tip and the world's only mainland breeding colony of the northern royal albatross. Options to see the birds also include boat trips.

🚗 45min from Dunedin

• Invercargill

• Bluff

oveaux Strait

Ruapuke Island

South Pacific Ocean

• Oban

Stewart Island Rakiura)

Stewart Island/Rakiura

Travel by ferry or plane from Invercargill to Stewart Island/Rakiura, tackling the 32km Rakiura Track before venturing to Ulva Island for an enjoyably noisy symphony of bird life.

⛴ 1hr from Invercargill (Bluff)
✈ 15min from Invercargill (Bluff)

7 Things to Know About
NEW ZEALAND

INSIDER TIPS TO HIT THE GROUND RUNNING

1 Four Seasons in One Day

It's not just a song by Kiwi-Australian band Crowded House. New Zealand's weather can be famously fickle, so it's important to dress in layers, and always have suitable apparel for cold and rain in the country's sub-alpine and mountain areas. Courtesy of a hole in the ozone layer, New Zealand's southern hemisphere sun is harsh and strong, so cover up, wear a hat and sunglasses, and apply sunscreen.

▶ See more about weather on p18

2 Be Physically Prepared

If you're planning on hiking, be prepared with a good level of fitness. Some visitors over-estimate physical abilities when venturing out in NZ's wilderness.

▶ See more about hiking safety on p244

3 Rush Hour NZ-style

In rural areas, road hazards sometimes include farmers moving cows or sheep. Slow to a crawl, or stop your vehicle altogether, and let the animals move unrestricted around the car.

▶ See more about road conditions on p243

4 Welcome to the Shaky Isles

New Zealand has around 20,000 earthquakes every year. Only 250 or so are actually felt, but significant seismic events have occurred in Christchurch (2011) and Kaikōura (2016). Adhere to local civic defence advice (civil defence.govt.nz).

Note: beaches on the North Island's east coast are sometimes affected by tsunami warnings. Many beaches have signs indicating safe inland areas to shelter.

5 Don't Try to See It All

There's a misconception that New Zealand is a 'small island nation', but in surface area it's actually bigger than the United Kingdom. Roads, especially on the South Island, are often more winding than international visitors are used to, and covering the kilometres can take longer than expected. Slow down, enjoy the journey and be realistic in your travel plans.

▶ See more about getting around on p242

6 Local Lingo

Learning a few words of Kiwi vernacular will help you get by and make friends along the way.

tramping The local word for hiking or bush walking.

'The Ditch' The Tasman Sea separating New Zealand and Australia.

jandals Rubber flip-flops, known as 'thongs' across 'the Ditch' in Australia.

yeah/nah Non-committal way for New Zealanders to say no (or maybe).

chur bro! A way of showing appreciation.

hokey pokey Vanilla ice cream studded with crunchy chunks of butterscotch; reputedly more popular in New Zealand than chocolate ice cream.

L&P (Lemon & Paeroa) A lemon-flavoured soft drink (soda) originally made from natural springs in the Coromandel town of Paeroa. It is now mass-produced by Coca-Cola Amatil, but is still refreshing.

chilly bin A portable drinks cooler, essential at a barbecue or at the beach.

ka pai 'All good' or 'well done' in te reo Māori.

sweet as The everyday Kiwi translation of 'ka pai'.

7 Respecting Māori Culture

Adhere to Māori protocols when visiting a *marae* (meeting house). A *karakia* (prayer) will be offered to bless the food, and you may be welcomed with a *hongi*, the Māori greeting of pressing together foreheads and noses. The *hongi* represents the mutual sharing of the breath of life.

▶ See more about etiquette on p247

Read, Listen, Watch & Follow

 READ

The Bone People
(Keri Hulme; 1984) Booker Prize–winning tale intertwining love, violence and Māori spirituality.

Dogside Story
(Patricia Grace; 2001) Māori family life in the remote Tairāwhiti region.

The Penguin History of New Zealand (Michael King; 2003) The definitive story of the development of Aotearoa.

Bewildered
(Laura Waters; 2019) A life-changing solo walk along NZ's 3000km Te Araroa trail.

 LISTEN

Polyunsaturated
(Nesian Mystik; 2002) Pioneering Polynesian-influenced hip-hop from a mixed Pacific Island crew.

Tally Ho! Flying Nun's Greatest Bits
(various artists; 2011) Essential 'best of' compilation from Dunedin's seminal Flying Nun label.

Make Way for Love
(Marlon Williams; 2018) Alt-country influenced songs of love and loss from the man with the best voice in the land.

Waiata Anthems
(various artists; 2019 & 2021) Top NZ musicians re-record their favourite songs in te reo Māori.

Solar
(Lorde, 2020; pictured) Lorde's woozily dreamy third album is the perfect accompaniment to a NZ summer.

WATCH

Whale Rider (2002; pictured top right) Magic realism, and Māori myths and spirituality on a remote east coast beach.

Boy (2010) Taika Waititi's gentle coming-of-age drama is set around the isolated East Cape.

Hunt for the Wilderpeople (2016; pictured bottom right) Taika strikes again with a warm-hearted rural comedy-drama.

Dawn Raid (2020) Documentary covering the global impact of the South Auckland–based hip-hop record label.

Cousins (2021) Māori family drama set across six decades.

MARKA/ALAMY STOCK PHOTO ©

MOVIESTORE COLLECTION LTD/ ALAMY STOCK PHOTO ©

 FOLLOW

100% PURE NEW ZEALAND
@purenewzealand
Tourism New Zealand's official Instagram account.

The Spinoff
(thespinoff.co.nz)
News, culture and opinionated podcasts.

Public Address
(publicaddress.net)
News and cultural commentary from well-established bloggers.

undertheradar.co.nz
Music news, gigs and ticket sales.

Lazy Susan
(search Facebook)
Crowd-sourced recommendations on dining countrywide.

Sate your New Zealand dreaming with a virtual vacation

AUCKLAND REGION

ISLANDS | RESTAURANTS | ACTIVITIES

Experience
the Auckland
region online

AUCKLAND
Trip Builder

Framed by two harbours, New Zealand's biggest city is a dynamic and multicultural gateway to a region of rugged surf beaches, urban thrills and island adventures, and a brilliant eating and drinking scene combining surprising vineyards and spectacular harbourside dining.

Orew

Silverda

Waimauku Huapai

Kumeū

Relax in stylish cafes, restaurants and bars along **Ponsonby Road** (p60)

🚌 *10min from Auckland's Ferry Building*

Muriwai Beach

Waitākere

Waitema Harbou

Negotiate cliff-top walking trails high above **West Coast surf beaches** (p50)

🚐 *1hr from Auckland's Ferry Building*

Bethells Beach/ Te Henga

Explore **Auckland's volcanic field** to discover the region's Māori history (p58)

🚌 *15-30min from Auckland's Ferry Building*

●Piha

Waitākere Ranges Regional Park

Huia

Manukau Harbour

Ⓝ 0
0

20 km

10 miles

Great Barrier Island (see Inset) (40km)

Inset

Experience pristine southern hemisphere night skies on **Great Barrier Island** (p54)
30min from Auckland Airport

Discover the **Hauraki Gulf** by kayak, yacht or island ferry (p44)
45min from Auckland's Ferry Building

Ascend the **Sky Tower** for isthmus views and action-packed thrills (p52)
10min from Auckland's Ferry Building

Motutapu Island

Rangitoto Island

Combine relaxed dining and maritime history on Auckland's **harbourfront** (p56)
5min from Auckland's Ferry Building

Learn about New Zealand art at the **Auckland Art Gallery** (p61)
15min from Auckland's Ferry Building

Tamaki Strait

○Maraetai

Enjoy the beaches, vineyards and restaurants of **Waiheke Island** (p44)
45min from Auckland's Ferry Building

○Whitford

Be immersed in cultural and culinary diversity along **Karangahape Road** (p49)
15min from Auckland's Ferry Building

○Clevedon

Explore bookable experiences in Auckland

Practicalities

ARRIVING

Auckland Airport Located 21km south of the city with adjacent international and domestic terminals a 10-minute walk from each other via a signposted footpath. SkyBus links to the CBD and inner suburbs (adult/child $17/2), while Super Shuttle provides a convenient minibus service linking the airport to city hotels ($15 to $25 per person depending on group size). Taxis to the CBD cost from $60 to $80 depending on traffic conditions, and ride-share services (Uber, Ola and Zoomy) are around $50.

HOW MUCH FOR A

Coffee
$5

Food truck meal
$15

Craft-beer pint
$13

WHEN TO GO

FEB–APR
Warm weather; festivals including Pasifika in March; ideal for island visits.

MAY–AUG
Weather cooling with festival highlights including July's Matariki.

SEP–NOV
Changeable spring weather. Wrap up for boat trips and West Coast beaches.

DEC–JAN
School holidays January. Some restaurants close over Christmas/New Year.

GETTING AROUND

Bus Link buses loop in both directions around three routes taking in most major sites. Visit the Auckland Transport website (at.govt.nz) to see where to purchase a prepaid AT HOP smart card and details of the City Link, Inner Link and Outer Link services.

Ferry Fullers (fullers.co.nz) runs regular passenger services to Waiheke and other Hauraki Gulf islands, and across the Waitematā Harbour to the heritage suburb of Devonport. Sealink (sealink.co.nz) operates vehicular ferries to Waiheke and Great Barrier Island.

Car It's definitely worth renting a car to explore the beaches and vineyards of West Auckland, and also to make the most of a stay on Waiheke Island.

EATING & DRINKING

Brunch Ease into the day with a flat white coffee and Peter Gordon's chilli-laced Turkish eggs at Homeland.

Global flavours Auckland's diverse multicultural future is revealed along raffish Karangahape Rd.

Beer Try craft brews with NZ hops including zesty Nelson Sauvin and citrusy Riwaka along the Auckland Beer Mile.

Vineyards Waiheke Island, West Auckland and Matakana are all essential expressions of the region's coastal terroir.

Must-try dish	Best one-stop dining destination
Snapper with chickpeas and green-shelled mussels Mr Morris (p60)	The brick-lined laneways of Ponsonby Central, including Bedford Soda & Liquor (p60)

CONNECT & FIND YOUR WAY

Wi-fi All Auckland public libraries offer free wi-fi hot-spots, conveniently also available outside of opening hours. For on-the-go access, purchase a SIM and Travel Plan from Vodafone or Spark. Both have branches in the arrivals hall of Auckland International Airport and around the CBD.

Navigation Google Maps is well-established and most Aucklanders will happily offer directions.

AUCKLAND'S NIGHT MARKETS

Eating at one of Auckland's nine night markets (auckland nightmarkets.co.nz) is a good way to dine cheaply from many international stallholders.

WHERE TO STAY

Book accommodation well ahead if you're attending a big concert or sports event.

Area	Pro/Con
City Centre	Good shopping and eating. Well located for Waiheke ferries and buses. Mainly hotels. Lacks charm.
Ponsonby	Bars, cafes, restaurants and shopping. Airbnbs, good hostels. Limited parking.
Parnell & Newmarket	B&Bs, smaller hotels. Good shopping and eating. Near the museum; short bus ride to city centre.
Mt Eden	Good boutique B&Bs, heritage village ambience. Convenient for Maungakiekie/One Tree Hill and Maungawhau/Mt Eden.
Devonport	Historic, quiet neighbourhood linked to downtown by ferry. Good restaurants and heritage B&Bs. Road access can be slow.
Waiheke Island	Holiday rentals, Airbnbs. Good restaurants and vineyards. Summer weekends and Christmas/New Year get busy.

MONEY

Buses Purchase an AT HOP smart card for 20% discount off standard bus fares.

01

Gourmet
WAIHEKE

WINE | FOOD | OUTDOORS

With its winemakers, chefs and craft brewers all inspired by Waiheke's relaxed ambience and sunny microclimate, the Hauraki Gulf's most popular island is an essential destination for travelling foodies. A longer flavour-packed sojourn of a few days is definitely recommended.

NEVILLE MARRINER/ALAMY STOCK PHOTO ©

How to

Getting here Catch downtown Auckland's passenger ferry or board the car ferry from Half Moon Bay.

When to go Try and visit midweek, and book ahead for accommodation on weekends and during school holidays.

Don't rush back to the mainland Waiheke's beachside villas, apartments and retro cottages are all options for an extended stay (staywaiheke.com).

Get on the bus The 50B bus route conveniently links most of Waiheke's tastiest destinations.

ANASTASIARAS/GETTY IMAGES ©

KRUG_100/SHUTTERSTOCK ©

Southern Europe or the Southern Hemisphere?

Enlivened by a Mediterranean micro-climate, Waiheke's vineyards combine a relaxed New Zealand ambience with a few surprising touches of sun-blessed European destinations. Wine varietals including tempranillo and albariño team with Spanish tapas and the architectural style of Antoni Gaudí at **Casita Miro**, while the quiet valley location, olive groves and legendary long lunches at **Poderi Crisci** channel a distinctly southern hemisphere version of Sicily.

Ascend the long tree-lined entrance to **Tantalus Estate's** elegant tasting room in Onetangi for excellent Bordeaux-style red wines, or pick up a rigger of locally brewed craft beer downstairs in

Island Zipline Thrills

Soar above vineyards with views of downtown Auckland on **EcoZip Adventures'** (ecozipadventures.co.nz) ziplines. The popular attraction is a short drive from the vineyards and restaurants of Onetangi, and experiences conclude with a bush walk through regenerating native forest. Packages include transport from Matiatia Wharf's ferry terminal.

Above left Restuarant, Tantalus Estate
Above Harbour, Waiheke Island
Left Vineyards, Waiheke Island

Alibi Brewing's brick-lined taproom. Wood-fired pizza and the Valhalla chardonnay are an ideal Mediterranean-style combination at **Man O' War's** secluded bay-front tasting room. After a swim off the wharf or a game of beach cricket, you'll definitely be celebrating a Kiwi summertime vibe.

Beachfront Dining

Onetangi is Waiheke's best swimming beach, and a brace of waterfront dining options also make a brilliant place to while away a few leisurely hours. Named after the first three digits of Waiheke phone numbers, **Three Seven Two** is a proud supporter of ingredients from around New Zealand and the Auckland region, with seasonal menus often including sustainable line-caught fish, venison and lamb, and farmhouse cheeses from prime North Island dairy country. Three Seven Two's summer-ready terrace is ideal for warmer months, and the wine list is a handy primer to the best of the island.

A Brewer's Guide to Waiheke

Mint As food truck Massive burgers combined with alfresco dining. Next to RAW grocery so you can pick up some Alibi beer while you wait. (@mintaswaihekeisland)

Fenice Who doesn't like pizza? Fenice is the perfect place to grab a 'zah. Nab a table out front and watch the hustle and bustle go by. (@fenicerestaurantwaiheke)

Indy's Curry Pot Mouth-watering Sri Lankan/fusion food with a 'roti-tating' menu of vegetarian and non-vegetarian flavours. (@indys_curry_pot)

Casita Miro It's all about shared dining here with tapas and *raciones* (larger plates) in a beautiful Mediterranean setting. (@casitamiro)

 ■ Recommended by Bernard Neate *head brewer at Alibi Brewing* @alibi_brewing_co

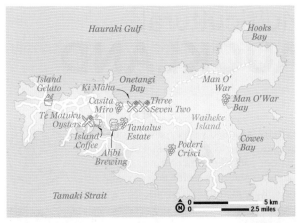

Hauraki Gulf

Hooks Bay

Island Gelato · Ki Māha · Onetangi Bay · Man O' War · Man O'War Bay

Casita Miro · Three Seven Two

Te Matuku Oysters · Tantalus Estate · Waiheke Island

Island Coffee · Poderi Crisci · Cowes Bay

Alibi Brewing

Tamaki Strait

N 0 / 0 — 5 km / 2.5 miles

Left Wine tasting, Casita Miro
Below Te Matuku Oysters

AUCKLAND REGION EXPERIENCES

Detour a couple of hundred metres along the beach to the corner location of **Ki Māha's** (the name broadly translates as 'towards abundance' from te reo Māori), where the restaurant's own wines and craft beers partner with Italian-infused plates of oysters, octopus, scallops and beef carpaccio. With a big selection of New Zealand artisan gins and Waiheke's best cocktail list, late afternoon and early evening sees Ki Māha morphing into the island's best spot for aperitivo drinks.

Seek Out Local Treats

Follow in the footsteps of savvy locals for this trio of Waiheke gourmet surprises. Combine homestyle baking from **Little Tart** – the cinnamon brioches are especially good – with Waiheke-roasted beans at **Island Coffee**, or detour nearby to **Te Matuku Oysters** for freshly shucked briny bivalves from the sheltered waters of the Te Matuku Marine Reserve. Of course, you'll want to add a splash of lemon juice and Tabasco sauce.

Waiheke's most refreshing summertime treats are at **Island Gelato's** shipping container in Oneroa. Leave room for a dessert of seasonal flavours including coconut latte or crisp apple.

02 Multicultural AUCKLAND

CULTURE | FOOD | FESTIVALS

Around 40% of Aucklanders were born overseas, and New Zealand's most cosmopolitan city is packed with experiences uncovering the diversity of the region also known as Tāmaki Makaurau. Go off the beaten track in flavour-packed dining precincts, explore contemporary art from locals with Māori or Pacific ancestry, and discover a world of food and culture at vibrant festivals.

PAUL KENNEDY/ALAMY STOCK PHOTO ©

🗺 How to

Getting here Local buses reach Auckland's multicultural inner suburbs, or it's an easy hop on ride-share services.

When to go Annual festivals include Pasifika (March), the Chinese New Year Lantern Festival (February), and the Māori and Pacific Islands dance extravaganza of Polyfest (also March).

The world comes to town CultureFest (late March or early April) showcases the food, music and dance of more than 70 nationalities that call Auckland home.

KRUG.100/SHUTTERSTOCK ©

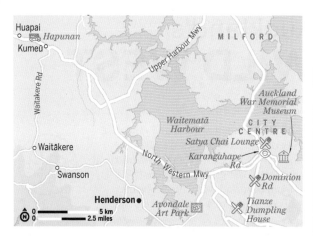

Left Samoan dancers, Pasifika
Below Auckland War Memorial Museum

Best of Multicultural Auckland

Hapunan Auckland's (other) best food truck! Try the Filipino beef 'Kare Kare' in a peanut and annatto sauce. Also has a permanent location in Kumeū.

Tianze Dumpling House Try the sizzling eggplant stuffed with pork or the clams noodle soup. Get adventurous. It's all good!

Avondale Art Park An ever-evolving outdoor gallery exhibition of Auckland's finest graffiti and street artists.

Sacred Tattoo From traditional to classic and modern, the tattoo art created here is world-class.

The Ghost of Freddie Cesar Troy Kingi's 2020 album is influenced by his father's love of 1970s funk and soul.

■ **Recommended by Otis Frizzell**
artist and co-owner of The Lucky Taco food truck. @otis.frizzell @theluckytaco_nz

Discovering Diversity

Auckland's volcanic field Ascend the *maunga* (mountains) of Tāmaki Makaurau's volcanoes to discover the region's historic Māori *pā* (fortified settlements), before exploring the world-leading Māori galleries at the **Auckland War Memorial Museum**, itself crowning the **Auckland Domain** atop the volcanic crater known as Pukekawa. Held across the city in June, the annual Māori New Year festival **Matariki** (matarikifestival. org.nz) grows in spectacle and importance each year.

Karangahape Rd Peruvian flavours (**Madame George**), Spanish cuisine (**Candela**) and modern Filipino food (**Bar Magda**) all span the globe along Auckland's most multicultural thoroughfare, while modern Pacific Islands art and culture is showcased at the **Tautai Contemporary Pacific Arts Trust** (tautai.org). Detour to nearby **Cross St** for Pacific-influenced street art, and add a 'K Rd' coda of art, music and contemporary installations at **Artspace Aotearoa**.

Dominion Rd Embark on a regional Chinese culinary adventure along Dominion Rd, segueing from mouth-numbing Sichuan flavours at **Eden Noodles** to *xiao long bao* (soup dumplings) at **Jolin Shanghai** and Muslim-influenced flatbreads and cumin-laced lamb skewers at **Xi'an Food Bar**. Welcome to one of Auckland's most dynamic dining scenes.

Sandringham Spice up an Auckland sojourn in this Indian and Sri Lankan precinct a few blocks northwest of Dominion Rd. An essential after-dark destination is the **Satya Chai Lounge** for Indian street food and New Zealand craft beers.

03 Auckland's
WILD WEST

BEACHES | BIRDS | WALKING

▬▬▬ Detour on a day trip or an overnight adventure to the surf beaches and bush-clad forests of West Auckland's Waitākere Ranges Regional Park. Piha, Bethells Beach/Te Henga and Muriwai all offer wild and windswept West Coast grandeur, while the region's gourmet bounty of food, beer and wine offers reward after negotiating clifftop trails or hiking to a hidden lake.

JUSTIN FOULKES/LONELY PLANET ©

🗺 How to

Getting here Piha is around 40km from central Auckland. North of Piha, Muriwai is a similar distance from downtown.

When to go Visit on a weekday for less crowds and easier parking.

You'll need wheels Rent a car as public transport is limited. Bush and Beach (bush andbeach.co.nz) offers guided tours.

FYI Between Titirangi and Piha, stop at the Arataki Visitor Centre for views, natural history displays and bush-walking information.

STARGRASS/SHUTTERSTOCK ©

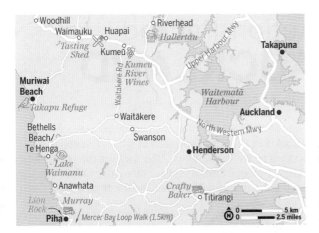

Left Lion Rock, Piha Bay
Below Gannet colony, Muriwai Beach

Beaches, Bird Life & Clifftop Walks

Hike high above the Tasman Sea surf Even on a windy and grey day, Piha's **Lion Rock** is a spectacular sight, crowning the black-sand beach that's one of Auckland's most popular surfing locations. Always swim between the flags under the watchful gaze of surf lifeguards. On a fine, blue-sky day, tackle Piha's **Mercer Bay Loop Walk** for brilliant coastal views high above the beach's southern edges.

Negotiate sand dunes to a hidden lake Framed by towering sand dunes – popular with West Auckland locals for summer sandboarding – the walk to **Lake Waimanu** near Bethells Beach is a classic West Coast experience. After the 11km loop trail (you may need to take your shoes off to wade through the shallows), continue to the wide open expanses of the rugged beach also known as Te Henga.

A surf-side seabird spectacle Perched on the cliffs above Muriwai's arcing surf beach, the **Takapu Refuge** gannet colony is enlivened by thousands of takapu (Australasian gannets) from September to March. Chicks are usually born from December to January, and by March the fledgling birds have established the confidence and skills to embark on the 2000km journey west to Australia.

Build up your own skill base by negotiating a blokart (land yacht) on Muriwai's surf-lined sandy racetrack (muriwaisurfschool.co.nz).

Best of the West

Between West Coast beach-hopping, check out these eating and drinking favourites.

Crafty Baker Superior pies and pastries in Titirangi village.

Murray Tacos, coffee and cool beats combine at this Piha surf shack.

Kumeu River Wines World-renowned varietals on the outskirts of Kumeū include superb chardonnay.

Tasting Shed West of Kumeū, and perfect for a lunch of Mediterranean- and Asian-inspired shared plates.

Good from Scratch Locavore cookery classes in a rural setting near Muriwai.

Hallertau Complete the day with craft beers brewed on-site at this Riverhead beer garden.

04 Action-Packed AUCKLAND

ACTION | VIEWS | OUTDOORS

▬▬▬ Elsewhere in New Zealand, Queenstown, Rotorua and Taupō are renowned adventure sports hubs, but Auckland also offers spectacular ways to combine adrenaline-fuelled fun with views of the harbour city. After tackling the heights of the Sky Tower and the Auckland Harbour Bridge, embark on outdoor adventures on Hauraki Gulf islands, or negotiate canyons and waterfalls on the rugged West Coast.

CHAMELEONSEYE/SHUTTERSTOCK ©

🗺 How to

Getting here In central Auckland on the corner of Victoria and Federal streets, the Sky Tower is impossible to miss.

Stretch your Kiwi budget Discounted combo deals including the SkyWalk, SkyJump and the Auckland Bridge

Climb and Bungy are available (bungy.co.nz).

Sporting and movie-making excellence Both adjacent to the Sky Tower, the All Blacks Experience and Weta Workshop Unleashed offer entertaining insights into New Zealand's rugby and cinema success.

TRAVELLIGHT/SHUTTERSTOCK ©

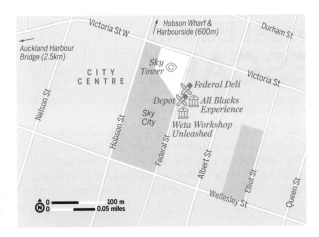

Left Sky Jump, Sky Tower
Below Auckland Harbour Bridge

Sky-High Thrills

Are they mad? That could be your reaction as you consider taking on Auckland's **SkyWalk**. At a height of 192m – around the same elevation as Maungawhau/Mt Eden – a 1.2m-wide walking platform encircles the **Sky Tower**. Yes, participants are secured with a harness, but there are no safety rails or handholds, just a very, very long drop to the streets below. Stellar city and harbour views come as standard. Ascending the Sky Tower to an enclosed viewing floor is also an option if you're not keen on Auckland's most extreme adventure. Good luck with those see-through glass floor panels. An optional way to descend to the **Federal St** dining precinct – recommended highlights are **Depot** and the **Federal Deli**, both from Kiwi chef Al Brown – is the **SkyJump**, a controlled 11-second 85km/h wired descent from the tower's observation deck.

Harbour Bridge adventures Maybe in the future it will be possible to walk or ride a bike across the Auckland Harbour Bridge, but right now the only way to get up close and personal with the iconic span linking the central city to the North Shore is on a guided bridge climb or by taking a leap of faith with **Auckland Bridge Bungy**. Look forward to plunging 40m towards the waters of the Waitematā Harbour, and brilliant views of downtown Auckland and the city's unique isthmus location.

Adventures Beyond the CBD

Auckland Sea Kayaks Kayak tours across the harbour to Rangitoto Island and half-day adventures to the extinct volcano of Motukorea/ Browns Island.

AWOL Canyoning Adventures Canyoning and abseiling adventures near Piha Beach and in the forests of the Waitākere Ranges Regional Park.

Explore Group Hands-on harbour adventures on an authentic America's Cup match-racing yacht. Also longer two- to five-night cruises exploring the Hauraki Gulf.

Fullers 360 Ferries to the islands of the Hauraki Gulf for hiking to the forested summit of Rangitoto or visiting the bird sanctuary of Tiritiri Matangi. Departures from downtown Auckland's Ferry Building.

05 Great Barrier ESCAPE

STARGAZING | WALKING | SUSTAINABILITY

Discover a different side to Auckland on Great Barrier Island. Known to Māori as Aotea, the forested island was designated a Dark Sky Sanctuary by the International Dark-Sky Association in 2017. Learn about Aotea's green-tinged sustainable ethos on guided walks to harbours and hot springs, before experiencing the after-dark spectacle of pristine southern hemisphere night skies.

EVGENY GORDETSKY/SHUTTERSTOCK ©

🗺 How to

Getting here Flights to Great Barrier Island take around 30 minutes from Auckland Airport.

When to go For better weather and to avoid busier weekends and school holiday periods, try to visit the island midweek from February to April.

Making it easy Book packages incorporating car hire, flights and accommodation with **Go Great Barrier Island** (greatbarrier islandtourism.co.nz).

Essential treat A lamb burger from Great Barrier's Swallow food caravan.

JULIE MACHADO/SHUTTERSTOCK ©

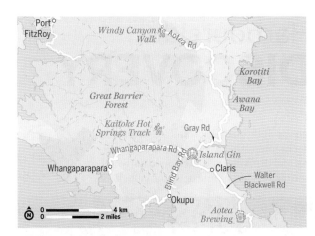

Left View from Mt Hobson, Great Barrier Island
Below Stargazing

Stargazing & Forest Walks

Night-sky experiences Depending on the progression of the astronomical year, Aotea's celestial highlights could include sightings of Jupiter, Venus and Saturn, and softly glimmering displays of the Magellanic Clouds and the Milky Way. Dark Sky Ambassadors Hilde Hoven and Deborah Kilgallon are superb guides to the pollution-free night skies above their adopted island home, setting up **Good Heavens'** (goodheavens. co.nz) powerful telescope amid the undulating sand dunes along the graceful arc of Medlands Beach. Their authoritative commentary incorporates astronomical observations and also an understanding of the cosmos from a traditional Māori perspective, and stargazing participants are guaranteed a few wedges of quite probably New Zealand's best carrot cake. Booking ahead with Good Heavens for your first night on the island is recommended to allow for flexibility with weather conditions.

Exploring history and nature Discover the island's heritage, culture and flora while exploring Aotea's more remote west coast on a guided walk. Highlights include a morning boat ride to a historic 19th-century timber mill, and then a forest hike with views of the silvery expanse of Whangaparapara Harbour. Born and bred on Great Barrier Island, chatty walking guide Benny Bellerby from **StarTreks** (startreks.kiwi) also usually comes equipped with a few home-baked organic treats. Other island adventures to check out with Benny or independently include the **Kaitoke Hot Springs Track** and the spectacular **Windy Canyon Walk**.

Artisan Endeavours on Aotea

Aotea Brewing Visit its rustic taproom to sample craft beers brewed entirely off the grid, or fill up a recyclable flagon for a takeaway purchase of the hoppy Solar Charged American Pale Ale. Check Facebook for occasional weekend live music across summer.

Island Gin Packaged in bottles made of recycled glass, award-winning gin harnessing local botanicals and forest ingredients is distilled in a simple set-up on the edge of Medlands Beach. See @islandgin on Instagram for details of its summer-only tasting sessions, or try an Island G&T at Aotea's popular Currach Irish Pub.

06 Harbourside **DISCOVERY**

ART | HISTORY | RESTAURANTS

▬▬▬ Embark on a leisurely stroll through Auckland's redeveloped harbourside precinct, taking in interesting art and markets, waterfront destinations for eating and drinking, and the opportunity to get out on the water in a heritage yacht or vintage motor launch.

🗺 How to

Getting around Start at the Lighthouse, 500m from Auckland's Ferry Building at the end of Queens Wharf.

When to go Begin around 1pm to incorporate a 1.30pm harbour cruise at the Maritime Museum followed by drinks and a meal later in the day.

How long? You're looking at around 2km. How about a leisurely two to three hours?

What to drink Beers from Auckland craft breweries including 8 Wired, McLeod's and Liberty.

🏪 A Chef's Choice

Avondale Market Great food stalls and produce from Auckland's wide range of ethnic communities.

Hello Beasty Superb Asian fusion dishes and great music.

Sri Pinang Fabulous, authentic Malaysian food.

Besos Latinos Auckland's best margaritas and beautifully spiced Mexican cuisine.

■ **Recommended by Peter Gordon** *co-owner, Homeland* @homeland.nz

04 On summer weekends, **Silo Park** (silopark.co.nz) is a popular location for outdoor movies, food trucks and the occasional DJ gig. Take in views of the Auckland Harbour Bridge.

01 Combining a giant stainless-steel statue of British maritime explorer Captain James Cook and Māori design motifs, the **Lighthouse** by Michael Parekōwhai is a bold commentary on sovereignty and colonialism.

03 Cross **Te Wero Bridge** to the **Wynyard Quarter** dining precinct. Standout addresses include **16 Tun** (pictured opposite) for Kiwi craft beer and the **Auckland Fish Market** for diverse dining options.

05 Continue to **Homeland's** marina-side location for innovative dining harnessing hyper-local and indigenous Māori ingredients. Chef Peter Gordon also offers excellent cookery classes.

02 From the first *waka* (Māori voyaging canoes) to yachting success in the America's Cup, the **New Zealand Maritime Museum** showcases the country's seafaring history. Book for harbour cruises online.

Freemans Bay

16 Tun

Jellicoe St

Wynyard Quarter

Hobson Wharf

Princes Wharf

Queens Wharf

Auckland Fish Market

Beaumont St

Daldy St

Madden St

Halsey St

Besos Latinos

Viaduct Harbour

Pier 2

Marsden Wharf

Customs St W

Market Pl

Hello Beasty

Sturdee St

Hobson St

Lower Albert St

Queen Elizabeth Sq

Quay St

Tyler St

Britomart

Albert St

Queen St

Customs St

Nelson St

CITY CENTRE

Bowen Ave

Albert Park

Cook St

0 — 500 m
0 — 0.25 miles

FILIP FUXA/SHUTTERSTOCK ©

City of Volcanoes

EXPLORE MĀORI HISTORY AROUND AUCKLAND'S VOLCANIC FIELD

More than 50 dormant volcanoes punctuate the Auckland isthmus, and Tāmaki Makaurau's unique urban landscape is on the Tentative List to be awarded Unesco World Heritage status. Since 2014, guardianship of 13 of the region's Tūpuna Maunga (ancestral mountains) has been co-governed by 13 different Māori *iwi* (tribes) from around Auckland.

Left Maungakiekie/One Tree Hill, Cornwall Park
Centre Maungauika/North Head
Right Rangitoto Island

Māngere Mountain

Around 70,000 years ago, Māngere Mountain was created by a huge volcanic eruption, and in more recent centuries the *maunga* was home to the local Te Wai-o-Hua *iwi*. Almost 80 *rua* (food storage pits) punctuate the landscape, while *kai moana* (seafood) bounty was also plentiful. Fertile volcanic soils and easily defended terrain combined to make the landmark also known as Te Pane o Mataoho (the forehead of Mataoho, the Māori god of earthquakes and volcanoes) an important *pā* (fortified settlement).

Maungawhau/Mt Eden

Maungawhau's 50m-deep crater is known as Te Upu Kai a Mataoho (the food bowl of Mataoho), and local *iwi* placed food offerings there for the all-powerful god. Agricultural terraces frame the *maunga*, now protected by a raised boardwalk. Summit views take in Auckland's two harbours, and Tāmaki Makaurau's other volcanoes can also be sighted. Views into Mataoho's food bowl are spectacular, and the Sky Tower, Rangitoto Island and the Harbour Bridge are standout sights from Auckland's highest point.

Maungakiekie/One Tree Hill

Topped by an obelisk, Maungakiekie dominates the rolling farmland of Cornwall Park. On the road to the summit (closed to traffic), it's easy to make out the *pā tūāpapa* (agricultural terraces) that made Maungakiekie an important *pā* site. Sweeping summit views include the Manukau and Waitematā harbours, Rangitoto Island and

Tāmaki Makaurau's other important *maunga*. Historically, Auckland's second-highest mountain after Maungawhau was also a prized defensive location for Māori *iwi*.

Maungauika/North Head

The legendary Polynesia explorer Kupe reputedly landed in nearby Te Haukapua (Torpedo Bay), and Devonport's Maungauika/North Head also features other echoes of history. Built in 1836, a navigation station marked the entrance to the Waitematā Harbour, while the Saluting Battery's impressive 8in gun was established in 1886 to protect against the (perceived) threat of a Russian invasion. To the west, Takarunga/Mt Victoria was also an important Maori *pā* site.

> Summit views take in Auckland's two harbours and Tāmaki Makaurau's other volcanoes.

Rangitoto Island

Rangitoto was formed around 700 years ago, and its volcanic origin is mentioned in Māori oral histories. Linked by a causeway, neighbouring Motutapu Island is around 178 million years old, and was used by local *iwi* for food cultivation. Footprints of an adult, child and dog have been discovered in a 30cm slab of volcanic ash. You can reach Rangitoto's forested volcanic cone along the **Summit Track**, a one-hour hike beginning at coastal mangroves, continuing through a lava field, and completing the experience more steeply through New Zealand's biggest pōhutukawa forest.

🔺 Best Ways to Explore Auckland's Volcanoes

Māngere Mountain Book in advance for a 90-minute guided *hikoi* (walk) with the Māngere Mountain Education Centre (mangeremountain.co.nz).

Maungawhau/Mt Eden Learn about Auckland's volcanic history at the Te Ipu Kōrero o Maungawhau Visitor Experience Centre (maunga.nz/maunga/maungawhau).

Maungakiekie/One Tree Hill Negotiate the sinuous 2km walk to the *tihi* (summit) for superb city views (maunga.nz/maunga/maungakiekie).

Maungauika/North Head Catch the Fullers ferry from downtown Auckland to Devonport and continue east along historic Torpedo Bay (maunga.nz/maunga/maungauika).

Rangitoto Island Journey from downtown Auckland with Fullers. Search 'Rangitoto' on doc.govt.nz for details of other longer walking tracks taking in Motutapu Island.

Listings

BEST OF THE REST

 Auckland's Multicultural Menu

Gemmayze St $$

Modern Lebanese dishes packed with seasonal ingredients are served amid the high-ceilinged art-deco ambience of Karangahape Rd's St Kevins Arcade. 'K Rd's' bohemian vibe also features many other good cafes and restaurants.

Azabu $$

Japanese-Peruvian Nikkei cuisine featuring the freshest of local seafood shines at Azabu's two locations: one in Ponsonby, the other near the beach on Mission Bay along Tāmaki Dr.

Ahi $$$

Ingredients from around Aotearoa are harnessed for fine dining with a relaxed Kiwi vibe. Ahi's takes on *kai moana* (seafood) is uniformly excellent, and ocean views reinforce you're dining in one of the world's great harbour cities. Ahi's Commercial Bay location also features a multicuisine food court that's ideal for lunch.

Hello Beasty $$

Japanese, Korean and Chinese flavours all blend seamlessly on Hello Beasty's innovative and modern menu. Ask for a table at the front of the restaurant to take in Viaduct Harbour's maritime vibe.

Cassia $$$

Often judged as central Auckland's best restaurant, Cassia's modern spins on traditional Indian flavours partner with a global selection of artisan gins, a well-curated beer list, and fresh and vibrant wine varietals including New Zealand riesling, pinot gris and sauvignon blanc.

Mr Morris $$$

Helmed by top New Zealand chef Michael Meredith, Mr Morris is a standout in downtown's Britomart Precinct. Local and sustainable ingredients underpin seasonal menus that often blend Asian and Pacific culinary influences to perfectly reflect the city's emerging cultural diversity.

Giapo $

Quite possibly the world's most inventive dessert treats are crafted at this artisan ice-cream shop in central Auckland. Follow co-owner Giapo Grazioli on Instagram (@giapokitchen) to see what intensely creative surprises he's currently dreaming up.

Ponsonby Central $$

From Venezuelan and Turkish to Chinese and Korean, global flavours abound at this essential destination along Ponsonby's eating and drinking strip. Highlights include the tiki bar meets Shanghai ambience of the Blue Breeze Inn, and excellent cocktails and gourmet meatballs at Bedford Soda & Liquor.

SARAWOOTP/SHUTTERSTOCK ©

Ice cream, Giapo

Craft Beer & Cocktails

Galbraith's Alehouse $$

A sunny beer garden, excellent food – including Auckland's best Sunday roasts – and a stellar selection of Kiwi beers make Mt Eden's Galbraith's a perennial contender for the city's best pub. During cooler months, secure a spot inside around the cosy fire.

Auckland Beer Mile $$

Eight different bars, brewpubs and taprooms feature along this 4.5km route (facebook. com/aucklandbeermile) showcasing a hoppy celebration of Auckland's craft-beer scene. Highlights include Churly's for robust IPAs and house-made charcuterie, and 40 taps and visiting food trucks at the Beer Spot.

Hoppers Garden Bar $$

Artisan gin, craft beer and a top selection of New Zealand wines all combine with street-food-inspired snacks in Hoppers' brick-lined Ponsonby courtyard. A retractable roof ensures it's popular throughout the year.

Freida Margolis $$

Freida's corner location in Grey Lynn is a top spot to combine cocktails, craft beer and diverse sounds from the owner's expansive collection of vintage vinyl. Formerly a butcher – look for the West Lynn Organic Meats sign.

Caretaker $$$

Descend to this stylish cellar bar in central Auckland's Britomart Precinct and let the savvy bartenders magic up a cocktail.

 Walk Across the Country

Coast to Coast Walkway

Catch public transport to Onehunga and embark on this 16km urban stroll across Auckland's narrow isthmus to link the Manukau and Waitematā Harbours, where you can refuel at the restaurants and bars of Viaduct Harbour.

Mission Bay, Tāmaki Dr

 The Best of New Zealand Art

Auckland Art Gallery Toi o Tāmaki

Emerging Māori and Pacific artists combine with works from iconic New Zealand painters including Ralph Hotere, Colin McCahon and Frances Hodgkins in this elegant French Renaissance–style building on the edge of central Auckland's Albert Park.

 Day Trips

Matakana

Journey one hour north of Auckland for Matakana's popular Saturday morning farmers market, barrel-aged beers from 8 Wired Brewing, and the vineyards of the emerging Matakana wine region. (matakanawine.co.nz)

Tāmaki Dr

Catch the TāmakiLink bus along Tāmaki Dr for swimming, eating and drinking at popular city beaches including Mission Bay and St Heliers.

 Family Favourite

Sea Life Kelly Tarlton's Aquarium

Be surrounded by sharks and stingrays as you walk through transparent tunnels, or get up close to king and gentoo penguins in the Antarctic Ice Adventure.

 Scan to find more things to do in the Auckland region online

NORTHLAND

BEACHES | CULTURE | HISTORY

Experience Northland online

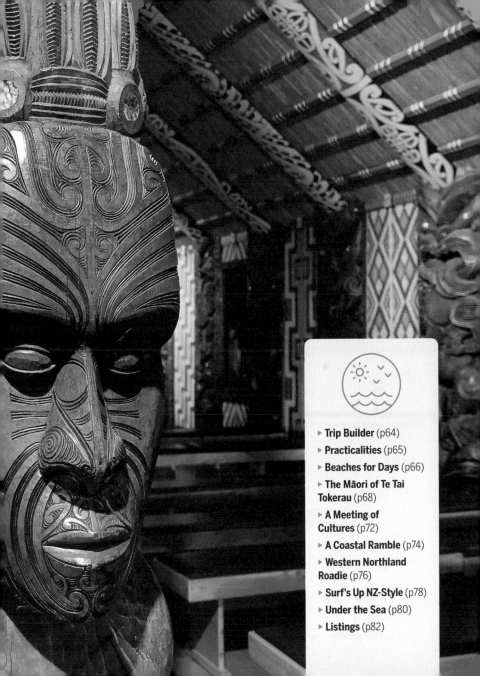

NORTHLAND
Trip Builder

South Pacific Ocean

Take a tiki tour of New Zealand's subtropical, northernmost region, nicknamed the Winterless North. Te Tai Tokerau is a stronghold of Māori culture and history, spectacular beaches and ancient forests, and some surprising modern and contemporary art.

Dive at the marine reserve of the **Poor Knights Islands** (p80)
⛴ *Whangārei*

Hike the **Cape Brett Track** in the Bay of Islands (p75)
🚗 *1¾hr from Whangārei*

Find out about Māori and colonial history at **Waitangi** and **Russell** (p68)
🚗/⛴ *1hr from Whangārei*

Be dazzled by all things Hundertwasser in **Whangārei** and **Kawakawa** (p72)
🚗/🚌 *2½-3hr from Whangārei*

Learn to surf at **Waipu Cove** or **Tutukaka** (p78)
🚗 *30-40min from Whangārei*

Cape Brett

Kerikeri ●
● **Russell**
Paihia
Lake Omapere

Hokianga Harbour
Opononi ○
Omapere ○

Sandy Bay

○ Kaihu

Kamo ●

Ngunguru Bay

● **Ruakākā**
Bream Bay
Waipu ●
Hen & Chickens Islands

○ Wellsford

Warkworth

Tasman Sea

Explore bookable experiences in Northland

Ⓝ 0 — 50 km
0 — 25 miles

Practicalities

ARRIVING

Whangārei There's a small local airport that has several flights per day from Auckland (30 minutes), and long-distance buses travel to/from Auckland and the Bay of Islands/Kaitāia.

MONEY

Northland isn't a low-budget destination. Save money by staying at campsites.

FIND YOUR WAY

The Whangārei i-Site Visitor Information Centre has helpful information on attractions around Northland.

WHERE TO STAY

Town	Pro/Con
Whangārei	A small city with great art and dining. Not so near the beach.
Paihia	Plenty of accommodation but very busy in summer.
Russell	More peaceful than Paihia. Take the ferry or drive the long way around.
Rawene	Sleepy and historic but without the tourist crowds or amenities of the east coast.

EATING & DRINKING

With a long coastline east and west, a fertile subtropical climate and a lot of dairy farming land, fresh seafood, dairy products and veggies feature prominently on Northland menus. Stylish waterfront restaurants in historic buildings in Whangārei and the Bay of Islands serve modern Kiwi seafood dishes, pizza, Mexican-inspired fare, and top-notch ice cream (pictured).

Must-try ice cream
NZ Fudge Farm (p82)

Best subtropical wine
Marsden Estate (p83)

GETTING AROUND

Car You'll need your own wheels beyond the major hubs.

Ferry Ferries run between Paihia and Russell and Rawene and Kohukohu.

Bus Long-distance buses travel from Auckland up the east coast and through Whangārei and the Bay of Islands. Local buses are limited to Whangārei.

NORTHLAND FIND YOUR FEET

DEC–FEB
Hot and humid days, warm nights; tourist crowds in the Christmas school holidays.

MAR–MAY
Warm days and sea temperatures, uncrowded beaches, decreasing daylight hours.

JUN–AUG
Rainy and humid, with cool nights. Did we mention the rain?

OCT–NOV
Diminishing rain, warm days but still a bit chilly at the beach.

07 Beaches
FOR DAYS

OUTDOORS | RELAXATION | NATURE

▬▬▬ With a subtropical climate and a long eastern and western coastline, Northland's beaches are numerous and nothing short of spectacular. Whether you're looking for a small shady bay for a swim and a snooze on the sand or somewhere more expansive for a long walk, you can find it in Northland.

How to

Getting here Follow SH1 up the east coast (and north to Cape Reinga) or SH12 down the west coast to find your own beach paradise.

When to go December to March have the warmest sea and air temperatures. Outside busy high summer you might even have the beach to yourself. Winter beach walks can be impressively solitary.

Beach lingo Use local vocab at the beach and you'll blend right in. Jandals = flip flops/thong shoes. Togs = bathing suit/swimming costume. Bach = a basic beachside holiday home (on the North Island).

Life's a Northland Beach

A tale of two coasts Like much of New Zealand, the beaches on the east and west coasts of Northland are dramatically different from each other.

As well as the east coast being more developed –

Bream Bay, the Tutukaka Coast, the Bay of Islands and the Karikari Peninsula are major tourist areas – the beaches here are picture-perfect, in an idealised white-sand, gentle-surf, shady-cove kind of way.

But don't dismiss the west-coast beaches. The currents

are stronger and the surf rougher, so extra caution is needed. **Ninety Mile Beach**, which runs 88km (go figure) from Cape Reinga to Ahipara, is an invigorating stretch of sand for a walk or dune activities. **Baylys Beach** near Dargaville is a local favourite surfing spot (see p79).

CRISTINA R./SHUTTERSTOCK ©

🖋 Birds of the Beaches

When you're on Northland's beaches, keep an eye out for conservation projects aimed at protecting and growing populations of local and migratory seabirds.

Sand dunes and estuaries in particular are rich habitats for coastal birds, so heed any warnings to keep out of certain areas.

Keen bird-watchers and wildlife enthusiasts can look out for oystercatchers, New Zealand dotterels, Caspian terns, fairy terns and little penguins. Bartailed godwits also spend time in Northland's Paren-garenga Harbour, Whangārei area and Kaipara Harbour during their annual 10,000km migration.

Island-hop There's more to the Bay of Islands than Paihia and Russell – don't forget the 144 islands themselves.

Island-hopping tours take travellers to island beaches that would be hard to access any other way. Some are reserves with restricted access but many are not.

Tours offer a range of activity levels so you can opt to kayak or paddle board or just relax on the sand.

Above Ninety Mile Beach

08
The Māori of Te
TAI TOKERAU

CULTURE | HISTORY | LANDMARKS

Te Tai Tokerau, Northland, is where much of New Zealand's early colonial-era history played out. The region is rich in Māori history but this isn't a forgotten thing of the past – Māori account for around one-third of Northland's population, much higher than the national average, and their culture is strong.

🖰 How to

When to go Any time's a good time, but Waitangi is abuzz on 6 February, the national holiday of Waitangi Day.

Should you attend a cultural show? Some travellers wonder whether or not Māori cultural shows are too touristy or contrived to be worthwhile.

The decision is up to the individual, but attending a show at a location with deep and rich ties to Māori culture – such as Waitangi – is an informative way of learning more.

Sleep at a marae Swap the hotel for a cultural exchange at a *marae* (meeting house).

Northland is often called the cradle of New Zealand because it is here that many significant events have happened: Polynesian explorer Kupe is said to have landed in the Hokianga Harbour around 1000 years ago; the founding document of modern New Zealand, the Treaty of Waitangi, was signed in the Bay of Islands in 1840; and some of the first battles of the New Zealand Land Wars occurred in Northland in the 1840s.

Treaty, yeah The **Treaty of Waitangi/ Tiriti o Waitangi** continues to loom large in modern-day politics and interactions between Māori and Pākehā New Zealanders. The treaty ceding sovereignty of the lands of New Zealand was signed between representatives of the British Crown and some Māori leaders on 6 February 1840 at

📖 A Great Migration

Many tribal stories credit Kupe with being the first Polynesian to arrive in Aotearoa when he landed in the Hokianga Harbour around 1000 years ago. Travellers can learn more about this migration and the myths and legends surrounding it at Opononi's Manea: The Footprints of Kupe Experience.

Above left Māori warriors commemorating Waitangi Day
Above Te Whare Rūnanga
Left Hokianga Harbour

what is now the Waitangi Treaty Grounds. To learn more about New Zealand history, if you go nowhere else in the country, make sure to spend at least half a day (preferably longer) at Waitangi. The extensive grounds include interactive museums, a carving studio, a ceremonial *waka* (canoe), a small beach, the British-style Treaty House, the incredible **Te Whare Rūnanga** (Carved Meeting House), a cafe, and great views across the Bay of Islands from around the 34m Flagstaff.

The Hellhole of the Pacific In the 21st century, pretty, sleepy **Russell** is about as far from its old moniker of 'Hellhole of the Pacific' as it's possible to be. But a stroll around the village will reveal why the town was so named in the 1830s. There's also plenty of evidence of how colonisers tried to 'civilise' the town through Christianity. Check out the Russell Museum, the Pompallier Mission and Printery, and Christ Church Cathedral, still displaying bullet holes from a shootout in 1845.

ⓘ How to Recognise a Pā Site

A *pā* was a fortified Māori settlement, usually upon a hill. *Pā* sites are common around Northland and road journeys are all the more interesting if you learn to distinguish a *pā* from, well, just a regular old hill. *Pā* were usually located on volcanic hills. The slopes were terraced, and that's the giveaway sign that a hill was once a *pā*. One of the most extensive and significant you can visit is Ruapekapeka Pā, the site of the final battle in the War of the North in 1846, part of the New Zealand Land Wars. It's southeast of Kawakawa.

Far left Rangikapiti Pā (p82)
Left Christ Church Cathedral, Russell
Below Ceremonial *waka*, Waitangi
Treaty Grounds

While away an hour or two A road trip through
Northland reveals many small-town museums
providing intimate, hyper-local insights into the
region's history and long-standing interactions
between Māori and settlers. Some little
museums worth a visit include the Mangawhai
Museum, the Kauri Museum in Matakohe, the
Dargaville Museum, Clendon House in Rawene,
Museum @ Te Ahu in Kaitāia, Hokianga Museum
and Archives Centre in Omapere, and the Waipu
Museum.

On a mission Learn how European missionaries
lived, how they attempted to convert local Māori
to Christianity, and how they tried to control
what they considered the unsavoury influences
of certain settlers (the type giving Russell its
hellhole nickname!) on the new colony of New
Zealand at mission sites throughout Northland.
The Kerikeri Mission Station, the Waimate
Mission, and Russell's Pompallier Mission and
Printery display exhibits in renovated 19th-
century buildings.

A Meeting of Cultures

LOCAL AND INTERNATIONAL ART BLOSSOM IN NORTHLAND

Northland was home to one of the 20th century's greatest European avant-garde artists. More than two decades after his death, Friedensreich Hundertwasser has played a role in uniting diverse artistic traditions in the city of Whangārei.

Left Hundertwasser Art Centre, Whāngarei
Centre Friedensreich Hundertwasser
Right Hundertwasser Toilets, Kawakawa

FIONA GOODALL/GETTY IMAGES ©

Austrian-born artist Friedensreich Hundertwasser settled in Kawakawa, Bay of Islands, in the 1970s, turning a patch of farmland into forest and blending in with the rural locals. The avant-garde artist who is known for Central European architectural masterpieces such as the Hundertwasserhaus, an apartment block in central Vienna, was asked to draw up plans for an art centre in Whangārei in the 1990s. But his aesthetic – all wavy lines, colourful tiles and gold domes – was a little too avant-garde for the conservative Whangārei of three decades ago, and his art centre wasn't built during his lifetime.

In the years after Hundertwasser's death in 2000, committed art enthusiasts refused to let his ambitious architectural plans die with him. It took a couple more decades, pandemic-related delays, a bitter public campaign and a referendum and the support of former prime minister John Key but, in February 2022, the Hundertwasser Art Centre and Wairau Māori Art Gallery opened in Whangārei's Town Basin.

The incredible gold-domed building is chequered with black-and-white tiles, undulating pathways and a carpet of 'tree tenants' – Hundertwasser's term for plants integrated into architectural designs – on the roof. That's just the outside, which would be marvellous enough regardless of what lay inside. Inside are two separate galleries, one displaying a collection of 80 original Hundertwasser works (the only permanent display outside Austria) and the other a Māori-curated collection of Māori art. The latter is the first public gallery dedicated solely to displaying the finest contemporary Māori art and represents a pivotal moment in curatorial practices

in Aotearoa. Hundertwasser's original plans for the art centre in Whangārei included space for the display of Māori art and that has been honoured in the posthumous incarnation.

The long-overdue project has breathed fresh life into the contemporary arts scene in Whangārei, or at least given it its rightful visibility. The Town Basin and Hatea River areas now boast artistic and architectural attractions that move Whangārei from a 'drive-by' pit stop en route to the Bay of Islands to a stand-alone destination in its own right.

> The incredible gold-domed building is chequered with black-and-white tiles, undulating pathways and a carpet of 'tree tenants' on the roof.

The Hātea Loop walkway connects the Hundertwasser Museum and the Town Basin with other areas of the city along the shores of the Hātea River and the end of Whangārei Harbour. Along the way is a sculpture walk, dotted with sculptural artworks that celebrate the people, history and environment of Whangārei. The Hihiaua Cultural Centre preserves, creates, displays and promotes Māori arts and culture in a purpose-built glass-and-wood building. The laser-cut weathered-steel whorl of the Camera Obscura on the east bank of the river takes an ancient photographic technique and imbues it with place-based significance. And the striking Te Matau ā Pohe bridge, which opens periodically to let boat traffic pass beneath, resembles the traditional Māori fish hook of Pohe, the local chief who first welcomed colonial settlers to Whangārei.

Whangārei may not have been ready for Hundertwasser in the 1990s, but his legacy, and that of the indigenous New Zealand artists he shared this land with, is proudly on display in the 21st century.

Kawakawa: More Than a Loo Stop

Whangārei doesn't get all the Hundertwasser fun. The Bay of Islands town of Kawakawa, where Hundertwasser spent the last two decades of his life, has been graced with the presence of the Hundertwasser Toilets since 1999, a project the artist saw to fruition in his lifetime. They're probably the only public loos you'll ever want to linger in, as you sit (or stand) and admire the colourful tilework, repurposed glass bottles embedded in the walls and other quirky details.

The nearby Te Hononga Hundertwasser Memorial Park does provide a reason to linger in Kawakawa a little longer.

09 A Coastal RAMBLE

OUTDOORS | NATURE | EXERCISE

▬▬▬ Getting active and enjoying the views in Northland can be as simple as following a coastal trail. Whether you're looking for a quick walk to stretch the legs or a multiday hike while camping or staying in huts along the way, Northland's long coastline offers plenty of options. Pack those hiking shoes but don't forget the togs, either.

TRISTANBALME/SHUTTERSTOCK ©

🗺 **How to**

Getting here Many walks around Northland don't require meticulous end-to-end planning of transport transfers. Shuttles can be arranged for the longer routes that do.

When to go Northland's subtropical climate makes walking in the summer rather hot, whereas winter brings rain. Walk in spring and autumn for optimum conditions.

City strolling No time for a longer walk? Whangārei's scenic Hātea Loop connects the Town Basin marina with the Te Matau ā Pohe bridge at the end of Whangārei Harbour.

TILL KLIMA/GETTY IMAGES ©

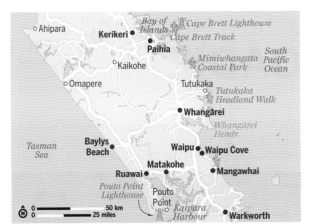

Left Waipu Cove to Mangawhai Heads coastal track
Below Cape Brett Lighthouse

Island walks Walking around some of the islands in the Bay of Islands is a great way to enjoy sweeping views of the picturesque bay. The day walks on Moturua Island and Urupukapuka Island are administered by DOC. There are many archaeological sites on pest-free Urupukapuka.

Headland views Walks around headlands offer panoramas from multiple angles. The Tutukaka Headland Walk to the lighthouse takes around one hour return, while various tracks around the Whangārei Heads offer views of the ocean, Mt Manaia and Whangārei Harbour.

Clifftop trails If you can arrange a drop-off or pick-up at either end (or can commit to the three- to four-hour return walk), the Waipu Cove to Mangawhai Heads coastal track is worthwhile. Follow the cliffs along the coast, stopping at points of interest such as shady pōhutukawa groves and Waipu's own pancake rocks.

Coastal and marine parks Walking through protected land or past marine areas provide extra wildlife-spotting opportunities. The Mimiwhangata Coastal Park north of Tutukaka offers various short walks and the chance of spotting wood pigeons, Australian eastern rosellas, kākā (parrots), and even brown kiwi at night.

Dune bashing The large sand dunes of the west coast offer a different kind of walking experience. Walk across the dunes to the Pouto Point Lighthouse at the entrance to the Kaipara Harbour, or up and across the dunes along the long stretch of Ninety Mile Beach (and then slide down again!).

🏠 Bag a Hut

An alternative way of seeing the famous Hole in the Rock, other than the standard boat trip, is to take the **Cape Brett Track**.

This is a rugged, challenging 16-km track from Rāwhiti to the Cape Brett Lighthouse at the end of the Cape Brett Peninsula. It's an eight-hour walk and is usually done over two days, as it can be quite tiring to do in one.

Spend the night at the serviced Cape Brett Hut, which has bunks, toilets and cooking facilities.

It's a good introduction to hiking huts if you're travelling further south in New Zealand on longer multiday hikes.

10 Western Northland ROADIE

NORTHLAND EXPERIENCES

NATURE | OUTDOORS | CULTURE

Take the road less travelled on a road trip between Dargaville and Kaikohe that takes in the ancient kauri trees of the Waipoua Forest, the sparkling Kai Iwi Lakes, the grand Hokianga Harbour and low-key hot springs at Ngawha.

RAIMUND LINKE/GETTY IMAGES ©

🗺 Trip Notes

Getting here From Whangārei, head southwest towards Dargaville, from where SH12 winds through the Waipoua Forest (pictured above) and out to the Hokianga Harbour, before continuing inland to Kaikohe.

When to go In summer the fresh waters of the Kai Iwi Lakes beckon, but in the cooler months the hot thermal baths at Ngawha Springs are inviting.

Refuelling Fill up at a petrol station in Dargaville before heading north. There are some stations along SH12 but having a full tank will let you take relaxed detours.

◎ Lakes, Forests & Hot Springs

Give the busy east coast SH1 a miss and instead take your roadie (road trip) along the quieter, arguably even more scenic SH12 between Dargaville and Kaikohe over two to three days.

At Kaikohe, the road forks northeast to the Bay of Islands or northwest to Kaitāia and Cape Reinga beyond.

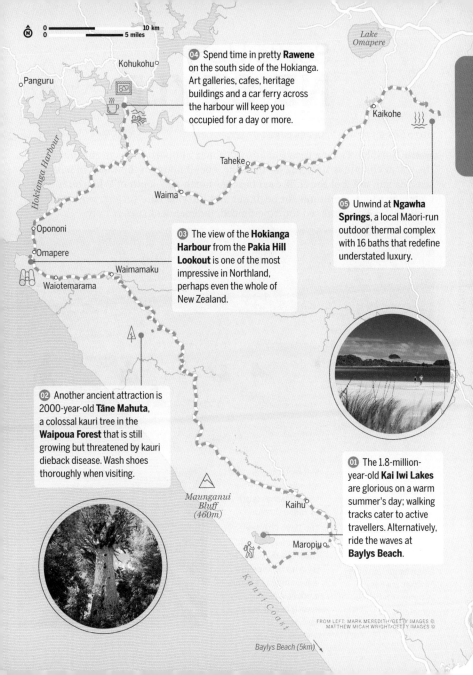

N 0 ─── 10 km
0 ─── 5 miles

Lake Omapere

Kohukohu

Panguru

04 Spend time in pretty **Rawene** on the south side of the Hokianga. Art galleries, cafes, heritage buildings and a car ferry across the harbour will keep you occupied for a day or more.

Kaikohe

Hokianga Harbour

Taheke

Waima

Opononi

Omapere

Waiotemarama

Waimamaku

03 The view of the **Hokianga Harbour** from the **Pakia Hill Lookout** is one of the most impressive in Northland, perhaps even the whole of New Zealand.

05 Unwind at **Ngawha Springs**, a local Māori-run outdoor thermal complex with 16 baths that redefine understated luxury.

02 Another ancient attraction is 2000-year-old **Tāne Mahuta**, a colossal kauri tree in the **Waipoua Forest** that is still growing but threatened by kauri dieback disease. Wash shoes thoroughly when visiting.

Maunganui Bluff (460m)

Kaihu

Maropiu

01 The 1.8-million-year-old **Kai Iwi Lakes** are glorious on a warm summer's day; walking tracks cater to active travellers. Alternatively, ride the waves at **Baylys Beach**.

Kauri Coast

FROM LEFT: MARK MEREDITH/GETTY IMAGES ©, MATTHEW MICAH WRIGHT/GETTY IMAGES ©

Baylys Beach (5km)

11 Surf's Up
NZ-STYLE

OUTDOORS | SPORT | ADVENTURE

Northland's long coastline provides many opportunities to surf but the warm climate is the icing on the cake: spend hours in the water in most seasons and not feel the chill. Surf beaches north and south of Whangārei offer consistent conditions for beginner and intermediate surfers, while the east coast is best reserved for experienced, independent surfers only.

GRANT ROONEY PREMIUM/ALAMY STOCK PHOTO ©

🗺 **How to**

Getting here Road-tripping around coastal Northland is the best way to find both popular and remote beaches for a surf.

When to go Northland beaches are busy in summer because conditions are good for surfing and swimming.

Mobile, temporary surf schools operate from some beaches (such as Waipu Cove).

The Cove Fish Fry Keen surfers should check out the Cove Fish Fry, a non-competitive, non-commercial surfing event held at Waipu Cove in early to mid-March each year.

STACEY KAMMERER/SHUTTERSTOCK ©

Left Children's surf lesson, Waipu Cove
Below Ruakaka Beach

A Beginner's Guide

The east coast of Northland is ideal for beginners, both north and south of Whangārei. Sandy Bay, north of Tutukaka, gets a big swell, but when it's on the lower end it's good for beginners.

Best, though, is Waipu Cove, because the sand banks there make the swell more gentle. The surf schools at Tutukaka and Waipu Cove make these the best places for beginners because not only will you learn surfing skills, you'll learn safety tips and the etiquette of surfing, too.

Nothing annoys an experienced surfer more than a beginner getting in the way because they don't know the etiquette. Surf schools will teach you how to avoid difficult situations.

■ **Recommended by Simon Egginton**
surfing instructor at Tutukaka Surf School. @tutukakasurf

Advanced surfers If you well and truly know your way around a wave, head to **Pataua** (Ngunguru Bay), **Ocean Beach** (Whangārei Heads) or **Baylys Beach** (west coast). The surf at these beaches isn't for the faint of heart and you've got to know how to get on your feet. Some experienced surfers consider the left-hand breaks in New Zealand, specifically parts of Northland, to be among the best in the world.

Body boarding If you're travelling with kids or would rather not surf proper, body boarding is a great alternative. Body boards are lighter and more portable than surfboards, and great for general splashy play. Beaches with smaller waves ideal for body boarding fun: **Matapouri**, **Woolleys Bay**, **Waipu Cove** and **Ruakākā Beach**. For safety's sake, don't skip the flippers.

Best of both worlds While some surf spots are reliably better for beginners or advanced surfers, others cater to differing levels depending on the conditions. Tutukaka's **Sandy Bay** gets big waves when there's a northerly or northeast swell and **Shipwreck Bay** at Ahipara offers 5m waves for experienced surfers, but both places host surf schools catering to beginners.

12 Under THE SEA

OUTDOORS | WILDLIFE | ADVENTURE

Warm waters, offshore islands, marine reserves and some incredible wrecks make Northland an unmissable destination for keen divers. It's often said that the Poor Knights Islands, off the east coast of Whangārei, are the best subtropical diving destination in the world. Take a refresher course or rent some gear and find out for yourself.

How to

Getting here The east coast, between Whangārei and the Far North, is the best base for diving. Outfitters operate largely out of Tutukaka and Paihia.

When to go Summer and early autumn provide warm water (relatively speaking!) and good visibility.

Open-water courses Northland is an ideal place to get PADI certified and dive schools offer everything from entry-level courses to instructor courses.

Snorkellers tag along Boat trips out to ocean diving spots often offer snorkelling, too.

It's Better Down Where It's Wetter

It's a wreck Learn about the dramatic history of Greenpeace's *Rainbow Warrior* protest ship before diving to see it at its final resting place in Matauri Bay. Open-water divers (or those who'd like to learn) can check out the intact wreck of the HMNZS *Canterbury* at Deep Water Cove. The *Tui*, off Tutukaka, was sunk deliberately to create a reef.

Those Poor Knights Twenty-two kilometres northeast off the coast of Whangārei, and sometimes visible from shore, are the Poor Knights Islands. They're surrounded by the Poor Knights Islands Marine Reserve. Fishing or disturbing the marine life or land is strictly verboten, but swimming and diving is A-OK and highly recommended.

Hen & Chicks The islands east of Bream Bay are a

JULIAN GUNTHER/GETTY IMAGES ©

🐾 Only Fearless Divers Need Apply

Experienced divers with an appetite for unusual, dramatic and even kind of creepy dive spots aren't short of options in Northland.

Beneath the surface at the Poor Knights Islands are a huge range of dramatic underwater landscapes to explore, from kelp forests and sponge fields to a tumbling staircase and sheer cliffs plunging 100m to the sea floor.

If the name 'Sonic Boom Cave' doesn't send shivers down your spine (or perhaps even if it does), this spot in the Bay of Islands lets you feel the force of the ocean through your whole body. The cave is named after the sound created when waves hit the top.

Above Scorpion fish, Poor Knights Islands Marine Reserve

fixture on the ocean-scape but they don't just make a pretty scene: you can dive there, too. Trips to the Hen & Chicks are less commercialised than other dive spots along the coast so may be appealing to independent, fully trained divers.

Coastal snorkelling If full-on scuba diving isn't for you, snorkelling from the beach is possible in many places. Choose a sheltered spot without waves, near rock pools. Whale Bay, Whangaumu Bay and Matapouri Bay on the Tutukaka Coast are good spots.

Listings

BEST OF THE REST

From on High

Mt Parihaka

Presiding over Whangārei, volcanic Mt Parihaka (241m) has the remains of one of the largest ever Māori *pā* and a viewing platform at the summit. The views look out over Whangārei city and harbour.

Mt Manaia

The strenuous climb to the top of 420m Mt Manaia, at the Whangārei Heads, passes through regenerating native forest. Stay a while at the top to enjoy views of Whangārei Harbour, Bream Head and the Hen & Chicken Islands.

Cape Reinga

The journey to the northernmost tip of the North Island is nothing less than a pilgrimage. See and feel the meeting of oceans from Cape Reinga Lighthouse.

Flagstaff at the Waitangi Treaty Grounds

The spot where the Treaty of Waitangi was signed in 1840 offers calm views across the Bay of Islands, down to Paihia, and across to Russell.

Kairara Rock (Duke's Nose)

Look out over Whangaroa Harbour after the short but steep climb up Kairara Rock. Sections of rock scrambling and ropes make this a better option for travellers without small children.

Rangikapiti Pā

Work off those fish and chips from the Mangōnui Fish Shop with a hike up Rangikapiti Pā. Enjoy views over Mangōnui Harbour, Coopers Beach, Doubtless Bay and the Karikari Peninsula.

Sweet Treats

Bennetts of Mangawhai $$

Shop for handmade chocolates at this boutique chocolatier before dropping into the connected cafe for a very special hot chocolate or mochaccino drink.

NZ Fudge Farm $

With a wide range of creative fudge flavours and ice creams that are definitely in the running for the title of New Zealand's best, this Town Basin Whangārei establishment will satisfy any sweet tooth.

Craft Shops

Burning Issues Gallery

This gallery at Whangārei's Town Basin sells and displays contemporary handmade glass, ceramics and sculpture, as well as jewellery. Watch glass being blown and fired in the workshop at the back.

Pipi Gallery Mangawhai

Browse or buy local pottery, ceramics, glass, garden art, jewellery, gifts and flower bouquets in Mangawhai Town, not far from Bennetts chocolate shop.

NICRAM SABOD/SHUTTERSTOCK ©

Lighthouse, Cape Reinga

Quarry Craft Shop and Gallery

The cooperative shop at the Quarry Arts Centre in Whangārei displays the work of more than 30 artists and is an ideal one-stop shop for local arts and crafts. You can also take a workshop at this arts institution.

 Waterside Pubs

Duke of Marlborough Hotel $$

The wrought-iron patios and balconies of the Duke have been sheltering patrons in Russell since 1827. In fact, this place held the first liquor license in New Zealand, back when Russell was nicknamed the 'Hellhole of the Pacific'.

Parua Bay Tavern $$

With views of the Whangārei Heads and plenty of outdoor space for the kids to play, the Parua Bay Tavern is a local favourite, especially in the summer.

The Quay $$$

Pick an outdoor table for the best views of the international yachts at Whangārei Marina as you drink and dine.

 Shop Local

Canopy Night Market

Operating on Friday evenings in summer, Whangārei's Canopy Night Market sells street food with an international, multicultural twist.

Whangārei Growers Market

Give the impersonal supermarkets a wide berth and instead buy fresh local produce from one of the oldest farmers markets in New Zealand. Held on Saturday mornings in the Water St car park, more than 100 stallholders set up shop here.

Old Packhorse Market

This indoor market in Kerikeri sells fresh and artisanal food and a wide range of

Duke of Marlborough Hotel

delicious breads and pastries from Northland producers on Saturdays. Sunday markets sell a wider range of bric-a-brac, clothing and jewellery.

 Subtropical Wineries

Marsden Estate

Sample award-winning wines in Kerikeri's oldest winery. Marsden Estate is named after Reverend Samuel Marsden, who planted the first vines in the Bay of Islands in 1819, long before NZ's viticulture boom of the 1990s.

Karikari Estate

Located on the Karikari Peninsula in the Far North, Karikari Estate is NZ's northernmost winery, with subtropical conditions far removed from those of temperate Hawke's Bay or Marlborough. The cellar door is open for tastings year-round.

Okahu Estate

Outside of Kaitāia, Okahu Estate was influential in NZ's wine renaissance of the 1990s. Sample award-winning syrah and chardonnay here.

 Scan to find more things to do in Northland online

CENTRAL NORTH ISLAND

VOLCANOES | NATURE | CULTURE

Experience Central North Island online

CENTRAL NORTH ISLAND
Trip Builder

The central North Island is a land of contrasts. Golden beaches give way to rich soil, nourished by the mighty Waikato River. Waterfalls dot the landscape along with volcanoes and forests, all sacred. Visit for an insight into the land and its people.

Auckland ●

Discover contemporary Māori art and design in **Raglan** (p90)
🚗 2hr from Auckland

Kāwhia

Float on a subterranean river in **Waitomo** (p92)
🚗 2½hr from Auckland

Tasman Sea

North Taranaki Bight

Trek among volcanic peaks on the **Tongariro Alpine Crossing** (p114)
🚗 4hr from Auckland

New Plymouth ●

Mt Taranaki (Mt Egmont) ⛰

Stratford ●

Cycle along old cobblestones on the Ōhakune **Old Coach Road** (p113)
🚗 5hr from Auckland

Hāwera ●

Explore bookable experiences in Central North Island

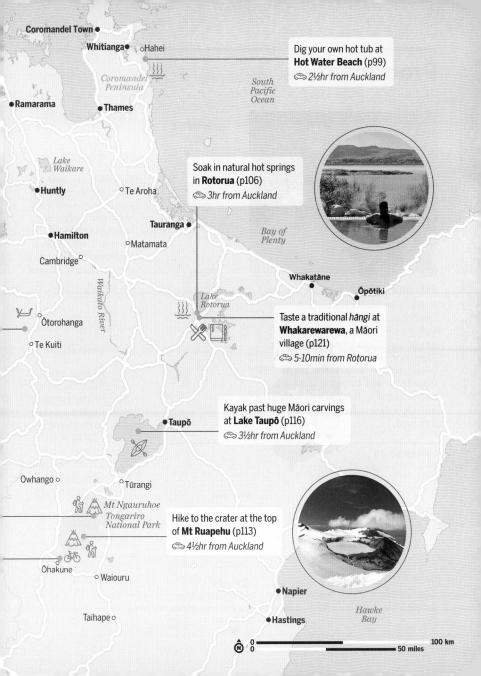

Coromandel Town ●

Whitianga ● ○ Hahei

Coromandel Peninsula

South Pacific Ocean

Dig your own hot tub at **Hot Water Beach** (p99)
🚗 2½hr from Auckland

● **Ramarama**

● **Thames**

Lake Waikare

● **Huntly**

○ Te Aroha

Soak in natural hot springs in **Rotorua** (p106)
🚗 3hr from Auckland

Tauranga ● ■

Bay of Plenty

● **Hamilton**

○ Matamata

Cambridge ○

Waikato River

Whakatāne ●

Ōpōtiki ●

○ Ōtorohanga

Lake Rotorua

Taste a traditional *hāngi* at **Whakarewarewa**, a Māori village (p121)
🚗 5-10min from Rotorua

○ Te Kuiti

Kayak past huge Māori carvings at **Lake Taupō** (p116)
🚗 3½hr from Auckland

● **Taupō**

Owhango ○

○ Tūrangi

Mt Ngauruhoe Tongariro National Park

Hike to the crater at the top of **Mt Ruapehu** (p113)
🚗 4½hr from Auckland

Ōhakune

○ Waiouru

● **Napier**

Taihape ○

● **Hastings**

Hawke Bay

Ⓝ 0 ─────────── 100 km
    0 ─────────── 50 miles

Practicalities

STEVE TODD/SHUTTERSTOCK ©

ARRIVING

Auckland International Airport The major transport hub for the region. Hire a car from Auckland – drive time is under two hours to Hamilton, and approximately three hours to Tauranga or Rotorua. You can also take an intercity bus. You can get connecting domestic flights to Tauranga, Rotorua or Taupō via the national carrier, Air New Zealand. Flights are available to these regional airports at least once a day.

HOW MUCH FOR A

Hot-springs visit
$35

Fish & chips
$10

Hāngi
$40

GETTING AROUND

Car Renting a car gives you access to remote springs, secluded nature walks and more rural destinations. To visit attractions like the Waitomo Caves, Hobbiton, or the Green and Blue Lakes in Rotorua, a car is essential, unless you are doing a tour.

Intercity buses You can get between the major cities by bus for a relatively affordable price. However, it can be challenging to access all the major attractions by public transport and the local bus networks are limited in some places.

WHEN TO GO

DEC–FEB
Hot. Spend your time at the beach or swim in the river.

MAR–MAY
Still warm, but getting cooler. Great time for hiking and seeing the autumn leaves.

JUN–AUG
Cold with more rain. Ski season starts in July; enjoy the hot springs.

SEP–NOV
Warm days with some rain. Waterfalls are most impressive after the rains.

EATING & DRINKING

This volcanic region is the only place in the country where you can try a *hāngi* cooked in thermal steam. Visit a Māori village and enjoy a traditional meal of steam-cooked meat and vegetables while learning about the local culture. Or head to the coast for fresh snapper or fish and chips on the beach. The central North Island is also the heart of dairy farming in New Zealand so try the local ice cream and cheese.

Must-try ice cream
Duck Island, Hamilton
(p118)

Best creamed paua
Eze Feedz, Mt Maunganui
(p119)

CONNECT & FIND YOUR WAY

Wi-fi Local cafes usually have free wi-fi, however, it's best to buy a local SIM card at the airport for data. There is good data connection in towns, but be prepared to lose signal when driving on remote roads.

Navigation Routes are well-signposted and easy to follow, with good signage for major attractions.

WHERE TO STAY

The central North Island is predominantly farmland and forests, with a few small cities and towns, each with their own personality. Use a couple of these as a base to explore the region.

Place	Pro/Con
Rotorua	Best place to see geothermal sites. Can be very touristy. Strong sulphur smell.
Mt Maunganui	Seaside town. Can be expensive and is a popular stop for cruise ships.
Raglan	Bohemian, surf town. Accommodation can be a bit rustic. Remote.
Hahei	Beachside village. Can get very busy during the summer.
Taupō	Central hub for the major attractions in the region.
Ōhakune	Ski town with good access to Tongariro National Park. Can be a party town during ski season.

DESERT ROAD

Check that the Desert Road is open before heading south from Taupō in winter. It's often closed due to ice and snow.

MONEY

You can pay by credit card in most places, even in small towns. Restaurants may be more expensive than you think. Fish and chips, burgers and bakeries are good options for cheaper meals.

13 Art & Creativity
IN RAGLAN

ART | BEACHES | ACTIVTIES

Beyond Raglan's easy-going surf-town vibe and an excellent cafe and restaurant scene, there's a diverse and vibrant community of artists, designers and craftspeople. After delving into the town's creative side, set out on relaxed walks to waterfalls and through native bush, or get active on a kayak, paddle board or surfboard around the region's spectacular beaches and coastline.

PETER UNGER/GETTY IMAGES ©

📸 How to

Getting here Raglan is 45km west of Hamilton. Busit's route 23 (one hour) departs from Hamilton's Transport Centre.

When to go
For the best weather and to avoid holidays and busy weekends, visit Raglan midweek from February to April.

Sky-high & sustainable Take in Tasman Sea views with an overnight stay in one of Solscape's rammed-earth domes or stylish eco-cottages.

Essential purchase Super-comfortable handmade shoes or sandals from Soul Shoes.

MARTIN VILNAS/GETTY IMAGES ©

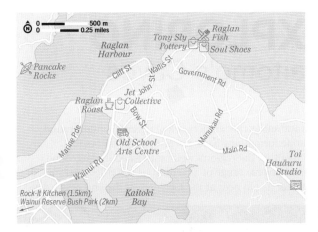

Left Bow St, Raglan
Below Wairēinga/Bridal Veil Falls

☼ Best Outdoor Experiences

Wainui Reserve Bush Park Experience peaceful nature walks through this bush reserve, cared for by local volunteers, with birdsong all around you.

Wairēinga/Bridal Veil Falls A popular proposal spot. Go on a short meandering walk and be greeted at the end by a beautiful plunge waterfall.

Surf Breaks This is what Raglan is known for – amazing surf! Catch the legendary left-hand break at Manu Bay, beginner waves at the beach, or challenge yourself on a big swell day at Whale Bay.

Water Sports Hire a kayak to explore Pancake Rocks, or a stand-up paddle board and make your way down to Rock-It Kitchen for lunch.

Welcome to Arty Whāingaroa

Discover local art Work from six of Raglan's diverse band of artists and craftspeople is showcased at **Jet Collective's** interesting hybrid of gallery and retail store. Inspired by living around the spectacular harbour known to Māori as Whāingaroa, ceramics, painting, textiles and mixed-media works all feature. It's just a short walk to the best coffee in town at **Raglan Roast's** hole-in-the-wall laneway location.

Raglan Creative Market On the second Sunday of each month, the **Old School Arts Centre** hosts this excellent event from 10am to 2pm. Look forward to a relaxed vibe, with food stalls selling organic and vegan treats, and plenty of local arts and crafts. A few food trucks usually make the short journey from the nearby big smoke of Hamilton.

Contemporary Māori design Meet local Māori artist Simon Te Wheoro at his **Toi Hauāuru Studio**. Highlights include *pounamu* (greenstone) carvings, *hei-tiki* (pendants) and Raglan-inspired surf wear. If you're keen on the ultimate reminder of a visit to Aotearoa, Simon is also skilled at the art of *ta moko* (Māori tattoo). Contact him in advance via his website (toihauauru.com).

Raglan's historic wharf Browse for both rustic and modern designs at **Tony Sly Pottery**, and stylish leathergoods including footwear, bags and satchels at **Soul Shoes**. Also essential is a harbourfront feast of seafood and chips at **Raglan Fish**.

■ **Recommended by Tesh Randall** *co-founder of Raglan Food Co*

@raglanfoodco
@latesharandallauthor

14 EXPLORING
Waitomo's Caves

CAVES | ACTION | SCENERY

 Waitomo's idiosyncratic subterranean network of caverns, underground streams and soaring limestone formations has been attracting visitors for over a century, and complementing the region's well-established underground experiences is an exciting and diverse range of adventurous activities guaranteed to give you bragging rights over a cold beer at the local pub at the end of the day.

LUKAS BISCHOFF PHOTOGRAPH/SHUTTERSTOCK ©

🗺 How to

Getting here Waitomo is 70km south of Hamilton. **BL Tourism** (bltourismgroup.com) offer transfers from nearby Ōtorohanga, a stop on the Northern Explorer train.

When to go With most attractions underground, visiting the caves is possible year-round.

Book accommodation in advance for Christmas/New Year and Easter.

Waitomo's quirkiest accommodation Formerly an advertising sign – no, really – the cosy HuHu Chalet is ideal for couples, and Waitomo's best restaurant (of the same name) is right next door. Search on Airbnb.

MARCEL STRELOW/GETTY IMAGES ©

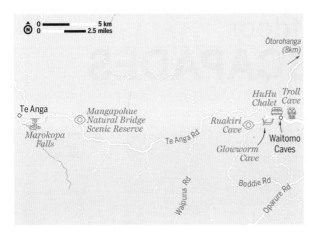

Left Ruakuri Cave
Below Glowworm Cave

Waitomo Three Ways

Subterranean spectacles Entered via an innovative 15m-high spiral staircase – there is also full access for wheelchairs – exploration of Waitomo's **Ruakiri Cave** takes in around 1.5km of the cave's entire 7.5km-long system. Underwater streams and waterfalls weave in and out of crystalline banks of limestone, and the cave is regarded as an intensely spiritual place by local Māori. Waitomo's iconic and most historic experience is boarding a boat to ride on an underground river to the galaxy-like spectacle of the nearby **Glowworm Cave**.

Adrenaline-fuelled action File under 'Only in New Zealand'. From rock climbing, abseiling and underground ziplines to the extreme fun of 'Black Water Rafting' – floating on a subterranean river on an inner tube while wearing a wetsuit – Waitomo's innovative tourism entrepreneurs offer plenty of ways to combine Aotearoa's adventure sports DNA with the region's natural beauty. **Waitomo Adventures**, **Glowing Adventures**, **Caveworld** and the **Legendary Black Water Rafting Company** all offer diverse underground thrills, and booking ahead online often secures a good discount. Good luck with jumping off those underground waterfalls.

Post-action relaxation Waitomo Adventures HQ also incorporates a good cafe, and its day spa and massage services both hit the spot after clambering and squeezing through a few subterranean tight spots. For younger travellers, Waitomo Adventures' **Troll Cave** is a fun blend of adventure and problem-solving.

Best Scenic Detours

Mangapohue Natural Bridge Scenic Reserve
Kick on 26km west of Waitomo to this duo of natural limestone arches created over millennia by the waters of the Mangapohue Stream. On a wheelchair-accessible pathway, it's a five-minute walk from the road through a narrow gorge shrouded with moss and ferns. Glowworms shimmer and shine after dark, but you'll need a torch to safely make the walk.

Marokopa Falls
Continue for another 6km to the Marokopa Falls, always spectacular in spring after the winter rains. The 30m-high cascade is reached by a 15-minute return track from the roadside car park.

Outdoor
ESCAPADES

HIKING | BIKING | SCENERY

▬▬▬ Amid Waikato's dairy pastures and the craggy and forested spine of the Coromandel Peninsula, this area, an easy drive from Auckland or Hamilton, offers plenty of ways to get active, taking in bush and river scenery, learning about New Zealand's gold-mining past, and discovering a sustainable future focused on protecting the country's endangered native wildlife.

🗺 How to

Getting around Renting a car is the most efficient and enjoyable option. Hire bikes in Paeroa, Waihi, Arapuni and Tirau.

When to go Spring and summer from November to April offers the best weather and drier trails.

Walk across Coromandel's northern tip Coastal and farmland views are highlights of the 3½-hour 10km hike between Fletcher Bay and Stony Bay on the Coromandel Coastal Walkway. Arrange shuttles in Coromandel Town with Coromandel Adventures.

Map showing Coromandel Town, Wharf Road, Whitianga, Coromandel Forest Park, Firth of Thames, Kauaeranga Kauri Trail, Papakura, Cafe Melbourne, Thames, South Pacific Ocean, Coromandel Forest Park, Refinery, Paeroa, Waihi, Waikato River Trails, Hauraki Rail Trail, Karangahake Gorge, Ngāruawāhia, Tauranga, Hamilton, Matamata, Pokaiwhenua Bridge, Lake Karapiro, Sanctuary Mountain Maungatautari, Tirau, Putāruru, Arapuni. Scale 20 km / 10 miles.

Mountain Adventures & Riverside Biking

On two legs Best accessed from the Waikato towns of Cambridge or Te Awamutu, **Sanctuary Mountain Maungatautari** (sanctuarymountain.co.nz) is a superb example of New Zealand's dedication to protecting the country's indigenous species. Almost 50km of pest-proof fencing has been erected around Maungatautari's forested volcanic cone. The project is best explored on the Over the Mountain trail, or the gentler Wairere Traverse. Both take around six hours. Northeast of Thames, the **Kauaeranga Kauri Trail** (Pinnacles Walk) winds through the Coromandel Forest Park to reach the summit of the Pinnacles (759m) after around four hours.

Be immersed in spectacular views of the Coromandel Peninsula before returning, or book ahead to overnight in the Department of Con-servation's Pinnacles Hut (doc.govt.nz).

TOMEK FRIEDRICH/SHUTTERSTOCK ©

☕ **Best Pre- & Post-Action Cafes**

Refinery Fire up the turntable with a record from the overflowing bins of vintage vinyl and team Paeroa's best coffee with a gourmet sandwich. The overflowing Cubano should see you through the best of the Hauraki Rail Trail.

Cafe Melbourne Located in a restored brick-lined bus depot in Thames' historic Grahamstown precinct. Check out the various food stores in the adjacent Depot development for artisan bread and picnic fixings.

Wharf Road Coromandel Town's best global flavours are served in Wharf Road's shaded garden. Enlivened with punchy chilli oil, the *cilbir* (Turkish eggs) are a brunch classic. Craft beers and Kiwi wines, too.

On two wheels New Zealand has gone cycle-trail-crazy, and a couple of options around the Waikato and the Coromandel Peninsula are perfect for day-long adventures. The **Hauraki Rail Trail** (haurakirailtrail. co.nz) stretches south from Thames to Matamata, but the most scenic section is the eastern bush-clad spur along the Ohinemuri River through the former gold-mining area of the Karangahake Gorge. New Zealand's longest river is the backdrop to the **Waikato River Trails** (waikatorivertrails. co.nz). Meandering along tree-lined Lake Karapiro, the 11.5km section linking the Pokaiwhenua Bridge to the hamlet of Arapuni is a popular option along the trails' full extent of 104km.

Above Kaka, Sanctuary Mountain Maungatautari

16 Discovering
COROMANDEL

BEACHES | HISTORY | ROAD TRIP

The Coromandel Peninsula is criss-crossed by hilly highways and framed by meandering coastal roads. Explore the region's marine landscapes from low-key resort towns, combine gold-mining history and ziplining action around Coromandel Town, or embark on a DIY adventure exploring the peninsula's remote northern tip.

 📖 **How to**

Getting here On the opposite side of the Firth of Thames, Coromandel Town is 230km east of Auckland. Self-driving a rental car is definitely the best way to explore the peninsula.

When to go Summer weekends and school holidays (especially) get very busy. Try and visit midweek.

Best bivalves En route to Coromandel Town, stop at the Coromandel Oyster Company, or enjoy platters of smoked and chilli mussels at the Coromandel Mussel Kitchen.

History & Adventure

Lined with heritage buildings dating from the region's 19th-century gold-mining era, charming **Coromandel Town** is the ideal base for exploration further north to more remote and rugged parts of the Coromandel Peninsula. Cafes and a smattering of design stores and galleries hint at the various arty types living in the surrounding hinterland, and the legacy of pioneering conservationist and artist, the late Barry Brickell, is showcased on the outskirts of town at **Driving Creek**. It's where gold was discovered in 1852, and now worthy of at least half a day discovering Driving Creek's cafe, pottery workshops and the forested combination of the **Driving Creek Railway** and **Coromandel Zipline Tours**. One-hour rides on Driving Creek's quirky narrow-gauge train take in spirals, tunnels and switchbacks to end at the

 Coromandel by Ferry

Departing from downtown Auckland's ferry building, **Fullers** runs scenic day-trip ferry sailings across the Firth of Thames to the Coromandel Peninsula. Free shuttles transport passengers on the 10km road journey to historic Coromandel Town, and it's also possible to visit **Driving Creek** for its bush railway and ziplines.

Above left Cathedrall Cove (p98)
Above Kayaking to Cathedral Cove (p98)
Left Driving Creek Railway

'Eye-full Tower' and views across the Firth of Thames to Auckland. Eight separate zipline sections negotiate an exciting downhill route through the **Driving Creek Conservation Park**, and plenty of information on its sustainable guardianship of the regenerating native forest is included during the exciting experience.

Coastal Walking & Natural Spa Pools

From the coastal town of **Hahei**, tackle the rolling 30- to 40-minute walk to nearby

Cathedral Cove. The iconic stone arch, often enlivened with a natural waterfall shower, is at its best early or late in the day – avoiding the inevitable crowds for such a popular destination – and there's good snorkelling en route amid the sheltered waters of Gemstone Bay. Rent snorkelling gear from **Cathedral Cove Dive & Snorkel** in Hahei. During summer, **Cathedral Cove Water Taxi** operates a 10-minute shuttle along the coast from Hahei beach to Cathedral Cove

Best Marine Adventures

Explore the coastal caves and rock arches of the **Te Whanganui A Hei Marine Reserve** with Hahei-based **Cathedral Cove Kayak Tours**.

Zip around the marine reserve and check out **Cathedral Cove** from the water on an exciting boat trip with **Ocean Leopard**, **Sea Cave Adventures** or **Cave Cruzer**.

Sail from Whitianga to Cathedral Cove on **Boom Sailing's** catamaran.

Learn to surf with the Kiwi-Brazilian team at **Surf n Stay** at Whangamatā. There's good self-contained accommodation, too.

Join a guided tour or hire a kayak or paddle board from **Surfsup** in Whangamatā to circumnavigate the wildlife sanctuary of **Whenuakura** (Donut Island).

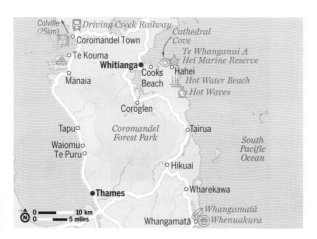

Left Catamaran, Boom Sailing
Below Spades to dig a natural hot tub, Hot Water Beach

that's both scenic and convenient. After exploring the cove, journey 10km south to **Hot Water Beach** and dig your own natural hot tub near the rocky outcrop in the middle of the beach. Two hours either side of low tide is recommended to experience the beach's thermal springs, and tide times are listed online (thecoromandel.com). Hire a spade at the nearby **Hot Waves** cafe while you're digging into its legendary Big Breakfast.

Remote Road-Tripping

An intrepid option on mainly unsealed roads is this loop around the northern part of the Coromandel. From Coromandel Town, depart north past Ōamaru Bay and Amodeo Bay to the hippyish vibe of sleepy **Colville**. Cross the peninsula and continue down the east coast via Whangaahei Bay, Waikawau and Kennedy Bay, before negotiating **Tokatea Hill** back to Coromandel Town. It's only 70km, but count on around two hours' driving time. Optional extensions are detouring further north from Whangaahei Bay to remote **Fletcher Bay**, an end-of-the-road location with a DOC campsite and backpacker accommodation, or taking the unsealed northern spur to Port Charles where there's motel-style accommodation and a cafe at the **Tangiaro Kiwi Retreat**. New Zealand's national bird is often heard in the surrounding forest.

TOMAS PAVELKA/SHUTTERSTOCK ©

North Island's Gold-Mining Heritage

GOLD-INFUSED HISTORY AMID STELLAR FOREST SCENERY

Explore the historic 19th-century shopfronts and streetscapes of Thames and Coro-mandel Town before learning about the past, present and future of Coromandel gold-mining amid the scenic Karangahake Gorge and in the interesting town of Waihi. The award-winning Waihi Gold Discovery Centre is one of New Zealand's best regional museums.

Left Martha Mine, Waihi
Centre Karangahake Gorge Windows Walk
Right Cornish Pumphouse, Waihi

The Attraction of £500

Back in 1852, £500 was a substantial amount of money, equivalent to more than $60,000 today, and definitely enough to attract prospectors from around New Zealand to be the first to discover gold in the Hauraki region. Scores of wannabe miners, especially from the then-capital of Auckland, descended on the remote rivers of the Coromandel Peninsula in a concerted effort to win the reward and become the luckiest and richest bloke in town.

NZ's First Gold Discovery

Leading the charge was Charles Ring, recently returned from the California goldfields with his brother Frederick. In October 1852, after negotiating access with local Māori, they found gold flakes on the banks of Driving Creek, now just a short distance from Coromandel Town. Alluvial gold deposits in the river ran out after a month – foreshadowing the future emergence of a different kind of gold-mining around the Coromandel – and the discovery of gold in Central Otago in 1861 saw gold fever take hold around Queenstown and Arrrowtown on the South Island.

A Golden Era for Thames

After gold was again discovered nearby in 1867, Thames became the centre for Coromandel gold-mining, but now using a more mechanised and industrial process to extract gold from the region's quartz-laden rock faces. With a population of 15,000 in 1870, Thames was one of New Zealand's most important towns. Banks and a stock exchange lined the main street, and the value of annual gold production surged to more than £1 million by

1871. Mining schools opened in Thames, Coromandel Town and Waihi, and over 100 pubs and three theatres ensured Thames' hard-working residents enjoyed their downtime.

Martha's Time to Shine

In 1878, gold was discovered in Pukewa Hill near Waihi, and from 1878 to 1911, the town's Martha Mine was one of the world's most important gold mines. More than 170km of tunnels criss-crossed inside the hill, employing more than 600 men, and ore from the mine was transported by train to nearby Waikino, where the Victoria Battery was Australasia's largest quartz crushing plant. Further along the Ohinemuri River rail line linking Waihi to Paeroa, other mining batteries were in the hills lining the rugged Karangahake Gorge, but Waihi's Martha Mine was always the biggest game in town.

> The value of annual gold production surged to more than £1 million by 1871.

Martha's Possible Future

A six-month miners' strike in 1912 greatly impacted Martha's operations, and after a downturn in global gold prices, the massive 600m-deep mine was closed in 1952. Following a revival in gold prices, Martha was reopened in the 1980s as an opencast pit mine measuring 1km by 700m, and mining continued until a major landslide in 2015. Martha is still watched over by the skeletal floodlit structure of Waihi's Cornish Pumphouse, and local tour guides reckon there's still 'millions of dollars of silver and gold' in the mine. Based on those numbers, a future reopening is likely on the cards.

📖 Unearthing Coromandel's Gold-Flecked History

Gold Discovery Centre Learn about Waihi's 143-year gold-mining journey at the interactive Waihi Gold Experience.

Waihi Gold Mine Tour Get 'inside the fence' and get the lowdown on a modern-day working gold mine.

Martha Open Pit Walkway Look down into this massive open-pit gold mine right in the middle of Waihi township.

Victoria Battery & Tramway Explore this heritage site in Waikino where ore from Martha Mine was processed from 1897 to 1952.

Karangahake Gorge Windows Walk Negotiate this historic gold-mining area high above the Onhinemuri and Waitawheta Rivers.

■ **Recommended by Eddie Morrow** *General Manager, Waihi Gold Discovery Centre*

17 Culture & History in
HAMILTON

CENTRAL NORTH ISLAND EXPERIENCES

GARDENS | ART | HISTORY

Often overlooked as a tourist destination, New Zealand's fourth-largest city offers a trio of standout museums and cultural experiences, and there's also an excellent restaurant scene. Before heading west to the arty surf town of Raglan, east to Hobbiton, or south to the Waitomo Caves, spend at least a day experiencing the rural heartland city also known as Kirikiriroa.

NATALIACATALINA.COM/SHUTTERSTOCK ©

📍 How to

Getting here Hamilton is an easy 90-minute drive south of Auckland.

When to go Hamilton is not a key destination for travellers, so visiting year-round is fine. July and August can be colder and more rainy.

Cross the river Check out the emerging dining scene in Hamilton East – standouts are Hayes Common and GG's Cafe.

ARCHITECT: IVAN MERCEP

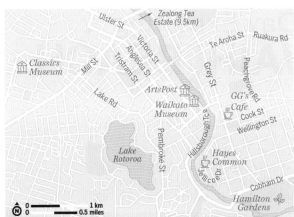

Left Hamilton Gardens
Below Waikato Museum, Hamilton

World-class gardens A brilliant destination for all travellers, but especially enjoyable for families, the **Hamilton Gardens** (hamiltongardens.co.nz) are spread over 50 spectacular hectares southeast of the city centre. Themed displays recreate Italian Renaissance, Japanese and Chinese gardens, while the surprising Surrealist garden is a confounding, intriguing and thoroughly entertaining experience inspired by dreams, magic realism and the subconscious. The Te Parapara garden highlights traditional foods and natural remedies harnessed by New Zealand's indigenous Māori.

Superb Māori galleries Celebrating a riverside location in the CBD, the essential highlight of the **Waikato Museum** (waikatomuseum.co.nz) are the galleries showcasing *taonga* (treasures) from the Tainui *iwi* who call the broader Waikato region home. The magnificent *waka taua* (war canoe), Te Winikawaka, is housed in a spacious atrium with river views. Check online for a rotating schedule of special exhibitions. Adjacent to the museum, **ArtsPost** is a gallery and retail space focused on work from local artists.

A surprising transport museum Just off SH1 on the northern edge of the city, the **Classics Museum** (classics museum.co.nz) is a treasure trove of more than 100 cars from earlier decades. Seriously cool vehicles that could be just the ticket for exploring New Zealand include retro Corvette and Maserati sports cars, and the so-crazy-this-might-just-work amphibious Amphicar from the 1960s. Look for the giant jukebox facade out front and you're in the right place.

Treat Yourself to High Tea

Surrounded by dairy farms 12km northeast of Hamilton, the tea bushes framing the entrance to the **Zealong Tea Estate** come as a real surprise.

Tea plantations usually feature at higher elevations in warm countries, and Zealong is uniquely New Zealand's only tea estate, but also the world's largest organic tea-growing enterprise.

On offer from Zealong's modern HQ are guided walking tours along the Tea Trail, highlighting the heritage and culture of tea around the world. At an elegant teahouse with estate views, Zealong's experts conduct ceremonial tea tastings, while optional high teas showcase delicious tea-infused sweet and savoury treats.

18

A Day Exploring
WAIHI BEACH

BEACHES | WALKING | EATING

Bordering both Waikato and the Coromandel Peninsula, Waihi Beach is a classic beach town. Swimming is good in Waihi's (usually) gentle eastcoast surf, and easy walks provide stellar views along the coast. Good dining options include an absolute beachfront cafe, and the Surf Shack, once described by Lonely Planet as serving 'quite possibly the best burgers in New Zealand'.

STARGRASS/SHUTTERSTOCK ©

🗺 Trip Notes

Getting here By car, Waihi Beach (pictured) is 90 minutes from Hamilton, and two hours from Auckland.

When to go Spring and summer are the best times, but try and visit on a quieter weekday during school holidays and at Easter.

Say g'day To Ruby the canine hostess at the excellent self-contained apartments at Waihi Beach Paradise Resort.

☀ Waihi's Summer Vibe

The garden bar at the **Waihi Beach Hotel** (waihibeach hotel.co.nz) is a popular summertime destination. New Zealand bands, often with a laid-back reggae vibe, perform throughout the warmer months – check the website to see who's playing – and a craft beer from Hamilton's Good George Brewing is ideal after a day's exploring. As the pub's own website says, 'Kiwi as, bro!'

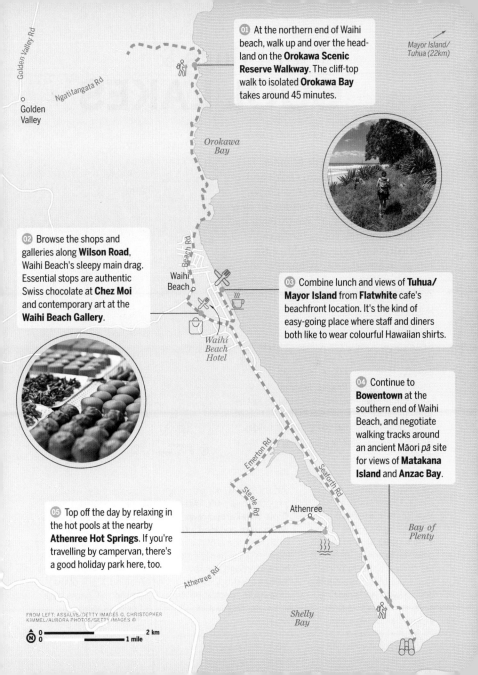

01 At the northern end of Waihi beach, walk up and over the headland on the **Orokawa Scenic Reserve Walkway**. The cliff-top walk to isolated **Orokawa Bay** takes around 45 minutes.

Mayor Island/
Tuhua (22km)

02 Browse the shops and galleries along **Wilson Road**, Waihi Beach's sleepy main drag. Essential stops are authentic Swiss chocolate at **Chez Moi** and contemporary art at the **Waihi Beach Gallery**.

03 Combine lunch and views of **Tuhua/ Mayor Island** from **Flatwhite** cafe's beachfront location. It's the kind of easy-going place where staff and diners both like to wear colourful Hawaiian shirts.

04 Continue to **Bowentown** at the southern end of Waihi Beach, and negotiate walking tracks around an ancient Māori *pā* site for views of **Matakana Island** and **Anzac Bay**.

05 Top off the day by relaxing in the hot pools at the nearby **Athenree Hot Springs**. If you're travelling by campervan, there's a good holiday park here, too.

Golden Valley Rd
Ngatitangata Rd
Golden Valley
Orokawa Bay
Beach Rd
Waihi Beach
Waihi Beach Hotel
Emerton Rd
Steele Rd
Seaforth Rd
Athenree
Athenree Rd
Bay of Plenty
Shelly Bay

N
0   2 km
0   1 mile

19 Hot Springs & **COOL LAKES**

THERMAL SPRINGS | LAKES | OUTDOORS

▰▰▰ The central North Island is home to beautiful volcanic lakes and hot springs. From Rotorua to Taupō, you can experience the wonders of New Zealand's volcanic heritage through its waters. Submerge yourself in steamy thermal waters surrounded by lush forests or spend a day swimming and boating on the shores of one of New Zealand's beautiful lakes – the choice is yours.

🗺 **How to**

Getting here Some of the springs and lakes in the central North Island are remote, so driving is easiest.

When to go The best time for swimming in the lakes is from November through to March. Just be aware that it can get busy from Christmas through to mid-January when the schools are on holiday.

Off-season perks Relax in a hot spring after hiking or skiing.

Discover Rotorua's volcanic waters See New Zealand's volcanic heritage come to life in its waters. Around between Rotorua, there are several opportunities to see bubbling mud pools, boiling lakes and spurting geysers. The best way to experience the volcanic waters is by walking through a geothermal park. **Wai-O-Tapu**, **Whakarewarewa**, **Waimangu** and **Hell's Gate** (p121) are some of the most impressive, with meandering tracks through steamy forests offering views of mud pools, sulphur pools and even a hot-water waterfall.

Submerge yourself in thermal springs While seeing the boiling lakes and rivers is an amazing experience, soak in a hot spring to truly immerse yourself in volcanic New Zealand. Many of the geothermal parks have thermal springs, but one of the most impressive is

DMITRY PICHUGIN/SHUTTERSTOCK ©

A Free ♨ Geothermal Experience

For a free peek at Rotorua's geothermal wonders, head to Kuirau Park, just a few minutes' walk from the city centre.

The meandering paths take you past steaming lakes and boiling mud pools, just a few metres away from cars and houses. Despite its central location, it's a remarkable place to visit, the leafy surroundings are peaceful and you'll find yourself walking through clouds of steam.

While the water in the pools is too hot for bathing in, you can finish your walk by soaking your feet in the free public foot bath in the park.

Waikite Valley Thermal Pools (p121), about 25 minutes' drive from central Rotorua, which uses the water from Te Manaroa, a natural boiling spring.

Explore the volcanic lakes
The beautiful, colourful lakes in Rotorua and Taupō are the result of New Zealand's volcanic activity. Not far from central Rotorua, you'll find the Blue and Green Lakes (**Lake Tikitapu** and **Lake Rotokākahi**). Spend a few hours boating, swimming or fishing on the Blue Lake and marvel at the colours of the Green Lake – just keep in mind that it is sacred *(tapu)* and you cannot enter the water.

Above Pohutu geyser, Whakarewarewa geothermal park

20 Food from the Forest
& THE SEA

FOOD | FISHING | CULTURE

Discover the traditional flavours of New Zealand through tasting authentic Māori *kai* (food). Try the *kai moana* (seafood) gathered from the Bay of Plenty. Taste the rich flavours of roast meats and vegetables slow-cooked in the warm earth for a *hāngi*. Food is sacred to Māori, connecting the people to land and the sea.

NAURIS KRESLINS/SHUTTERSTOCK ©

🗺 How to

When to go Whitebait is generally available between September and November while crayfish is available year-round.

Costs *Hāngi* cost from $15 at a food truck to $50 for dinner. Pies can be cheaper.

Top tip It can be challenging to find local foods at restaurants. Instead, head to festivals and events, where there are often food trucks offering a range of traditional Māori foods.

KIM HOWELL/SHUTTERSTOCK ©

ERIAN SCANTLEBURY/GETTY IMAGES ©

Far left *Hāngi*
Below *Kina*
Left Preparing a *hāngi*

Underground feasts Preparing a *hāngi* is both a labour and ritual. Traditionally, food is wrapped in leaves or placed in woven baskets and lowered into a pit. The pit is covered and the meat and vegetables cook slowly, gently flavoured by the smoke from the fire and the plants used to make it.

In areas with geothermal activity like Taupō and Rotorua, holes are dug in the ground and the thermal steam is used to cook the meat. You can sample a *hāngi* at **Te Puia** and **Whakarewarewa** (p121) in Rotorua.

Kai moana – the food of the sea, lakes and rivers As an island country, New Zealand has an abundance of *kai moana*. Crayfish (a rock lobster) is very popular, although can be expensive. Other delicious, more affordable, options include the large, green-lipped mussels and plump scallops. Paua (a black abalone) and whitebait (tiny seasonal fish) are usually served in fritters. Food trucks at markets and festivals are great ways to try these authentic indigenous foods.

Catch your dinner Reward your fishing efforts by cooking your catch. If you go fishing, chances are you'll bring back a snapper, gurnard or terakihi. Have them filleted and smoked or cooked by a chef at a local restaurant. Ask your charter operator or hosts for their recommendations before you go fishing so you can arrange with restaurants in advance.

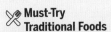

Must-Try Traditional Foods

Creamy paua Black abalone cooked in cream and served on loaded fries, baked in a pie or with fry bread.

Ika mata Fresh fish marinated in lemon and coconut cream in the traditional style of the Cook Islands.

Hāngi Tender lamb, chicken or pork cooked in an underground oven with root vegetables and stuffing.

Fry bread Deep-fried pockets of dough, crunchy on the outside, and light and fluffy on the inside.

Kina Sea urchin, usually eaten raw and best for more adventurous eaters. Try *kina* shots at festivals and events for a small taste of this local delicacy.

■ **Recommended by Jasmine Hayward** *owner of Eze Feedz, specialising in authentic Maori and Pasifika food, Mt Maunganui.* @ezefeedz

21 A Traditional
KIWI SUMMER

BEACHES | CAMPING | FAMILY-FRIENDLY

Experience summer like the locals do – by heading to the beach. Camp near the water and wake up to incredible views or hire a bach in Tauranga, near the coast. Enjoy seemingly endless warm days, explore the region's coastline, and cool down with ice creams from the local dairy. Barbecue your dinners or opt for the Kiwi classic, fish and chips on the beach.

PHOTOS BRIANSCANTLEBURY/SHUTTERSTOCK ©

📖 How to

Expect to pay From $15 to $30 per night for a campsite. The nightly rate for cabins and baches varies depending on season, number of bedrooms and location.

Weather Temperature highs in New Zealand range from 22°C to 28°C between January and March.

Essential supplies The sun can be harsh in New Zealand so be sure to apply sunscreen regularly. Insect repellent can also be useful to protect against mosquitos and sandflies in the evenings.

JOSHUADANIEL/SHUTTERSTOCK ©

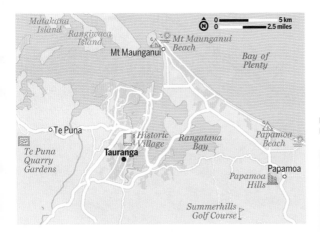

Left Holiday park, Mt Maunganui
Below Mt Maunganui

Camping by the sea Spending a week or more camping at the beach is a Kiwi favourite during the summer. There are many campsites with good facilities or, if you want something a bit more remote, pick a DOC campsite where you can camp on the beach. Some favourite campsites include **Papamoa Beach** and **Mt Maunganui**, where you can wake up with the long, sandy beach on your doorstep.

Break up your days at the beach with creamy ice cream from the local dairy and watch the sunset with fish and chips and beer on the beach.

A home away from home The traditional Kiwi bach is a small, simple house near the beach with basic facilities. Nowadays, a bach is a holiday home which families rent for a few days (or weeks). Search popular sites bookabach.co.nz or bachcare.co.nz to find your summer home by the sea. Spend your days at the beach and cook your dinner on the barbecue in the evenings.

A holiday highlight Spend at least a day (or more) exploring Mt Maunganui, a seaside town just outside of Tauranga city centre. Walk around the *maunga* (mountain) or hike to the top if you're feeling more adventurous. Then walk down the main street and relax in one of the many local eateries, or prepare a picnic and enjoy it on the sandy beach.

◎ **Things to Do in Tauranga**

Admire outdoor art at Te Puna Quarry Gardens, then pop into the nearby Cider Factorie for a drink in picturesque surroundings.

Play a round of golf at Summerhills Golf Course or just go for a walk and enjoy the panoramic views of the Bay of Plenty. Make time for lunch at the kiosk.

Explore the *pā* sites in the Papamoa Hills, looking out over the coast.

Take a V8 motorcycle trike tour of Mt Maunganui to see some of the offbeat local spots in style.

Learn about colonial history at the Historic Village in Tauranga – and sample the doughnuts while you're there.

■ Recommended by Vince Taylor & Annette Kennedy
Papamoa locals

22

Adventures Among
VOLCANOES

HIKING | SKIING | CYCLING

Explore the rugged volcanic landscape of Ruapehu and Tongariro. Challenge yourself on strenuous hikes among craters and lake, cycle through forests and snowboard down volcanoes. Seek out waterfalls and savour the bits of luxury hidden in unexpected places.

🗺 How to

Getting here By car, Ruapehu is around five hours from Auckland and four from Wellington. The Northern Explorer train also stops at the Chateau Tongariro. Intercity buses are also available.

When to go February to April for hiking and July to October for skiing and snowboarding.

Getting around Renting a car is easiest; however, there are regular shuttles up the mountain from Whakapapa and Ōhakune from late June to October.

Take to the Slopes

Experience skiing or snowboarding on a volcano. With three ski areas to choose from, **Mt Ruapehu** has well-maintained trails, snowy basins and spectacular views. **Whakapapa** is New Zealand's largest ski field and its Happy Valley ski area is great for kids. **Tūroa** boasts the country's longest vertical drop (722m) and **Tūkino**, a club-operated field, is a great option for avoiding the queues.

Cycle the Old Coach Road

A fascinating day ride, the **Ōhakune Old Coach Road** connects Ōhakune and Horopito. Originally used by horse-drawn coaches, the route is steeped in history, passing through farmland and forest in Tongariro National Park.

Find old railway tunnels and bush camps, marvel at the remarkable views of Mt

❋ Party in the Peaks

Experience the mountain at its most festive in early August for the annual Ohakune Snowball. If you want to cap off a ski trip with drinks and DJs, dress up and let loose at the local favourite, the Powderhorn Chateau. The event usually sells out, so book in advance.

Above left Tongariro Alpine Crossing
Above Cycling, Tongariro National Park
Left Snowboarder, Mt Ruapehu

Ruapehu and see the remnants of the original cobblestone road as you ride. The trail also passes two historic railway viaducts including **Hapuawhenua**, at 45m high and 245m long. This route is suitable for families and is easiest to cycle from Horopito to Ōhakune.

Trek Through Volcanic Peaks & Dramatic Landscapes

The **Tongariro Alpine Crossing** is widely regarded as the top single-day hike in New Zealand and one of the best one-day treks in the world. Traverse the South and Red Craters, offering panoramic views across lava flows and steam vents, before descending past emerald-coloured lakes and tussock-covered slopes to shady, green forest.

The 19.5km trek includes steep climbs and most people choose to do it in the summer. However, if you are after a challenge, walk the crossing between July and October for snow-covered landscapes and magnificent views, all without the summer crowds. Guides are necessary in the winter months, with training and equipment provided.

 High Tea with Mountain Views

Tongariro is one of New Zealand's most iconic hotels, usually referred to by locals simply as the **Chateau**. The building is impressive, situated in Whakapapa Village surrounded by snowy peaks and two national parks.

In winter, visitors are greeted by high ornate ceilings, chandeliers and a roaring fire, and you can relax in a lounge with a drink. Reward yourself after a day on the slopes or hiking with high tea in the Ruapehu Lounge, with spectacular views of Mt Tongariro. Or, if you're in the area on a Sunday, stop by for a traditional Sunday lunch in an elegant setting.

Bookings are available at chateau.co.nz.

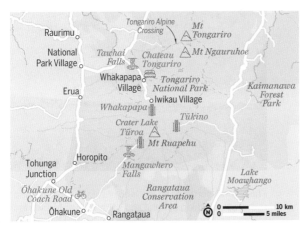

CENTRAL NORTH ISLAND EXPERIENCES

Left Ruapehu Lounge, Chateau Tongariro
Below Tawhai Falls/Gollum's pool

Discover Alpine Waterfalls... & Gollum's Pool

Majestic waterfalls are sometimes just a short walk from the road. Follow the sign on Ōhakune Mountain Rd and take a 10-minute stroll from the car park to the wonderous **Mangawhero Falls**, surrounded by beech forest. In winter, icicles form around the falls.

In Tongariro National Park, **Tawhai Falls** drops 13m over the edge of an ancient lava flow. The falls cascade into a beautiful pool, the filming location of Gollum's pool in the *Lord of the Rings*.

Gaze into a Crater Lake

A startlingly blue crater lake sits at the top of Ruapehu, the highest volcano in New Zealand. For those looking for a challenging hike, walking to the top is an unforgettable experience. When you reach the crater, have a picnic next to the geothermal lake and soak in your stunning surroundings.

Just keep in mind that there is no track and the route can be unstable, so is best suited to hikers with a good level of fitness. There are no markings so consider going with a guide, particularly in winter.

Stories of the Earth

THE PEOPLE AND THE LAND ARE ONE

Places and myths about them are often inextricably intertwined, explaining how natural features formed and why the world is the way it is. Māori legends tell the stories of the mountains, rivers and lakes that dominate the North Island, illustrating the heritage and power of this fiery land.

Left Lake Taupo
Centre Boiling Lake, Kuirau Park
Below Ngātoro-i-rangi carvings, Mine Bay

STEWART WATSON/GETTY IMAGES ©

The central North Island is a land of volcanoes, lakes and rivers, all with deep cultural and spiritual significance to Māori. There are many stories about how that landscape formed and, according to Māori tradition, the mountains were once warriors of great strength. Here are a few stories from just a few of the landmarks in the central North Island.

Filling Taupō with Water

One of the largest crater lakes in the world, **Lake Taupō** was formed nearly 2000 years ago by a huge volcanic eruption. The lake is so large that when you stand on one side, you cannot see across to the far shore.

One of the Māori legends of Lake Taupō tells how the crater filled with water. When the early Polynesian explorer and priest Ngātoro-i-rangi first saw Taupō, it was a huge, barren bowl in the earth. In an effort to promote growth, he uprooted a totara tree and threw it into the dirt. The wind caused him to miss his mark and, after striking a hard bank, the tree landed upside down, its branches piercing the earth.

Fresh water welled up, forming Taupō Moana – 'The sea of Taupō'. This tree is said to still be visible under the water about 70m off the shore at Wharewaka Point. After giving thanks, Ngātoro-i-rangi threw strands from his cloak into the water where they became the native fish of the lake.

Tongariro's Victory

Tongariro, the great mountain, was one of seven mountains surrounding Lake Taupō. Pihanga was

the only female mountain in the range, and she was exceptionally beautiful. The other mountains were all in love with her and fought each other for her favour. As they battled, the land beneath them erupted with fire, smoke and hot rocks, and the ground shuddered beneath them.

Eventually, Tongariro was victorious, winning Pihanga's devotion and the right to stand next to her. The defeated mountains had a single night to move away from the couple and at dawn remained fixed in their new locations forever.

Kuirau Park's Boiling Lake

With its boiling mud pools and steaming rivers, it's not surprising that many local legends take place in Rotorua. In the centre of town is **Kuirau Park**, named after a woman from a tragic tale. The park is known for its boiling lake; however, according to this story, the lake was cool in the past.

> Lake Taupō is so large that when you stand on one side, you cannot see across to the far shore.

The first people to live on its shores were a couple, Tamahika and Kuirau. One day when Kuirau was bathing in the lake, a *taniwha* (sea monster) grabbed her and dragged her down into the depths of the lake.

The gods saw this and were angry, so they made the waters of the lake boil. The *taniwha* was destroyed but Kuirau was also killed, and since that time the lake and the park around it have taken her name.

🗺️ Stories in Stone

The journeys of the explorer Ngātoro-i-rangi took him through the central North Island and the Bay of Plenty, past Lake Tarawera, past Taupō and to the peaks of Tongariro. His magic also brought cold and frost to the mountaintops and fire to the volcanoes.

In Mine Bay on Taupō, you can see 14m-high carvings of Ngātoro-i-rangi by Māori artist Matahi Brightwell. The carvings are impressively detailed and were recently retouched by the artist. They are also only visible from the water. Go with a guide to learn some of the history of the artwork and the stories of the legendary explorer.

Listings

BEST OF THE REST

 Favourite Feeds

Duck Island Ice Cream, Hamilton East $

High-quality artisan ice cream made locally with a wide range of flavours. Available by the tub from retail stores, but having scoops from the freezer is better. Offers a good range of vegan options.

Gothenburg, Hamilton $$$

Enjoy tapas with a river view in Hamilton. The wide selection of food provided to diverse groups and vegetarians are catered for. A great spot for a drink and a bite with friends.

Surf Shack, Waihi Beach $$

A family favourite with a play *marae* (meeting house) and child-friendly options. Head there for brunch or try the burgers if you're there later in the day.

Luke's Kitchen, Kūaotunu $$

The go-to for traditional, wood-fire pizza and fresh, organic coffee. There's also a good selection of seafood, salads and cabinet food. Relax with live music and views during the summer.

Blue Ginger, Whitianga $$

Asian-fusion at its best with dumplings, stir-fries and fresh salads on the menu. Blue Ginger takes pride in using local seafood and produce; be sure to try its special, seasonal dishes.

Port Road Project, Whangamatā $$

The bestselling item on the menu is paua fritters, and for good reason – order them when you go. Add some meat and Middle Eastern–inspired dishes to make it a feast.

Falls Retreat, Karangahake Gorge $$$

Slow food made with seasonal, organic produce in a picturesque setting. The menu changes frequently, but is always delicious, and the location feels like you're miles away from the world.

ULO's Kitchen, Raglan $$

Noodle and rice-based dishes influenced by Japan and flavours from around the world. A relaxed vibe with friendly staff and indoor and outdoor seating. Try the cocktails (or mocktails) when you visit.

Rock-It Kitchen, Raglan $$

Have breakfast or lunch in an old woolshed nestled among native plants. The menu is seasonal and uses local, organic produce. An unpretentious spot that embodies Raglan's laid-back atmosphere.

The Chateau, Tongariro $$$

Visit this New Zealand institution (p114) for high tea with a view or an elegant dinner. The surroundings are as important as the food, so admire the sparkling chandeliers and luxury from a bygone era.

SKYIMAGES/GETTY IMAGES ©

Gothenburg, Hamilton

Eze Feedz, Mt Maunganui $

Taste authentic Māori and Pasifika food you can normally only get at someone's house (usually for a celebration). Try creamed paua on chips, fry bread and even *hāngi*.

Atticus Finch, Rotorua $$$

A modern bistro with seats spilling onto the pavement. Food is designed to be shared so go with a group, order some wine and take your time lingering over your meal.

Factory Smokehouse & Grill, Rotorua $$

If you're craving a burger, these may be the best in Rotorua! Also try the smoked meat, smothered with rubs and sauces, all made in-house. Excellent gluten-free options available.

Pauly's Diner, Taupō $

On those hungry days head to Pauly's for a burger and chips (or potato and gravy if you prefer). Portions are large, the meals are satisfying and the milkshakes are a must.

Master of India, Taupō $$

Generous portions of Indian-style curries served with fluffy naan bread. Flavours are authentic and the service is warm, friendly and helpful. Try the banquet if you're in a group and hungry.

Raw Balance Vegan Deli & Health Shop, Tūrangi $

A convenient option for a healthy meal on the go with a wide selection of plant-based meals. Try the juices, smoothies and raw desserts. A must for vegetarian and vegan travellers.

Blind Finch, Hamburgeria & Bakehouse, Ōhakune $$

Head here for lunch for pies, sourdough sandwiches and gourmet burgers. A good range of food to choose from – the banh mi is another popular choice and the pastries are well worth trying.

Star & Garter, Coromandel Town

Local Watering Holes

Pourhouse, Hahei $$

Have a drink in the peaceful gardens of this small brewery. Taste its craft beers, sip a glass of wine in picturesque surroundings. There are also light meals on offer.

Good Merchant, Matamata $$

Have a pint (or two) of locally produced craft beer with some snacks to share. Sample some of the beer on tap and enjoy the friendly, relaxing atmosphere. Stay for a meal if you're hungry – the portions are generous.

Star & Garter, Coromandel Town $$

Sip your drink and soak up your surroundings in this historic building. Choose from a range of local beer and wine. Head outside to the garden bar if it gets hot inside.

Powderkeg, Ōhakune $$$

Drop in for a mulled wine or beer after a day out on the slopes. Enjoy the cosy ambience and warm fires, and grab a pub-style meal. There's also live music from time to time.

Anann – Pineapple Pub, Te Puke $$

Chill with friends and a cold beverage at this quirky, pineapple-themed bar. Make yourself comfortable in the cosy environment and admire the interesting decor. A great place to meet locals.

Hop House, Tauranga $$

Spend a leisurely afternoon drinking boutique wine or craft beer in this historic pub in central Tauranga. In summer sit outside in the beer garden. The Sunday lunch is a local favourite.

 Adventure Activities

Canyonz, Thames

Abseil down canyons deep in the Coromandel, with waterfalls thundering nearby. Cool off by leaping into deep pools and slipping down water slides. An exhilarating outdoor adventure.

Redwoods Treewalk, Rotorua

Explore a redwood forest while suspended on walkways perched high in the branches of 115-year-old trees. For an extra special adventure, join the magical night walk, illuminated with lanterns hanging from the trees.

Kaituna Cascades Rafting, Rotorua

Discover the thrill of white-water rafting on the Kaituna River, surrounded by native bush. Float through deep-water canyons and raft over rapids, including a waterfall. A challenging and exhilarating experience.

 Family-Friendly Fun

Julians Berry Farm & Café, Whakātane

Spend a morning berry-picking, then head to the cafe and enjoy a coffee while over-looking the berry fields. Children love the berry ice creams and the on-site animal farm, playground and minigolf course.

aMAZEme, Rotorua

Get lost in a hedge maze with your family and friends. Race the kids to the middle, get stuck in the dead end and play the other games and activities on-site when you finish.

Hobbiton

Step into the world of *The Hobbit* and experience life in the Shire for yourself. Take a guided tour through the movie set and finish with a drink at the Green Dragon Inn.

Aratiatia Rapids/Aratiatia Dam spillway, Taupō

Watch thousands of litres of water flow from the Aratiatia Dam through a narrow gorge, then see the dam gradually fill back up. An especially fun activity for families.

 Unique Art & Designs

ArohArt, Thames

Browse the selection of authentic Māori art in ArohArt's carefully curated collection. Choose from the beautifully crafted jewellery, carvings and clothing for meaningful gifts that reflect the spirit of Aotearoa New Zealand.

Puawai Jade, Rotorua

Discover the beauty of New Zealand *pounamu* (jade) and watch as it's carved into intricate patterns. Learn the meanings behind the Māori symbols and consider sharing this traditional gift with a loved one.

Hobbiton

Ahu Boutique, Rotorua

For a hint of local flair, check out the Māori-inspired fashion in this small boutique. Admire the colourful prints, artistic fabrics and sophisticated classics. There is also intricate jewellery on display.

 Geothermal Parks & Hot Springs

Wai-O-Tapu

Choose one of three walks through a surreal landscape of geothermal wonders. Stroll past colourful pools of bubbling water, exploding geysers and the largest mud pool in New Zealand.

Waimangu Volcanic Valley

Wander through native bush and discover volcanic lakes in the former home of the pink-and-white terraces (now destroyed). Take the lake cruise for a unique perspective of the valley.

Hell's Gate

Marvel at the geothermal sights then relax in a mud pool, sulphur bath or hot spring. Take the opportunity to learn about the healing properties of the geothermal mud and waters.

Waikite Valley Thermal Pools

Submerge yourself in thermal waters in hot pools filled from a boiling river. The water is cooled to varying temperatures, so pick the one that relaxes you the most. Bliss on a cold winter's day.

Kuirau Park

Follow walkways over boiling mud pools and steaming streams in the centre of Rotorua. Marvel at the bubbling lakes and soak your feet in the free foot bath at the end of the path.

BOB HILSCHER/SHUTTERSTOCK ©

Te Puia, Rotorua

 Māori Culture & Heritage

Te Puia, Rotorua

Discover Māori culture, art and food surrounded by geothermal activity. Take the tour to learn about Te Puia's histoy and lineage and take a peek into how Māori people lived before European settlement.

Whakarewarewa Living Village, Rotorua

Have a rare glimpse of traditional Māori life in a fully functional village surrounded by geothermal sights. Experience a Māori cultural performance and try a geothermal *hāngi* meal at the on-site cafe.

Mataatua: The House That Came Home, Whakātane

Discover ancient Māori rituals and traditions in the restored Mataatua Wharenui. The fully carved house is the ancestral home of the Ngāti Awa people and provides a fascinating setting to hear their stories.

 Scan to find more things to do in Central North Island online

LOWER NORTH ISLAND

RURAL | CULTURAL | SCENERY

Experience
Lower North
Island
online

LOWER NORTH ISLAND
Trip Builder

The lower North Island is a prime example of the unique concentration of diverse landscapes for which New Zealand is famed: rolling farmland, snow-capped mountain chains, surf-ready beaches and wild river gorges all sit within short driving distance.

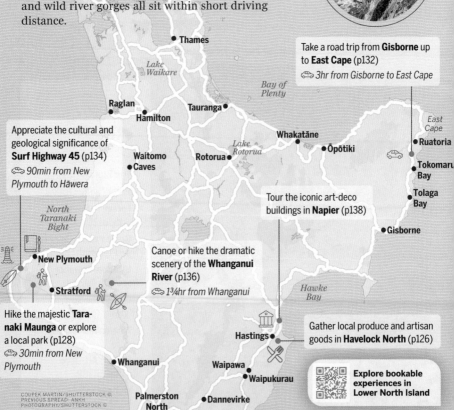

Thames

Lake Waikare

Bay of Plenty

Take a road trip from **Gisborne** up to **East Cape** (p132)
🚗 *3hr from Gisborne to East Cape*

Raglan
Hamilton
Tauranga

East Cape

Appreciate the cultural and geological significance of **Surf Highway 45** (p134)
🚗 *90min from New Plymouth to Hāwera*

Waitomo Caves
Rotorua
Lake Rotorua

Whakatāne
Ōpōtiki

Ruatoria
Tokomaru Bay
Tolaga Bay

North Taranaki Bight

Tour the iconic art-deco buildings in **Napier** (p138)

New Plymouth

Canoe or hike the dramatic scenery of the **Whanganui River** (p136)
🚗 *1¾hr from Whanganui*

Gisborne

Stratford

Hawke Bay

Hike the majestic **Taranaki Maunga** or explore a local park (p128)
🚗 *30min from New Plymouth*

Hastings

Gather local produce and artisan goods in **Havelock North** (p126)

Whanganui
Waipawa
Waipukurau

Palmerston North
Dannevirke

Explore bookable experiences in Lower North Island

Practicalities

ARRIVING

Wellington International Airport
Venturing north from Wellington, bear east towards sunny Hawke's Bay, or west toward scenic Taranaki – each a distinct launch pad for further exploration. Flights to Napier or New Plymouth run regularly.

MONEY

Cash is rarely needed, although it may be useful to have $10 to $20 for *koha* (donations) at certain Māori cultural sites.

FIND YOUR WAY

The Napier i-SITE is centrally located. New Plymouth's Puke Ariki is an i-SITE, museum and library with excellent wi-fi.

WHERE TO STAY

Place	Pro/Con
New Plymouth	Convenient for hiking, restaurants, beaches and galleries. Plenty of camping options.
Napier	Best nightlife in Hawke's Bay. Art-deco capital and close to airport.
Havelock North	Plentiful boutique options. Excellent cafes and restaurants, plus wineries.
Gisborne	Relaxed coastal vibe with lots of affordable options. Ideal base for surfers.
Whanganui	Voted NZ's most beautiful small city.

EATING & DRINKING

Fresh produce abounds in Hawke's Bay, with numerous farmers markets and opportunities to pick your own. Wineries in the region are also highly regarded, especially for red wine. Taranaki's Manaia is the bread capital.

Fish and chips A Kiwi classic in Ōpunake.

Feijoas A uniquely delicious fruit harvested around April and May (pictured left top).

Best coffee
Hawthorne Coffee Roasters (p141)

Must-try sparkling wine
Alpha Domus (p141)

GETTING AROUND

Car Necessary for regional sightseeing and those that wish to be time-flexible.

Bus Daily connections available between the main regional centres, with stops at most rural towns.

Bicycle Ideal for within the cities, or cycling around the Hawke's Bay wineries.

LOWER NORTH ISLAND FIND YOUR FEET

JAN–MAR
Surf's up on both sides of the country; busiest time for festivals.

APR–JUN
Shoulder season brings fewer crowds but still relatively mild temperatures.

JUL–SEP
Watch coastal storms and visit the blooming rhododendrons in New Plymouth.

OCT–DEC
Prime time for spotting lambs and daffodils as temperatures climb.

23 FORAGE
in Havelock North

PRODUCE | MARKET | ARTISAN

Hawke's Bay is a champion of wine, but the hot, dry climate earns the region another title: the Fruit Bowl of New Zealand. The fertile Heretaunga plains are a patchwork of orchards, vineyards and farmland, and there's no better place to sample the local fare than the serene village of Havelock North, nestled in the Te Mata Peak foothills.

How to

Getting around The village is compact, but wider exploration requires private transport. Cycling is a popular activity on the Bay's flat roads.

When to go Summer harvest begins in December with asparagus, strawberries and artichokes, while the Bay's famed stone fruit are late-summer staples.

Love figs? Te Mata Figs has a dedicated cafe paying homage to its namesake.

Got kids? Arataki Honey provides an educational, interactive and tasty experience.

Map: Ya Bon French Baker · Mangateretere · Te Awanga · Hastings · Clifton · Strawberry Patch · Black Barn Growers' Market · Havelock North · Birdwoods Gallery · Te Mata Peak · Red Bridge · Maraetotara Falls · Ocean Beach · Waimārama Beach store · 0 5 km · 0 2.5 miles

Local fare Start your weekend as the locals do: stocking up on fresh produce at the **Black Barn Growers' Market**. The market's rustic stalls, set under a leafy canopy and surrounded by vines, make an ideal backdrop for browsing and people-watching. Just don't be surprised if you end up with a locally roasted coffee or freshly baked goodie in your hands before long!

Strawberry fields Continue your day of foraging at the **Strawberry Patch**, a local institution where hand-picking your own berries is the order of the day. Pick-your-own is not the only drawcard here: the long queues – often visible from the road on a hot summers' day – are testament to the popularity of the home-made Real Fruit Ice Cream, a delightfully fresh take

Above Foraging for strawberries
Right Waimarama Beach

☼ Favourite Outdoor Picnic Spots

Take some locally sourced goodies to Ocean Beach, where a picnic can be paired with a swim and a stroll. Or trade the picnic on the beach with some much loved fish and chips from the Waimārama Beach store.

Alternatively, grab your bike and stock up on baked treats from Ya Bon French Baker (which also has a stall at the Black Barn Growers' Market), before heading out to the freshwater favourite, Maraetotara Falls, for a picnic and swim followed by a coffee or ice cream at Red Bridge before cycling back to town.

■ **Recommended by Liv Glazebrook**
local foodie
@kitchenoftreats

on the frozen treat that has long been a Kiwi classic.

Treat yourself If you're not too sweeted out, take a visit to the quaint oasis at **Birdwoods Gallery**. The sprawling lawn will keep kids occupied with space to play, while parents can enjoy the peace of the sculpture garden. The old-school sweet shop stocks every kind of sweet in traditional glass jars, while the cafe offers a basic but delicious menu. After your meal, check out the Gallery – a carefully curated gift shop in a beautifully restored chapel.

24

Go Sea to Sky in
NEW PLYMOUTH

HIKES | PARKS | MOUNTAINS

▬▬▬ 'Getting out there' has never been easier with an assortment of outdoor pursuits on New Plymouth's doorstep. Naturally, region-defining Taranaki Maunga invites inspection from all angles, but the plethora of world-class beaches, parks and gardens shouldn't be overlooked.

SIMONE BETZ/GETTY IMAGES ©

🗺 How to

Getting around New Plymouth offers a variety of urban trails and parks, easily walkable from the town centre. The national park is 30 minutes' drive from downtown.

When to go Temperatures are highest between December and March, making it a popular festival period, including the TSB Festival of Lights and WOMAD.

Hike carefully Check online for track conditions. Mountain weather changes notoriously quickly, so be prepared. Tell someone your plans.

WESTEND61/GETTY IMAGES ©

The Coastal Walkway

Frequented by pedestrians and cyclists, this popular coastal path hugs the foreshore for 13 uninterrupted kilometres, with ample access points and sites of interest. New Zealand–born artist Len Lye's iconic **Wind Wand** towers over the city waterfront, and stunning **Te Rewa Rewa bridge** mimics the mechanics of a breaking wave, framing Taranaki Maunga perfectly on a clear day.

MARTIN VLNAS/SHUTTERSTOCK ©

Pukekura Park

New Plymouth's famed gardens strike a perfect balance between hive of activity and peaceful sanctuary. The idyllic **Sports Ground** was a key filming location in Tom Cruise's *The Last Samurai*, as well as being voted one of the most beautiful cricket ovals in the world. Continue past ponds and waterfalls, crossing the picturesque

🚶 A Local Favourite

The riverside **Te Henui Walkway** runs perpendicular to the more famous **Coastal Walkway**, linking Fitzroy Beach to the leafy suburb of Welbourn. A preferred refuge for locals from the masses of beachfront tourists, the numerous reserves, gardens, and even two *pā* sites along the way make for a fascinating stroll.

Above left Taranaki Maunga
Left Poet's Bridge, Pukekura Park
Above Dawson Falls (p131), Egmont National Park

Poet's Bridge (whose namesake is in fact a racehorse) to visit the lakefront teahouse. The **Bowl of Brooklands** is surely one of the world's most beautiful concert venues (just ask Elton John), and adjacent **Brooklands Zoo** exhibits meerkats, monkeys and alpaca, among others.

Pukeiti Gardens

The expansive Pukeiti Gardens in the *maunga's* western foothills showcase a surprising collection of exotic rhododendron dells among thriving native bush. Visit between July and October to see more than 1250 species explode in colourful winter bloom.

Taranaki Maunga

With more than 300km of trail, there is something for hikers of all ages and skill levels in the near-perfectly circular boundaries of **Te Papakura o Taranaki** (Egmont National Park).

Dawson Falls Visitor Centre on the *maunga's* southeast slopes is a versatile starting point. Prepare to be enchanted

✿ The Festival of Lights

In the summer months, New Plymouth's Pukekura Park plays host to one of the most visually stunning events in the New Zealand calendar: the TSB Festival of Lights.

On summer days from December to February, the picturesque gardens hum with crowds seeking family-friendly fun and live performances. The true magic is revealed as night falls, with the park's trails, lakes and clearings transformed into an LED wonderland that must be seen to be believed.

Replete with acres of illuminated sculptures, interactive installations, rainbow waterfalls and futuristic tunnels, the festival still grows each year. Best of all – it's entirely free.

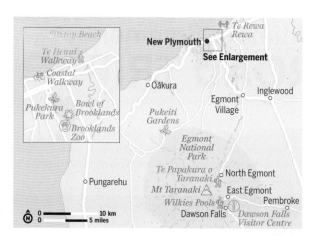

Left Pukekura Park
Below Te Rewa Rewa Bridge

as you make your way through 'goblin' forests, twisted labyrinths of young trees covered in ferns and mosses of every conceivable shade of green. Even the access road is magical, with voracious forest threatening to re-swallow the narrow strip of pavement. Notable short hikes beginning from the visitor centre include the family-friendly **Wilkies Pools** and the **Kapuni Loop Track** to the eponymous waterfall.

While the forested lower slopes provide shelter from inclement weather, the breathtaking upper slopes are best visited in clear, calm conditions. Despite its gentle appearance, summiting the *maunga* should be attempted only by fit and experienced hikers, due to its steep approach and volatile weather. On a clear day, the summit offers unmatched 270-degree views of the equidistant coastline.

For those not afflicted by summit fever, the multiday **Pouakai Circuit** takes hikers past the active erosion scar of Boomerang Slip, the towering Dieffenbach Cliffs and the ochre waters of the Kokowai Stream. For the time-poor, the **Pouakai Crossing** is a 19km subsection that can be walked in a single day and includes the Circuit's crown jewel: the reflective **Pouakai Tarn**.

25 Ultimate Summer **ROAD TRIP**

ROAD TRIP | BEACHES | CULTURE

Steeped in Māori culture and natural beauty, Tairāwhiti Gisborne is replete with golden sand beaches, pristine waters and tight-knit rural communities. The coastal highway beyond sun-drenched Gisborne offers a quintessential Kiwi road trip.

DAVID WALL/ALAMY STOCK PHOTO ©

☼ Local Beaches

Gisborne is 'the first place in the world to see the sun' and locals put that ample sun to good use at three stunning beaches. Waikanae is centrally located and ideal for swimming, Makorori (pictured above) offers the best snorkelling and diving, and Wainui is renowned for its surf and white sand.

ᨈᨅ Trip Notes

Getting around Venture north from Gisborne to the East Cape Lighthouse. Return, or continue around to Ōhope. Bolt through in a day, or travel slow by camping along the coast.

When to go Summer guarantees higher temperatures. Expect major crowds if your trip coincides with Gisborne's New Years' festival, Rhythm and Vines. Beyond Gisborne the region is sparsely populated.

Learn some te reo Māori The local *iwi* will appreciate it.

■ Recommended by Annabel Campbell
Gisborne artist
@annabelcampbellart

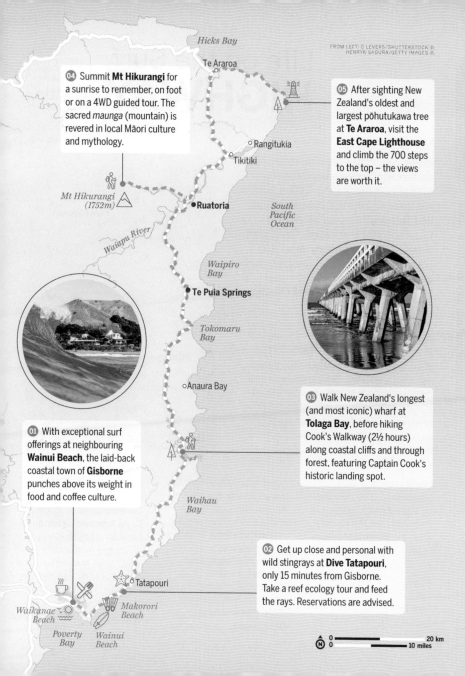

04 Summit **Mt Hikurangi** for a sunrise to remember, on foot or on a 4WD guided tour. The sacred *maunga* (mountain) is revered in local Māori culture and mythology.

Hicks Bay

Te Araroa

FROM LEFT: © LEVERS/SHUTTERSTOCK © HENRYK SADURA/GETTY IMAGES ©

05 After sighting New Zealand's oldest and largest pōhutukawa tree at **Te Araroa**, visit the **East Cape Lighthouse** and climb the 700 steps to the top – the views are worth it.

○ Rangitukia

○ Tikitiki

Mt Hikurangi (1752m)

● **Ruatoria**

South Pacific Ocean

Waiapu River

Waipiro Bay

● **Te Puia Springs**

Tokomaru Bay

○ Anaura Bay

03 Walk New Zealand's longest (and most iconic) wharf at **Tolaga Bay**, before hiking Cook's Walkway (2½ hours) along coastal cliffs and through forest, featuring Captain Cook's historic landing spot.

01 With exceptional surf offerings at neighbouring **Wainui Beach**, the laid-back coastal town of **Gisborne** punches above its weight in food and coffee culture.

Waihau Bay

02 Get up close and personal with wild stingrays at **Dive Tatapouri**, only 15 minutes from Gisborne. Take a reef ecology tour and feed the rays. Reservations are advised.

○ Tatapouri

Makorori Beach

Waikanae Beach

Poverty Bay

Wainui Beach

0 — 20 km
0 — 10 miles

26 Life on the Surf HIGHWAY

BEACHES | HISTORY | VOLCANO

Named for the generations of surfers who have combed the coast for the best breaks, the 109km Surf Highway 45 between New Plymouth and Hāwera offers far more than just swell and black sand. Geological wonders and historic cultural sites pepper the roadside as you cruise the green rolling hills under the watchful gaze of the hulking Taranaki Maunga.

How to

How long? It is 90 minutes of total driving time between New Plymouth and Hāwera.

When to go December to March offers the best swimming and surfing. Taranaki Maunga's sheer mass means it is frequently shrouded in cloud – take any opportunity you get for a clear photo!

Hungry? Consider stopping in for fresh fish and chips in Opunake, a classic Kiwi beachfront delicacy.

Map:
Tasman Sea
Waitara
Paritutu Rock
Puke Ariki Museum
Back Beach
New Plymouth
Oākura
Koru pā
Egmont Village
Warea
Okato
Cape Egmont Lighthouse
Parihaka
Mt Taranaki
Egmont National Park
Stratford
Oaonui
Te Namu pā
Eltham
Opunake
Opunake Beach
Pihama
Otakeho
Tāwhiti Museum
Manaia
Hāwera
0 10 km
0 5 miles
N

Local learnings Surf Highway 45 is bookended by **Puke Ariki** (p140) in New Plymouth and the visually stunning **Tawhiti Museum** (p140) in Hāwera, each providing fascinating cultural and geographical exhibits in engaging formats.

Geological wonders Taranaki's black-sand beaches are testament to the area's volcanic origins. At New Plymouth's west end, a short, steep climb up **Paritutu Rock** provides sweeping views of the city and nearby **Sugar Loaf Islands** (remnants of an ancient volcanic crater). Kids will love sliding down the steep dunes to neighbouring **Back Beach**, a popular spot for surfers and sunset-chasers.

Colonial history Today, **Cape Egmont Lighthouse** provides a postcard-ready photo, but its erection in 1877 was marred by events unfolding at nearby Parihaka, a prosperous Māori settlement believed to have been the country's

WALTER BIBIKOW/GETTY IMAGES ©

🌊 Local Surf Spots

Taranaki's semicircular coastline exposes it to 180 degrees of swell and wind directions – so on any given day you're bound to find a wave somewhere!

Around New Plymouth, Fitzroy and Oākura are quality beach breaks suitable for beginners and experts alike. Banks are constantly changing but look for the peaks around the river mouths. To the south, Opunake beach is a friendly beginner's wave that works best on a northerly wind.

Alternatively, search and you will be rewarded – numerous roads radiate from the Surf Highway to the coast, though many of these are rocky and for experienced surfers only.

■ **Recommended by Magnus Holding**
an enthusiastic surfer and photographer
@_mags.nz

largest. After *iwi* peacefully resisted the confiscation of their land to European settlers, the Crown forcefully disbanded the village, arresting resistance leaders. In 2017, the Crown formally apologised with pecuniary reparations, labelling its actions 'among the most shameful in the history of our land'.

Nowadays, the Parihaka site is home to the tomb of *iwi* leader Te Whiti, though development of a visitor centre was greenlit in 2020.

Other notable *pā* (fort) sites along the Surf Highway include **Oākura's Koru pā**, showcasing unique use of stone, and **Te Namu pā**, set on an imposing headland near Opunake.

Above Cape Egmont Lighthouse

27 Whanganui
JOURNEY

SCENERY | ADVENTURE | HISTORY

▬▬▬ A once critical transport route for Māori and early European settlers, the Whanganui River is now a recreational mecca of great cultural significance. Be transported through the untouched beauty of the Whanganui National Park on this ancient waterway, by canoe, jetboat or historic paddle steamer or stay on solid ground and cycle or hike the adjoining Mountains to Sea trail.

🗺 How to

Getting here Pipiriki, a common launch point, is 75 minutes' drive from Whanganui.

When to go Open year-round, but October through April means less chance of a rain-out. Hut and campsite reservations are essential (bookings.doc. govt.nz).

Marae visit The Tīeke hut/campground has a unique opportunity to visit a *marae*. Soak up the history and partake in a *pōwhiri* (welcome). Remember cash for a *koha* (donation): $10 to $30 each.

[Map showing the Whanganui region with locations: Whangamomona, Whakahoro, Raurimu, Whanganui National Park, National Park Village, Aotuhia, Bridge to Nowhere, Whanganui River, Ōhakune, Raetihi, Pipiriki, Matahiwi, Waverley, Whanganui River Rd, Parikino, Waitotara, Kai Iwi, Whanganui, scale 0–20 km / 0–10 miles]

Not just any river Springing from the volcanic slopes of Tongariro National Park, the 290km Whanganui River snakes its way through untamed wilderness before reaching the sea at Whanganui city.

It is New Zealand's longest navigable river and was officially recognised in 2017 as a legal person.

Far from gimmick, this novel recognition is due to the traditional symbiotic relationship between local *iwi* and the river (known to *iwi* as te Ata o Whangan-ui), and legally entrenches the river's long-term protection and restoration.

Back to the past The **Whanganui National Park**

was established around the river's upper reaches. The park is remote and rugged, so much so that original attempts to settle and cultivate the area were abandoned. The iconic **Bridge to Nowhere** remains a haunting relic of this bygone era, just a short walk from the river's banks. It was built in 1936 to

🚶 Whanganui Journey as a Walk

The Whanganui Journey is one of New Zealand's esteemed Great Walks, though in this case it's more of a paddle.

The most common starting points are Taumarunui and Ōhakune; however, destination trips to the Bridge to Nowhere often begin from Pipiriki. The 145km journey comprises a multiday canoe or kayak downstream, finishing up in Whanganui, a recently recognised Unesco World City of Design.

The trip can be completed independently, or through one of several tour companies providing guided excursions of varying lengths with equipment provided.

service a failed settlement of returned soldiers, but upon completion, only three farmers still remained. Today, the picturesque bridge is accessible via boat, mountain bike or on foot.

The riverside road connecting Whanganui city to Pipiriki, a common launch point for journeys on the river, is dotted with tiny settlements. These once relied on the river for transportation until the road was built in 1934.

The new addition of informative roadside billboards describing the region's history elevates this already stunning journey.

Above Canoeing, Whanganui River

■ With input from Jeremy Smith
*Heritage Manager of
the Napier Art Deco Trust
artdeconapier.com*

Napier: Art-Deco Capital

HOW AN EARTHQUAKE CAUSED THE CITY'S REBIRTH

Napier's catastrophic 1931 earthquake remains New Zealand's deadliest natural disaster, claiming at least 256 lives. Yet from tragedy, citizens seized the unique opportunity to rebuild with proud, contemporary flourish. The character precinct that literally rose from the ashes remains resplendent today, earning the title 'Art Deco Capital of the World'.

At 10.47am on 3 February 1931, the clock of Napier's band rotunda stopped forever. Moments later, the ground began to sway, and in just two and a half minutes, the grand seaside town of Napier was in ruins.

The 7.8-magnitude quake left all but a few of Napier's buildings completely destroyed. What the quake didn't flatten was quickly levelled by fires. Attempts to curb the spread of flames were hampered by burst water pipes. The destruction was immense, and few buildings, such as the historic Hawke's Bay Club building, were saved only by the grace of changing winds.

The Arrival of Art Deco

The Napier rebuild was a tonic to local unemployment in the midst of the Great Depression, and authorities issued a clear and simple edict: the new township must be safe, modern and cheap. There was also significant time-pressure, with many residents being temporarily housed in government-supplied canvas tents either on their properties or in 'tent towns' at local parks.

Despite not yet bearing its modern name, 'art deco', a prevailing trend that originated in Europe, satisfied many of the above criteria. Heritage Manager of the Napier Art Deco Trust, Jeremy Smith, explains that the art-deco movement 'celebrated the modern age, the machine and synthetic materials', with simple designs that captured an 'optimistic and energetic spirit'. Think basic geometrical motifs (including chevrons and zigzags) and bright, pastel colours. Decorative themes include suns and skyscrapers, as well as symbols of speed, power and flight.

Left Masonic Hotel
Centre National Tobacco Building
Right Art-deco detailing

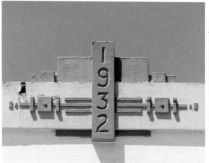

While art deco became the predominant style, the influence of Spanish Mission, Stripped Classical and Classical Moderne styles are also evident. Incredibly, 111 buildings were constructed in Napier's centre between 1931 and 1933. The character revitalisation was accompanied by the establishment of wider streets and the introduction of underground power and telephone lines. The earthquake also uplifted 225 hectares of former seabed into new land able to be developed.

> Incredibly, 111 buildings were constructed in Napier's centre between 1931 and 1933.

Art Deco Today

Today, the art-deco precinct is preserved and celebrated by the Art Deco Trust, established in 1985. Notable examples of art-deco architecture include the photographer-friendly National Tobacco Building; the Masonic Hotel, where Queen Elizabeth II once stayed; and the Auckland Savings Bank, where traditional Māori artistry features prominently. While Napier is the prize showpiece for art-deco buildings, many can also be seen in nearby Hastings.

Though much of the city's art-deco architecture is easily viewed on a casual stroll around Napier's city core, taking a guided tour with a volunteer from the Art Deco Trust (on foot, or in stylish vintage cars) enriches the experience with fascinating historical context and anecdotes. 'Three-hundred and sixty-four days a year, our local volunteers share their love of this great town on walking and vintage car tours,' says Jeremy. 'Our guides are dedicated, extremely knowledgeable and passionate about Napier's art-deco-era history and present-day stories.'

The Art Deco Festival

Every February, Napier's population practically doubles and the city steps back in time to celebrate the era of art deco.

The lynchpin of the Hawke's Bay social calendar, the festival features over 200 different events, including walking tours, vintage-car parades, fashion shows and concerts. Of course, era-appropriate costume is strongly encouraged.

Jeremy Smith revels in the atmosphere. 'People from across New Zealand flock to Napier to be a part of the festival – their fashion, cars, spirit and style brings magic to the streets. The spectacle is not one to be missed!'

For more information visit artdecofestival.co.nz.

Listings

BEST OF THE REST

 Rainy-Day Activities

Govett-Brewster Art Gallery/Len Lye Centre

Behind the mind-bending exterior lies New Plymouth's state-of-the-art contemporary art museum. Don't miss adjoining Monica's Eatery for breakfast or lunch.

Puke Ariki

A museum, library and i-SITE makes this waterfront complex a one-stop tourism shop in New Plymouth. The museum is free, interactive and well thought out.

Tawhiti Museum

An innovative local-history museum in Hāwera that feels more like a small theme park. Life-size figures and scale modelling brings history to life.

Historic Cape Lighthouse & Museum

Hard to miss with its replica lighthouse, this Taranaki museum provides detailed accounts of the region's history, including the infamous Crown seizure of Parihaka.

National Aquarium

Enjoy plenty of close encounters at this family favourite situated on Napier's stunning Marine Pde. Make sure you ask someone about the scandalous escape of Inky the Octopus!

 Regional Road-Trip Stops

Tui Factory

One of the country's ubiquitous beer brands brews in this iconic tower overlooking the Mangatainoka River. Explore the grounds, taste a beer and remember to check out the souvenir shop.

Manawatū Gorge Track

Stretch your legs mid-road trip and hike a portion of the scenic 11km track, surrounded by native forests, birds and the river far below.

Feilding Sale Yards

Pretend you're a farmer and attend one of the country's largest weekly livestock auctions. Don't worry, a real farmer will ensure you know what's going on!

NZ Rugby Museum

Have a ball at the official museum of the nation's beloved sport in Palmerston North, discovering its origins and anecdotes. Kids can test out their skills too!

Bell Rock Loop Track

To break up the winding drive from Napier to Gisborne, hike to the 'Pride Rock' of Hawke's Bay. Three hours return, medium intensity.

 Pastries & Coffee, Please

BABCO $

A perfect pit stop in Palmerston North, the Brick Artisan Bread Company has a cabinet loaded with fresh breads and pastries to die for. Don't miss the custard-filled beignets.

Six Sisters Coffee House, Napier

Knead $

A popular doughnut shop in New Plymouth's suburbs offering two releases daily to keep up with the demand. Has limited hours and a guaranteed queue, so plan your visit first.

Ozone Coffee Roasters $$

Industrial-style cafe in central New Plymouth with a bean-store. A spacious, relaxed environment to pull out your laptop.

Six Sisters Coffee House $$

Part of an extremely iconic row of villas on Napier's Marine Pde. The peanut butter cookie slice will rival the best you've ever had.

Hawthorne Coffee Roasters $

One of Havelock North's most esteemed coffee houses, Hawthorne serves a scone and a brew worth going back for.

Ya Bon French Baker $$

This stylish artisan bakery combines pastries, coffee and a fresh deli with goodies such as imported cheeses, chorizo and sourdough.

 ## Cycle the Bridge Pa Wine Triangle

Abbey Cellar

A winery that also houses a brewery, Abbey Cellar is an idyllic weekend spot to enjoy live music and platters in an outdoor picnic area.

Sileni Estate

Prepare to be wowed from the moment you turn into Sileni's long, majestic driveway. Equally impressive is its internationally recognised wine.

Alpha Domus

On its way to becoming a fully certified organic vineyard and winery, the tales behind the winery are as captivating as its wines.

Trinity Hill

Live music and food trucks make this winery particularly family-friendly; its sprawling lawn and outdoor games keep everyone entertained.

Oākura Beach

Oak Estate

Oak Estate has lovely outdoor seating around a photogenic barn house.

Coastal Swim & Surf

Muriwai Beach

Rural beach settlement with a stunning coastline. Arrive in style on the Gisborne City Vintage Railway.

Oākura Beach

New Plymouth's neighbouring surf town is an easy beach escape with a relaxed vibe; stay over at the Holiday Park right on the beachfront.

Mahia Beach

Majestic scenery, prime fishing and small-town vibes await. Climb to Mokotahi Lookout at sunset for magical views across the water.

Waimārama Beach

The best surf in Hawke's Bay, this is a popular weekend destination for locals. It has good swimming, golden sand and an expansive local store. Be mindful of dangerous currents.

Porangahau Beach

With plenty of water-sport hire options, the beach is only a few kilometres from a hill bearing the world's longest place name (85 characters!).

 Scan to find more things to do in Lower North Island online

LOWER NORTH ISLAND REVIEWS

WELLINGTON

CITY LIFE | CULTURE | CRAFT BEER

Experience Wellington online

Visit **Garage Project** and savour Wellington's eclectic urban craft-beer scene (p151)
🚶 5min from CBD

Ditch the crowds for endemic wildlife on secluded **Kāpiti Island** (p156)
🚌 80min from CBD plus ⛴ 20min ferry

Paraparaumu

Tararua Forest Park   *Mt Holdsworth*

Paekākāriki

Mt Hector

Visit **Martinborough** to enjoy artisanal food and wines (p152)
🚗 15min from CBD

Pukerua Bay

Mana Island   Plimmerton

Featherston

Tauherenikau

Go behind the scenes at the **Wētā Cave** and nearby filming locations (p146)
🚗 15min from CBD

Upper Hutt

Petone   **Lower Hutt**

Wellington

● Wainuiomata

Rub shoulders with locals in the artsy neighbourhood of **Newtown** (p148)
🚋 10min from CBD

Eastbourne

Explore the endless bays of Wellington's rugged **south coast** (p154)
🚲 2-4hr loop

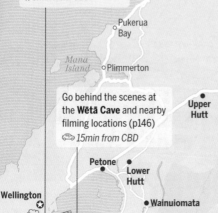

WELLINGTON
Trip Builder

Affectionately known as the world's 'coolest little capital', Wellington sits in a wild, windy horseshoe-shaped harbour. The city's beating heart is its compact, cosmopolitan centre, quickly giving way to rugged natural surrounds, meaning adventure is never far away.

Explore bookable experiences in Wellington

Practicalities

TOP: YUQCHEUNG/SHUTTERSTOCK ©
BOTTOM: ANTHIA CUMMING/GETTY IMAGES ©

ARRIVING

The airport is only 6km from the city, so ride-shares or taxis are most convenient. Cost-conscious travellers can bus but will have to walk the last 700m.

MONEY

Cash is obsolete. Save money by scoping food trucks and catch a local (free) gig or comedy show.

FIND YOUR WAY

Find free wi-fi at the waterfront, Te Papa Museum, the library and at most cafes.

WHERE TO STAY

Place	Pro/Con
Thorndon	Lacking charm, but convenient for sightseeing, Parliament, stadium events and transport hubs.
Oriental Bay	Postcard views of Wellington. Close to beaches, cafes and Mt Victoria.
Cuba St	Central to shopping, restaurants, nightlife (loud at night). Ideal without a car.
Newtown	Cheaper prices, neighbourhood feel. Diverse culinary options. Central to airport, city, beaches.

EATING & DRINKING

Cuba St (pictured top left) and its surrounds is the undisputed centre of Wellington's culinary universe. The laneways are laden with culinary secrets, waiting to be discovered. Don't miss Mt Cook's Hiakai for an innovative degustation emphasising native ingredients and traditional Māori cooking techniques: reservations are essential.

Best winery
Poppies of Martinborough (p158)

Must-try salted caramel cookies
Leeds Street Bakery (p153)

GETTING AROUND

Walking and public transport
The city is mostly walkable, and purchasing a pre-paid Snapper card will provide discounted bus and train fares.

Train The train station has connections to the Kāpiti Coast and Wairarapa, as well as functioning as a bus depot.

WELLINGTON FIND YOUR FEET

JAN–MAR
Visit artisanal Martinborough or swim in the crisp Pacific Ocean.

APR–JUN
Windy days induce craft-beer tours, shopping and cinema visits.

JUL–SEP
A solid line-up of indoor food, drink and cultural festivals.

OCT–DEC
Warmer, sunnier days pave the way for cycling and hiking.

28 Movie Magic in **WELLYWOOD**

TOUR | CINEMA | FILM SETS

Home to multiple world-class film studios and a lion's share of talented filmmakers, Wellington was recently named a world Creative City of Film by Unesco. 'Wellywood' heartily embraces its new cinematic reputation by offering public access to studios, shooting locations and even a homage to Los Angeles' vaunted Hollywood sign (with a characteristically breezy twist).

AMBLING IMAGES/ALAMY STOCK PHOTO ©

🗺 How to

Getting around Buses run regularly to Wētā Workshop in Miramar, and organised tours start from the city centre. Having a private car puts a DIY film location tour within easy reach.

Tours Wētā Studio Tours occur on-site, and tour companies Rover Rings Tours and Adventure Safari Ltd organise half- or full-day trips to film locations around greater Wellington.

Timing Consider coinciding your visit with the International Film Festival in November.

Behind the scenes Sleepy Miramar Peninsula is home to Oscar-winner Peter Jackson, as well as two globally renowned studios: **Wētā Workshop** (*Avatar, King Kong* and *Lord of the Rings*); and **Park Road Production** (*The Last Samurai, The Adventures of Tintin*). Wētā Workshop offers popular tours, giving behind-the-scenes insight into how props, costumes and miniature effects can create epic fantasy worlds on the silver screen. Don't miss the **Wētā Cave**, a mini museum replete with souvenirs.

On location *LOTR* fans may already know that much of the trilogy was shot in greater Wellington: Rivendell (Kaitoke Regional Park); the Paths of the Dead (Putangirua Pinnacles); Osgiliath Wood (Waitārere Forest); as well as various scenes in the city's parks. But geographic diversity, modern infrastructure and esteemed post-production

☆ Experience More Film

The iconic Aro Video in the inner-city suburb of Aro Valley is one of the few remaining video stores in the country. It holds an incredible collection of cult and arthouse films and you'd need years to work through its collection.

If you're in Wellington for some time, then I'd recommend joining the Wellington Film Society. It's a chance to watch eclectic films on the big screen at the Embassy Theatre. It's year-round, except during the New Zealand International Film Festival, the film festival that reportedly has the best per capita attendance in the world.

■ **Recommended by Brannavan Gnanalingam**
novelist, lawyer, columnist and (former) film reviewer based in Wellington.
@Brannavan

resources has made Wellington a stand-in for more than just Middle-earth. Other films shot here include *The Hobbit, Skull Island* and *What We Do In the Shadows*.

Popcorn time If you'd prefer not to peek behind the curtain, Wellington boasts many boutique cinemas. The inner city is home to the famous **Embassy Theatre**, which has been screening since 1926 (including the world premiere of *The Hobbit: An Unexpected Journey*). For a more retro movie-going experience, try Miramar's **Roxy Cinema** (and restaurant) – owned by Wētā Workshop's co-founders.

Left Wētā Workshop
Above Wētā Cave

29 Wellington's
MELTING POT

DIVERSE | VINTAGE | CULTURE

Though renowned for its annual block-party-style festival, the neighbourhood of Newtown is a worthwhile year-round destination. A cultural melting pot, the diverse suburb is dripping with community and humming with life. Escape the CBD and do as the locals do, experiencing the grit, colour and aromas of a community that reflects NZ's unique cultural patchwork.

How to

Getting here Most southbound bus routes from the city centre transit through Newtown.

Further exploration Weather permitting, hike the spine of the Southern Walkway from the Mt Victoria Summit to Wellington Hospital for some inner-city tranquillity.

Animal lovers Our furry friends at the SPCA (five minutes from the hospital) love cuddles, and also nearby is the Wellington Zoo, although its larger animals are a bit more standoffish.

Adventure on foot Though easily accessed by bus, Newtown is also the endpoint of a particularly scenic section of the Southern Walkway trail. Start at the popular **Mt Victoria summit**, but quickly trade the crowds for quiet solitude. Traversing the wooded ridgeline, the trail provides unbeaten views of the inner harbour and historic **Basin Reserve Cricket Ground**, and can include a short detour to the iconic 'Hobbits Hideaway' *Lord of the Rings* filming location.

Historically a blue-collar landing spot and now home to various diaspora, there's something for everyone in this unpretentious, effortlessly cool neighbourhood. From the vintage racks at Riddiford St's thrift stores to the fresh produce at the Saturday farmers market, there is also plenty to please the cost-conscious.

Fill your belly Naturally, the neighbourhood boasts authentic cuisine from all

☼ Newtown Festival

Every March, 11 blocks of Riddiford St (and numerous side streets) are closed to traffic and instead play home to 12 performance stages and over 400 festival stalls.

More than 80,000 visitors throng the streets each year, from those cloaked in costumes to those with young children in tow.

After its debut more than two decades ago, the event is a lock in every local's calendar, and captures the artistic and community-driven spirit for which the neighbourhood is famed (newtownfestival.org.nz/about-us).

corners of the globe. Highlights include the **Ramen Shop**, serving steaming bowls of well-priced goodness; and **Cicio Cacio**, which celebrates seasonal fare on its all-Italian menu.

There's also no shortage of quality vegan and vegetarian options. End the night with local live music at spacey **Moon Bar**, or choose from an extensive beer list at Latin-inspired **Bebemos**.

For the time-conscious, Newtown more than holds its own in Wellington's thriving coffee culture. Try a Double Brown among the work of local artists at **Black Coffee**, or enjoy a socially conscious brew at **People's Coffee**.

Above Newtown Festival

30 Not Just Beer
ESSENTIALS

ARTISANAL | HOPS | CULTURE

▬▬▬ Wellington's breweries are like its populace: innovative, fun and quirky. A close-knit brewing community has turned the 'coolest little capital' into the country's craft-beer epicentre. Discerning local clientele now expect quality and inventiveness at a minimum, so brewers increasingly strive to build experiences beyond just another pint to draw in the thirsty masses.

KRISTA ROSSOW/ALAMY STOCK PHOTO ©

🗺 How to

Getting around
Wellington's compact hospitality precinct is a pedestrian's paradise – seven official taprooms within five minutes of Cuba St! Craftbeercapital.com has a downloadable interactive map.

When to go A truly year-round pastime, with festivals in August (Beervana, the marquee event), October (Oktoberfest), December (Beers at the Basin), April (Hopstock – the fresh hop harvest) and May (BrewDay).

Like dogs? Most central breweries are dog-friendly.

KRISTA ROSSOW/ALAMY STOCK PHOTO ©

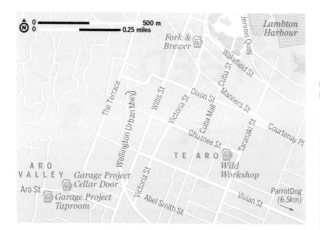

Left Brewery, Garage Project
Below Craft beer, Garage Project

Ringed by hills, Wellington's pedestrian-friendly CBD is its greatest asset. The city's army of urban microbrewers, challenged by limited space, have converted former industrial spaces into suds-producing powerhouses. Taprooms often share space with mash tuns, enabling guests to watch the magic (slowly) happen, final product in hand.

From small things... Excelling in a market that is deliciously saturated, pioneering brewery **Garage Project** was until recently little more than an ambitious upstart, brewing in a 50L kit out of a derelict former petrol station. The perennially innovative beer purveyors have since bloated to have multiple taprooms in central Wellington (and one in Auckland), and were recently named New Zealand's 2021 Champion Large Brewery.

Big things grow There's always a fresh invention in the Garage Project tanks. A recent venture that has quickly gained traction with Wellington beer lovers is the **Wild Workshop**: where weird and wacky recipes push the creative limits in Wonka-esque fashion. It's a dedicated space for wild, mixed culture and spontaneous ferments, meaning that unique flavours are quite literally divined from the very air and chattels of the workshop itself.

Even a trip to the washroom is a peek behind the scenes, as you overlook the spontaneous fermentation process. The shapeshifting menu features both beer and natural wine (from another project, 'Crushed'), meaning no two trips will ever be the same.

A Brewer's Insight

Brewers have so many materials to work with: malts, hops, yeast, fruits and ways to age...it's all ripe for play.

We're particularly proud of cult favourite IPA 'Pernicious Weed', recently releasing a 10% imperial edition for our 10-year anniversary. By contrast, we've just released 'Tiny', a non-alcoholic hazy IPA which required plenty of experimentation to perfect the flavour profile.

Further afield, I also recommend Fork & Brewer, an OG brewpub with an eclectic range of batch brews and guest taps, and ParrotDog, a retro brewpub serving tight, concise beers by Lyall Bay beach.

■ Recommended by Jos Ruffell
passionate dog walker and co-founder of Garage Project
@garageproject

31 An Artisanal **HOTBED**

VINEYARDS | LOCAL | TASTINGS

Martinborough has transformed from quiet countryside escape for Wellington's city slickers to hotbed for culinary artisans. With a climate and soil profile comparable to Burgundy, it is rightly heralded for its quality vineyards. But the sun-soaked village also boasts award-winning food, and boutique shopping around a thriving village square, not to mention gourmet olive oil straight from the grove.

DAVID WALL/ALAMY STOCK PHOTO ©

🗺 **How to**

Getting here Drive 70 minutes from Wellington, or take the train from Wellington to Featherston and transfer to the Martinborough bus. The township and vineyards can be navigated on foot, though bike or car is preferable.

When to go Visit during the long, dry summer, or for November's Toast Martinborough festival.

Well travelled? The streets were named for notable cities visited by the village's eponymous founder – how many have you visited?

AGEFOTOSTOCK/ALAMY STOCK PHOTO ©

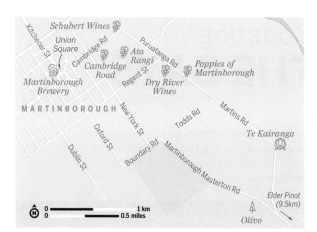

Left Te Kairanga
Below Olivo

🍷 Savouring a Pinot Noir

Pinot noir is the local speciality. It is a wine of subtle structure, and a character that is more feminine than masculine. It should have softness, elegance and a beautiful balance of black fruit with spice and oak.

Martinborough's climate provides growing conditions which focus on quality rather than quantity, and flavour rather than power.

Don't miss the pinot noir pioneers **Dry River Wines** and **Ata Rangi**, as well as local favourites the **Elder Pinot** and **Schubert Wines**. Visit **Poppies Martinborough** for the best pinot noir and platter pairing!

■ Recommended by Shayne Hammond *local viticulturist and general manager at Poppies of Martinborough poppiesmartinborough.co.nz*

What to taste Martinborough was once a humble service town for local sheep farmers. Over time, the primary industry has shifted from wool to wine, but the emphasis on local persists, attracting a second wave of culinary craftspeople to the village: coffee roasters, olive oil makers, restaurateurs and brewers alike.

Martinborough's trademark drop is a savoury, complex pinot noir, thanks to optimal growing conditions. The towering Tararuas create a dry climate, with free-draining alluvial soil. Hot days and cool nights ensure a lengthy ripening process, and the infamous Wellington wind keeps crop levels low, concentrating the fruit's flavour.

And where to taste it With a high density of small, family-owned wineries, **Puruatanga Road** on the village's north side is a must-visit. Here you'll find **Poppies of Martinborough**, where namesake winemaker Poppy Hammond is a charismatic fixture at tastings. After tasting, pair your favourite drop with a seasonal charcuterie, spotlighting local produce. Nearby **Cambridge Road** offers organically produced wine, while neighbouring **Te Kairanga** has an on-site gin distillery for those in search of the harder stuff.

Nowadays, Martinborough's artisanal pilgrims need not end their day at the cellar door. Continue the degustation with a tasting tray at **Martinborough Brewery**, or forego alcohol for a tour of **Olivo's** olive groves, studying the varieties and sampling the freshly pressed oils. Round out the day with a meal on picturesque **Union Square**.

32 Coasting
THE BAYS

VIEWS | CAFES | BEACHES

■■■■ Wellington's southern coastline is rugged and diverse, and with bays for days what better way to experience it than by bicycle? Soak up the impressive scenery and historic landmarks, re-energising at the plentiful cafe options along the way.

LIZ RITCHIE/SHUTTERSTOCK ©

🗺 Trip Notes

Getting around It costs about $75/60 per day to hire an e-bike/city bike.

What to wear Wellington is one of the windiest cities in the world, so it pays to dress warm and bring gloves. Consider bathers on a good day.

Route Using Oriental Bay as a reference point, explore the eastern bays around to the south coast, looping back to the city at Lyall or Island Bays.

🤿 Raw & Rugged

The treacherous and unforgiving waters off the south coast have sunk many a ship, resulting in a bounty of extremely popular local diving spots.

For non-divers, just watching the Cook Strait ferries battle white caps on a windy day makes for a nauseating sight.

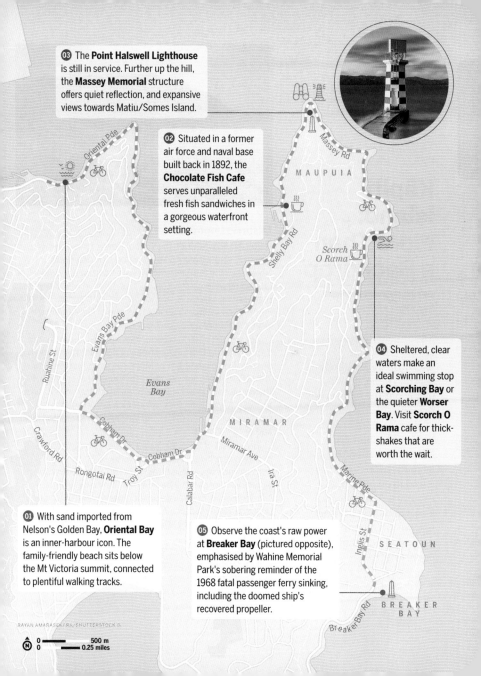

03 The **Point Halswell Lighthouse** is still in service. Further up the hill, the **Massey Memorial** structure offers quiet reflection, and expansive views towards Matiu/Somes Island.

02 Situated in a former air force and naval base built back in 1892, the **Chocolate Fish Cafe** serves unparalleled fresh fish sandwiches in a gorgeous waterfront setting.

04 Sheltered, clear waters make an ideal swimming stop at **Scorching Bay** or the quieter **Worser Bay**. Visit **Scorch O Rama** cafe for thickshakes that are worth the wait.

01 With sand imported from Nelson's Golden Bay, **Oriental Bay** is an inner-harbour icon. The family-friendly beach sits below the Mt Victoria summit, connected to plentiful walking tracks.

05 Observe the coast's raw power at **Breaker Bay** (pictured opposite), emphasised by Wahine Memorial Park's sobering reminder of the 1968 fatal passenger ferry sinking, including the doomed ship's recovered propeller.

MAUPUIA

Scorch O Rama

Evans Bay

MIRAMAR

SEATOUN

BREAKER BAY

Oriental Pde
Massey Rd
Shelly Bay Rd
Evans Bay Pde
Ruahine St
Cobham Dr
Crawford Rd
Rongotai Rd
Troy St
Cobham Dr
Miramar Ave
Calabar Rd
Ira St
Marine Pde
Inglis St
Breaker Bay Rd

0   500 m
0   0.25 miles
N

■ **With input from Leon Berard**
DOC ranger and avid bird photographer
@leonberardnz

Kāpiti Island: More Than a Backdrop

REGENERATION IN ACTION

Kāpiti Island is the horizon-defining backdrop for Wellington's coastal traffic, and its iconic outline is instantly recognisable on punnets of New Zealand's treasured Kāpiti Ice Cream. However, the island is more than just a backdrop: offering visitors a rich history, a neighbouring marine reserve and abundant natural photography opportunities.

Left Kāpiti Island
Centre Kārearea
Right Hihi

SAM LAWRENCE PHOTOGRAPHY/SHUTTERSTOCK ©

Historic Importance

Kāpiti Island was once the seat of power for expansive empires, strategically prized and fiercely defended. Nowadays the human residents are few, but the island is used for an equally vital purpose – one in which being regarded as a backdrop is not only advantageous, but also intentional. Today, Kāpiti Island is one of New Zealand's largest offshore predator-free islands.

According to Māori legend, the explorer Kupe created Kāpiti Island with a single stroke of his club. The island has been home to a number of Māori *iwi*, including the Ngāti Toa *iwi* and their notable chief Te Rauparaha, creator of the renowned *haka* 'Ka Mate' of All Blacks fame. A natural fortress, Kāpiti Island was strategically important as a foothold for control of the sea passage between the North and South Islands.

The arrival of Europeans saw settlers briefly use the island to rear livestock and hunt whales. Evidence of colonial industry persists, as 'try-pots' used to boil down whale blubber can still be found on the island's shores. Native species on the island soon became threatened by unsustainable resource management, and in 1897 the Crown designated the island a sanctuary. With that, the backdrop was set.

Pioneering naturalist Richard Henry soon took up residence and implemented initiatives that were successful in stabilising wildlife numbers. The Department of Conservation (DOC) has continued this work in recent years, eventually making Kāpiti the largest island in the world to have eradicated rats.

The Marine Reserve & Photography Opportunities

Since 1992 the waters around the island have also been protected. Leon Berard, the local DOC Marine Reserve Ranger, explains that the Kāpiti Coast is abundant in marine life thanks to nutrient-rich waters coming from the South Island's west coast. 'The marine reserve provides the highest level of protection to a marine area, allowing it to recover without fishing pressure', says Leon.

By day, Leon patrols for illegal fishing in the reserve and manages ecological monitoring. In his spare time, Leon is a passionate photographer of Kāpiti's abundant wildlife. After a century in the backdrop, Kāpiti Island has become a birder's dream, teeming with endemic species that are rare or extinct outside of protected areas, such as the 1200 little spotted kiwi that call the island home. Other noteworthy locals include the endemic hihi (stitchbird), kōkako, kākā, takahē and tīeke (saddleback).

> According to Māori legend, the explorer Kupe created Kāpiti Island with a single stroke of his club.

According to Leon, 'Photographic opportunities start the minute you leave the mainland', as you may see albatross while crossing through the marine reserve, or dolphins or whales. On the island, the best birding opportunities can be found in the tall forest around Rangatira or on the way to the summit, although the more open North End offers plenty of opportunities for chance sightings, including the kārearea (New Zealand falcon) and large flocks of kererū (wood pigeons).

What's more, the wildlife encounters on Kāpiti Island tend to be special, as the relative lack of human interaction means the birds are less shy. Perhaps, after a century in the backdrop, these local stars are ready for the limelight.

Visit the Island

Kāpiti Island is one of the country's largest offshore eco-sanctuaries. Access is restricted, so book your trip through one of two licensed operators: **Kāpiti Island Eco Experience** (kapitiislandeco.co.nz) or **Kāpiti Island Nature Tours** (kapitiisland.com). Overnight stays are possible and day trips begin from $80.

The ferry disembarks at centrally located Rangatira or at the North End. Take a guided walk of the island's natural and cultural history, or be your own guide.

The network of bush walks around Rangatira offer some of the island's best bird-watching opportunities, and access to the island's summit (Tuteremoana; 521m).

Listings

BEST OF THE REST

Start the Day Right

Comes & Goes $$

Made famous by its Instagram-worthy chicken Scotch egg, this trendy Petone eatery serves food as aesthetic as it is tasty, so don't forget your camera.

Maranui Cafe $$

A tried-and-true Wellington favourite, perched on Lyall Bay beach. Expect a wait – the queue winds down the stairs. Don't miss its thickshakes.

Pour & Twist $

The country's first fully manual coffee brew bar excels in visually curious concoctions. Take a moment to enjoy a freshly poured brew, learning about the process while you wait.

Leeds Street Bakery $

One of the staple culinary gems making up Hannah's Laneway Precinct; fresh bread, cookies and coffee are the way to go.

Customs $

Cosy and laid-back, specialising in excellent coffee and a simple menu of gourmet toast. Visit Thursday to Sunday for fresh doughnuts from Little Dough Co, but they sell quick!

Fidels $$

This Cuba St stalwart serves comforting home-style brunches, all day. The interior is dark, funky and close-quartered, with a more spacious back terrace.

Hangar $$

The selling points of this roastery-turned-cafe are its bold flavoured coffee flights and modern takes on classic brunches.

Family Fun in the City

Cable Car

A Wellington icon, this unique transport links Lambton Quay to the hill suburb of Kelburn for easy access to Space Place, the Botanical Gardens and Zealandia (via a free shuttle).

Zealandia

An urban eco-sanctuary seeking to protect and restore native flora and fauna. Take a guided tour or stroll independently, and have fun spotting wildlife in the lush surroundings.

Space Place

Discover space through interactive galleries, exhibits and a historic telescope. Don't miss the planetarium: try to coincide this visit with a talk about New Zealand's night skies.

Botanic Gardens

Explore 25 hectares of sprawling, beautifully curated gardens. With playgrounds, sculptures, lookouts and a duck pond the tranquil oasis makes for an easy escape from the CBD.

JACK DRIVER/SHUTTERSTOCK ©

Fidels

Te Papa Museum

The national museum provides free, interactive and constantly changing exhibits on topics such as Māori history, world wars and nature. Be sure to spot the colossal squid!

Wellington Chocolate Factory

Nestled in the city's core, WCF makes one of the most decadent hot chocolates around. Book a tour to learn the chocolatiers' secrets.

Wellington Zoo

Housing tigers, sun bears, otters and giraffes, the zoo is set on a beautiful Newtown hillside.

Coastal Day Hikes

Escarpment Track

Climb the 'Stairway to Heaven', traverse 9km from Paekākāriki to Pukerua Bay and be rewarded with sweeping views to Kāpiti Island. Local tip: north to south is easier.

Red Rocks

Explore Wellington's south coast with a 40-minute walk from Ōwhiro Bay to the aptly named Red Rocks. Watch out for seals.

Waterfront Walk

Walk, bike or blade your way around the city's scenic waterfront. Visit the Karaka Cafe to try a traditional *hāngi* meal. Hire a crocodile bike for a group adventure.

Castlepoint Lighthouse

A popular weekend getaway, Castlepoint is a wildly rugged coastal town featuring an easy, scenic walk with magnificent views of unique coastal formations and an iconic lighthouse.

Breweries & Local Drops

Choice Bros $$

Instagram-ready fairy lights line the alleyway to an old boxing gym, gloves and weights discarded in favour of David Bowie–inspired concoctions. Unmissable fried chicken.

Te Papa Museum

Waitoa Social Club $$

Recently expanded from its Hataitai flagship, the CBD location encourages conversation over plates from adjoining Little Penang, combining two of Wellington's favourite institutions.

HeyDay $$

Centrally located, with a pastel aesthetic that stands out on Cuba St, HeyDay offers fun arcade and yard games to keep any beer skeptics in the group occupied.

Fortune Favours $$

Residing in a former dip-strippers', its renovated interior is still heavily influenced by its past life. The upstairs terrace is particularly popular on Wellington's rare windless days.

Brewton $$

Take a train to Upper Hutt and be rewarded with multiple market-leading breweries, a distillery and a plethora of on-site, family-friendly activities.

Puffin $$$

Leading the charge on organic and minimal intervention wines, Puffin's plain facade hides an elegant speakeasy popular with the after-work crowd.

 Scan to find more things to do in Wellington online

NELSON &
MARLBOROUGH

BEACHES | DINING | NATIONAL PARKS

**Experience
Nelson &
Marlborough
online**

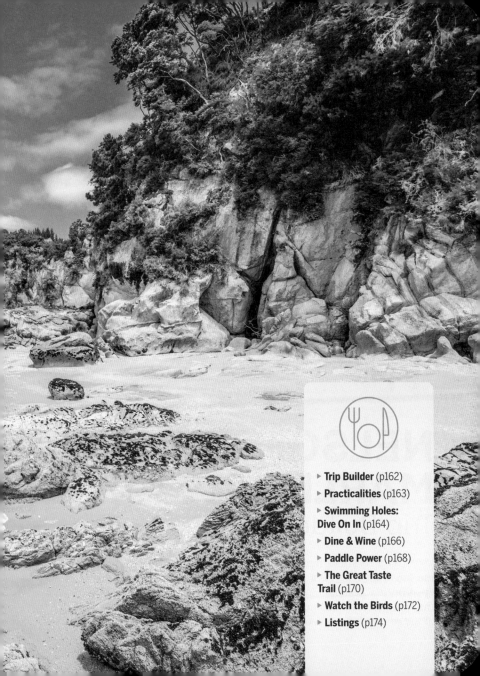

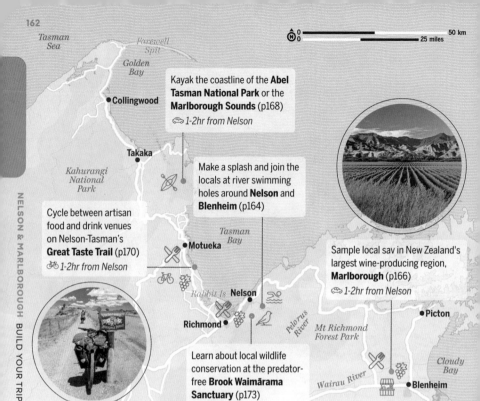

Tasman Sea

Farewell Spit

Golden Bay

● Collingwood

Kayak the coastline of the **Abel Tasman National Park** or the **Marlborough Sounds** (p168)
🚗 *1-2hr from Nelson*

Takaka ●

Kahurangi National Park

Make a splash and join the locals at river swimming holes around **Nelson** and **Blenheim** (p164)

Cycle between artisan food and drink venues on Nelson-Tasman's **Great Taste Trail** (p170)
🚲 *1-2hr from Nelson*

Tasman Bay

● **Motueka**

Sample local sav in New Zealand's largest wine-producing region, **Marlborough** (p166)
🚗 *1-2hr from Nelson*

Rabbit Is **Nelson** ●

Richmond ●

Pelorus River

Mt Richmond Forest Park

● **Picton**

Cloudy Bay

Learn about local wildlife conservation at the predator-free **Brook Waimārama Sanctuary** (p173)
🚗 *10min from Nelson*

Wairau River

● **Blenheim**

NELSON & MARLBOROUGH
Trip Builder

With coastline, mountains and fertile plains, the Top of the South is a microcosm of all that's great in New Zealand. Enjoy outdoor activities on the water or in the mountains and sample some of the country's finest food and drink.

Explore bookable experiences in Nelson & Marlborough

Practicalities

ARRIVING

 Nelson Airport is the region's main air hub. There's a smaller airport at Blenheim and an airstrip in Golden Bay. Arrive in Picton from Wellington on a Cook Strait ferry.

MONEY	**CONNECT**

MONEY
New Zealand residents enjoy local prices when staying in Department of Conservation huts and campsites in national parks.

CONNECT
Wi-fi is available in main towns and villages but don't count on it inside national parks.

WHERE TO STAY

Place	Pro/Con
Nelson	A small city with lots of accommodation and food options. Further from some outdoor activities.
Tākaka	Convenient for exploring Golden Bay and the northern Abel Tasman. Only one access road.
Picton	An attractive transport hub that's ideal for exploring Marlborough Sounds. Can get congested.
Blenheim	Wine central, with plenty of accommodation. Further from other activities.

EATING & DRINKING

Foodies have come to the right place. Nelson has a wide range of locally and internationally inspired restaurants. Blenheim's all about the wineries like Cloudy Bay (pictured left top; p176). Seafood lovers should head for little Havelock, the Greenshell Mussel Capital of the World (pictured bottom left).

Best seafood
Greenshell Mussel Cruise (p175)

Must-try platters
Tasman's Gravity Winery (p167)

GETTING AROUND

Car Beyond central Nelson you'll need a vehicle to explore very far.

Bus Limited long-distance buses and shuttles operate between Nelson and Golden Bay, Nelson and Murchison, and Nelson and Blenheim.

Train A scenic railway, the Marlborough Flyer, connects Picton and Blenheim.

NELSON & MARLBOROUGH FIND YOUR FEET

DEC–FEB	**MAR–MAY**	**JUN–AUG**	**SEP–NOV**
Summer brings long days and lots of sunshine, but many tourists and busy campgrounds.	Cooler but still pleasant days are ideal for outdoor activities.	Low season with cold nights and cool days, but accessible skiing at the Rainbow Ski Area.	Wet but increasingly warm, spring welcomes the godwits on their migration south.

33 Swimming Holes: DIVE ON IN

OUTDOORS | ACTIVE | NATURE

The Top of the South has some of New Zealand's clearest, least-polluted rivers. While hitting the beach on a hot summer's day is a favourite pastime throughout coastal New Zealand, locals at the Top of the South are just as likely to head to a river. To enjoy a cooling swim on a hot day without salty seawater residue, make a beeline to a river.

PETER UNGER/GETTY IMAGES ©

🗺 How to

Getting here Rivers snake from mountains to coast throughout the Top of the South. Swimming spots are accessible from main and back roads.

When to go The region's hot, dry summers make this season the ideal time for a swim but waterfalls are most impressive after rain.

Where not to swim Heed local safety warnings and respect Māori requests. The gorgeous Riuwaka Resurgence may look inviting but it's disrespectful to swim at the sacred spot.

CSNAFZGER/SHUTTERSTOCK ©

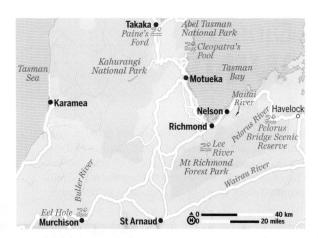

Left Pelorus Bridge Scenic Reserve
Below Cleopatra's Pools

Life's a River Beach

Make a splash Join the local youths and bomb, dive or (let's be honest) bellyflop from great heights. Jump from rocks at **Pelorus Bridge** (on SH6 between Havelock and Nelson), the **Lee River** (past Richmond) and **Paine's Ford** (Tākaka), or swing from ropes above swimming holes in the **Aniseed Valley** (Richmond), **Maitai Valley** (Nelson) and Murchison's **Eel Hole** on the Buller River.

Urban refreshment The Maitai River flows from the mountains east of Nelson city, and swimming spots along the river in the Maitai Valley are easy to reach from town.

En route On SH6 between Havelock and Nelson, the **Pelorus Bridge Scenic Reserve** contains a glorious stretch of clean river and wide pebbly beaches. It's a convenient place to take a walk and stretch the legs on a road trip between Blenheim and Nelson, and once you see the water you might be tempted to stay a while.

Family fun The gentle flow and shallow waters at Pelorus Bridge, the Lee River and the Aniseed Valley are ideal for kids and babies to splash about in.

≈ Bathe Like a Queen

A short walk from Anchorage Beach and Torrent Bay in the Abel Tasman National Park is a hidden freshwater swimming spot, **Cleopatra's Pools**.

Here the Torrent River forms a series of rock pools and small waterfalls surrounded by forest. When water levels are suitable, adventurous souls can slip and slide down the wet moss-covered rocks into the pools. Alternatively, lay out a towel and sunbathe on the surrounding rocks, like Cleopatra herself (without the milk).

Whether you plan to hike through the park or visit on a day trip via a water taxi, Cleopatra's Pools are a worthy detour.

34 Dine & WINE

FOOD | DRINK | ENTERTAINMENT

▬▬▬ Vineyards with views, restaurants, games and sculpture gardens make winery visits accessible for all. Wine novices, beer drinkers, families and even travellers who prefer a meal *sans* alcohol can experience the Nelson-Tasman-Marlborough region's culinary best by visiting wineries that offer more than typical wine tasting. Wine connoisseurs won't be disappointed by the range of sauvignon blanc available, either.

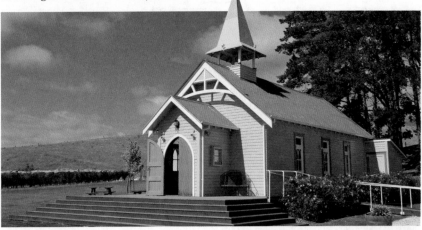

🗺 How to

Getting here The Marlborough region is home to around 30 wineries. Winery tour shuttle buses operate around Blenheim so nobody needs to drink and drive.

When to go Many wineries operate year-round, although some restaurants only operate in summer.

Short on time? If your itinerary doesn't allow for a full day of winery-hopping, drop in at the **Wine Station**, a self-service wine-tasting salon at Blenheim Railway Station.

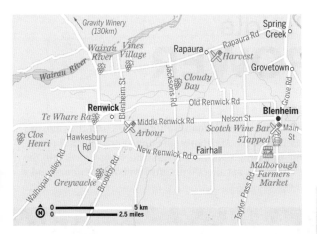

A Foodie's Weekend in Blenheim

Friday night Hang with the locals at **5Tapped**, a coffee and speciality beer bar. Follow with dinner at **Little Amigo's** Mexican food truck and finish at **Scotch Wine Bar**.

Saturday Head to **Vines Village** for breakfast. Then, jump in Explore Marlborough's van to visit some wineries, including **Cloudy Bay**, **Te Whare Ra**, **Clos Henri** (a converted chapel) and **Greywacke** (appointments required). After the tour, have dinner at **Arbour**, a vineyard restaurant that does nothing by halves.

Sunday Start with breakfast, coffee and a shop at the **Marlborough Farmers Market**. Visit Hedgerows for fresh strawberry frozen yogurt and a punnet of takeaway strawberries. Stop by the rustic shed at Bush's honey for the most delicate freshly cut honeycomb. End with dinner at **Harvest**, within the sprawling manicured gardens of **The Marlborough**, a luxury country estate.

■ **Blenheim itinerary recommended by Stephanie McIntyre**
certified sommelier and food and drink consultant, Blenheim. @outre_nz

Left Clos Henri
Below Platter, Cloudy Bay Winery

🍇 Grape to Glass & Paddock to Plate

Lawn games For a bit of old-world fun with your Kiwi drop, play a game of *pétanque* at Cloudy Bay Vineyards or Wairau River Wine, or croquet at Gravity Winery.

Wine with a side of art Gravity Winery in Mahana runs the Gravity Gallery, showcasing local art. The storytelling sculptures on the lawn at Wairau River Wines are Insta-worthy.

Turn up the temp in the kitchen Wither Hills, Wairau River Wines and Allan Scott Bistro, among others, tell the region's story through seasonally inspired menus and sharing platters.

Paddle
POWER

OUTDOORS | NATURE | SPORTS

The beautiful beaches of the Abel Tasman National Park and the (mostly) sheltered 1500km-long coastline of the Marlborough Sounds are the stuff of sea kayakers' dreams. Add some tumbling mountain rivers and scenic lakes into the mix and you have a region that suits kayakers with any level of experience and a thirst for adventure.

FRANS LEMMENS/GETTY IMAGES ©

📖 **How to**

Getting here Sea kayak rentals and tours of the Abel Tasman coastline operate from access towns south and north of the park. For the Marlborough Sounds, head to Picton or Havelock. Murchison is a whitewater kayaking hub.

When to go Conditions are best for water sports in the spring, summer and autumn.

Waka tours Paddle a modernised Māori *waka* (canoe) on a cultural tour of Abel Tasman.

JANA SHKOROVA/SHUTTERSTOCK ©

ANDREW PEACOCK/GETTY IMAGES ©

This is Where New Zealand Began

The Top of the South is really the best place in New Zealand
for kayaking.

Where to go The northern end of the **Abel Tasman National
Park** is particularly special because commercial activity is
very restricted here. The water taxis that operate in the rest
of the park can't go north past Tōtaranui. The area from Tata
Beach to Tōtaranui is a snapshot of the best sea kayaking in
New Zealand.

What to see These areas of the park are isolated and all
these plant species have sprung up that really shouldn't
be here, and that wouldn't survive anywhere else. You can
see grey spotted shags and reef herons, plenty of seals and
kororā (blue penguins), orca and southern right whales.

Layers of history This is where New Zealand began in
more ways than one: it's where the land of present-day New
Zealand split from Gondwanaland and it's where Māori and
Europeans first had contact. The historical human impact
here has been small, so it feels special.

■ Kayaking recommendations by
Lisa Savage
Golden Bay Kayaks, Tata Beach
@goldenbaykayaks

 **Pick Your River,
Lake or Bay**

Meeting Place The
inland Tasman village
of Murchison is on the
confluence of the Buller
and Matakitaki Rivers,
and is near the Mangles
and Matiri Rivers. It's an
ideal base for white-
water kayaking and
rafting adventures.

Nelson Lakes In
summer, rent kayaks
at Lakes Rotoiti and
Rotoroa, the two most
accessible lakes in the
Nelson Lakes National
Park. Paddle away from
shore to admire the
views of forested hills
turning to snowcapped
mountains.

Spot dolphins There's
no need to join a
motorised boat tour to
get up close to dolphins
in the Marlborough
Sounds. Dusky,
bottlenose and common
dolphins might just swim
alongside your kayak.

NELSON & MARLBOROUGH EXPERIENCES

36 The Great
TASTE TRAIL

CYCLING | EATING | SCENERY

The Nelson-Tasman region's Great Taste Trail provides 174km of on-road and cycle-path trails connecting some of the area's best food and drink experiences. Ride the full circuit over several days or pick shorter sections for day rides, refuelling at select pit stops along the way.

ROBERT CHG/SHUTTERSTOCK ©

🗺 Trip Notes

Getting here It's easy to rent bicycles in Nelson, Motueka and Māpua. Some rental services can even meet you at Nelson Airport with a bike.

When to go For comfortable riding conditions without sacrificing sunshine, cycle the Great Taste Trail in spring or autumn.

Ride the Mapua Ferry On Māpua's bicycle ferry cyclists far outnumber foot-travellers. The ferry connects Moturoa/Rabbit Island and Māpua so cyclists can avoid the hills of SH60.

☼ The Coastal Route

The two main sections of the Great Taste Trail are the Coastal Route and the Rail Route. The Coastal Route is arguably the more scenic of the two, winding its way between Nelson and Kaiteriteri via Richmond, Māpua and Motueka. Stop at vineyards, breweries and orchards en route.

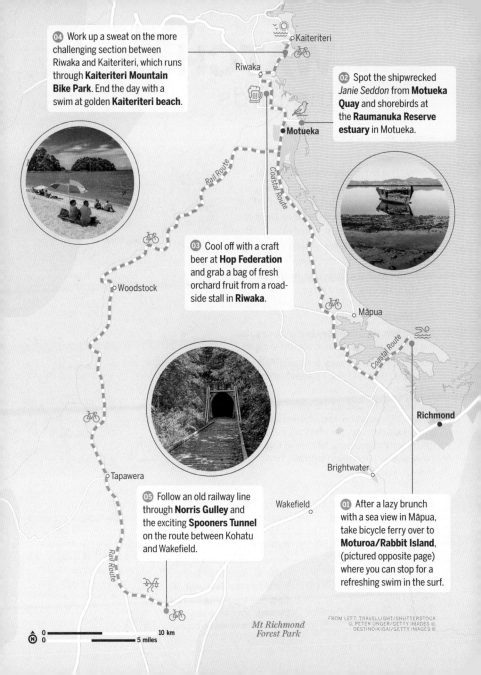

04 Work up a sweat on the more challenging section between Riwaka and Kaiteriteri, which runs through **Kaiteriteri Mountain Bike Park**. End the day with a swim at golden **Kaiteriteri beach**.

Kaiteriteri

Riwaka

02 Spot the shipwrecked *Janie Seddon* from **Motueka Quay** and shorebirds at the **Raumanuka Reserve estuary** in Motueka.

●Motueka

Rail Route

Coastal Route

03 Cool off with a craft beer at **Hop Federation** and grab a bag of fresh orchard fruit from a roadside stall in **Riwaka**.

Māpua

Coastal Route

○Woodstock

Richmond

05 Follow an old railway line through **Norris Gulley** and the exciting **Spooners Tunnel** on the route between Kohatu and Wakefield.

Brightwater

Wakefield ○

01 After a lazy brunch with a sea view in Māpua, take bicycle ferry over to **Moturoa/Rabbit Island**, (pictured opposite page) where you can stop for a refreshing swim in the surf.

○Tapawera

Rail Route

Mt Richmond Forest Park

FROM LEFT: TRAVELLIGHT/SHUTTERSTOCK ©, PETER UNGER/GETTY IMAGES ©, DESTINOIKIGAI/GETTY IMAGES ©

N

| 0 | | 10 km |
| 0 | | 5 miles |

37 WATCH
the Birds

BIRDS | WILDLIFE | NATURE

The birdsong around coastal Nelson-Tasman-Marlborough was once so loud that Captain Cook had to anchor his ship far offshore to hold a conversation. Hike and bird-watch in parks and sanctuaries where efforts are being made to restore New Zealand's birdsong and the habitats native birds need to survive and thrive.

📷 How to

Getting here Hike, take a bus tour or ride a water taxi to bird conservation areas across the region.

When to go Godwits appear at Farewell Spit, on their round-the-world tour, between September and March.

What to look for Godwits, Mongolian dotterels, gannets, little penguins, oystercatchers, shags, pīwakawaka (fantails), kākāriki, kākā, pāteke (brown teal), titipounamu, tūī, riroriro, kererū (wood pigeons), korimako (bellbirds), ruru (moreporks).

Dawn chorus In the **Abel Tasman National Park**, Project Janszoon and the Birdsong Trust work on pest eradication and to restore and maintain the native forest in which native songbirds thrive. Hikers on the Abel Tasman Coast Track will be woken by the sounds of the toutouwai (robin) and tīeke (saddleback), if they're lucky.

Wonderful waders Not all birds make their homes in the forests. **Farewell Spit** and the **Mangarakau Swamp** are home to wet-land and shore birds, some of which fly tens of thousands of kilometres in one stretch. The bar-tailed godwit is a remarkable little bird that flies between China, Alaska and New Zealand every year, and some of them make their seasonal home at Farewell Spit.

✍ An Urban Sanctuary

A purpose-built fence surrounds the Brook Waimārama Sanctuary, ensuring the area is free from introduced mammalian pests and officially 'bio secure'. This requires fence checking and maintenance 24/7 by staff and volunteers.

There has been a notable increase in endemic populations of birds and wildlife. Several 'lost' plants, including fungi, have been discovered in the sanctuary.

One of our biggest milestones for bird conservation has been the successful translocation of birds previously absent from the region, such as tīeke (South Island saddleback) and kākāriki karaka (orange-fronted parakeet), both of which are deemed critically endangered.

■ **Recommended by Ru Collin**
chief executive of the Brook Waimārama Sanctuary Trust, Nelson
@brooksanctuary

Cruise to a kiwi nursery
Motuara Island in Queen Charlotte Sound is used as a nursery for the rare rowi kiwi, who are raised until they're big enough to be returned to their native habitat in southern Westland. It's also home to tīeke, toutouwai and kākāriki. Cruise to the island from Picton and hike the half-hour track to the summit to enjoy views of the Marlborough Sounds.

Above Tīeke, Motuara Island

Listings

BEST OF THE REST

Waterfall Walks

Wainui Falls

Hike through bush on the edge of the Abel Tasman National Park to the impressive 20m-high Wainui Falls. An easy one-hour return walk but keep kids close.

Whispering Falls

At the end of the Aniseed Valley, the wispy Whispering Falls are best after a lot of rain. Follow the Hackett Track route through the Mt Richmond Forest Park.

Maruia Falls

Created by the huge Murchison earthquake of 1929, gushing Maruia Falls are a short drive from Murchison. Swing by on the way to the Shenandoah Hwy or the West Coast.

Brook Sanctuary Waterfall

Walk the easy loop track around the Brook Waimārama Sanctuary and find these lovely short waterfalls about halfway. This stream used to provide Nelson's main water supply.

At the Market

Nelson Art Market

Nelsonians' favourite Saturday morning activity, the Art Market in central Montgomery Sq offers local handicrafts, ready-to-eat food and fresh produce.

Isel Park Twilight Market

Historic Isel Park, in the Nelson suburb of Stoke, hosts the chilled-out Twilight Market on Thursdays during the summer, from late afternoon to late evening. Admire the enormous sequoia trees over a picnic dinner.

Nelson Farmers Market

Beside the Elma Turner Library, the Nelson Farmers Market on Wednesday mornings is the best place to get fresh local produce midweek.

Tākaka Village Market

Find fresh food, music, art and crafts in the heart of Golden Bay on Saturday mornings. Small Tākaka is known for its alternative cultural scene and this is an ideal place to see it in action.

Cosmopolitan Dining

Hawker House $$

Street food dishes from around Southeast Asia are served amid an energetic ambience. Team the zesty Vietnamese beef salad with Townshend's Sutton Hoo American Amber Ale from nearby Motueka, but leave room for dessert of cardamon-infused panna cotta.

Hopgood's & Co $$$

Mediterranean- and Asian-inspired dishes harnessing seasonal ingredients are the focus at this unpretentious restaurant. Relax and enjoy *pāua* (shellfish) dumplings with shitake and white radish. Five course tasting menus are $95.

Maruia Falls

ERNEST KUNG/GETTY IMAGES ©

Take to the Water

Pelorus Mail Boat

Help deliver the rural mail (which is just as likely to be a live animal than an envelope) on this local service-meets-tourist-attraction that's been running since 1919.

Greenshell Mussel Cruise

Three-hour cruise to mussel in on Kenepuru's aquaculture. Includes a tasting of steamed mussels and a glass of wine. Bookings essential.

Abel Tasman Water Taxis

Ideal for travellers without the time to hike through the Abel Tasman National Park, water taxis and cruises run up the coast of the park from Kaiteriteri. The cruise to Awaroa's white-sand beach is possibly the best.

Lake Rotoiti Water Taxi

Three-hour cruise to mussel in on Kenepuru's aquaculture. Includes a tasting of steamed mussels and a glass of wine. Bookings essential.

From Dizzy Heights

Days Track

Power up this steep track in the Tahunanui Hills for great views of Tahunanui Beach, Tasman Bay and the Western Ranges. Catch your breath on the mosaic community couches.

Centre of New Zealand

Once believed to be the geographical centre of the country, the trig point at the top of Botanical Hill offers sweeping views of Nelson, Tasman Bay and the mountains beyond.

Cullen Point Lookout

Stop on Queen Charlotte Drive to stretch your legs on the short walk to this lookout, overlooking Havelock and Pelorus Sound.

ROBERT CHG/SHUTTERSTOCK ©

Abel Tasman water taxi

Hawke's Lookout

Take a break from the twists and turns of the Takaka Hill road at Hawke's Lookout, with the Riwaka Resurgence right below and expansive views of Tasman Bay.

Fresh Fruit

Berry Lands

Throughout the summer, this huge fruit farm offers pick-your-own strawberries, raspberries, karaka berries, blackberries and more, as well as fresh fruit ice cream. Behind the tall hedges on the road between Richmond and Rabbit Island.

Blueberry Grove

Pick more varieties of blueberries than you even knew existed from this farm on the backroads of Hope. Summer only; bring your own containers.

Hedgerows

Pick up a punnet of hydroponically grown strawberries or a fresh fruit ice cream at this farm near central Blenheim.

 Scan to find more things to do in Nelson & Marlborough online

CENTRAL
SOUTH ISLAND

ADVENTURE | OUTDOORS | UNSPOILED

Experience
Central
South Island
online

CENTRAL SOUTH ISLAND
Trip Builder

Remote and unspoiled, Central South Island is home to some of NZ's most rugged and otherworldly scenery. The Southern Alps dominate the landscape and startlingly blue lakes hold the attention of all who pass. A destination for outdoor enthusiasts and nature lovers.

Cross swing bridges and turquoise water at Hokitika Gorge (p192)
🚗 4hr from Christchurch

Hike through the majestic Southern Alps (p184)
🚗 4hr from Christchurch

Kayak with icebergs in the Tasman Glacier Terminal Lake (p187)
🚗 3½hr from Queenstown

Gaze at the stars at Lake Tekapo (p182)
🚗 3hr from Christchurch

Mt Ryall
Grey River
Greymouth
Lake Brunner (Moana)
Hokitika
Lake Mahinapua
Lake Kaniere
Mt Rolleston
Arthur's Pass
Mt Murchison
Mt Bryce
Craigieburn Forest Park

Tasman Sea
Mt Whitcombe
Westland Tai Poutini National Park
Whataroa
Lake Mapourika
Mt Arrowsmith
Lake Coleridge
Franz Josef Glacier
Fox Glacier
Franz Josef Glacier
Albert Glacier
Aoraki/Mt Cook National Park
Fox Glacier
Tasman Glacier
Aoraki/Mt Cook
Rangitata River
Mt Hutt
Methven
Douglas Neve
Mueller Glacier
Lake Tekapo
Lake Pukaki
Burkes Pass

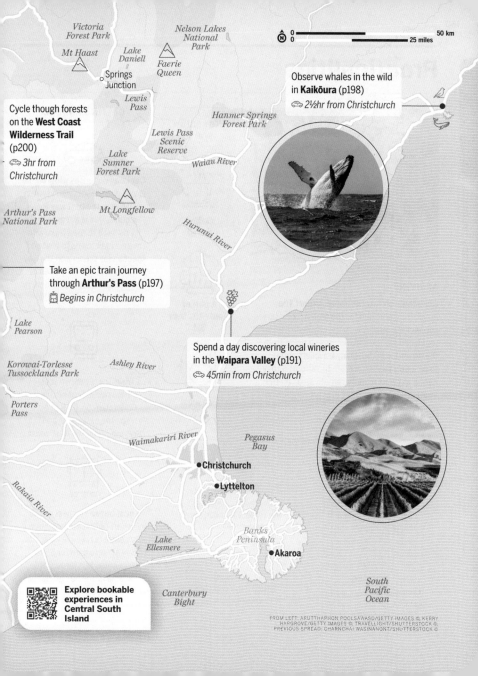

Victoria Forest Park

Mt Haast

Nelson Lakes National Park

Lake Daniell

Faerie Queen

Springs Junction

Lewis Pass

Observe whales in the wild in **Kaikōura** (p198)
🚗 2½hr from Christchurch

Cycle though forests on the **West Coast Wilderness Trail** (p200)
🚗 3hr from Christchurch

Hanmer Springs Forest Park

Lewis Pass Scenic Reserve

Waiau River

Lake Sumner Forest Park

Arthur's Pass National Park

Mt Longfellow

Hurunui River

Take an epic train journey through **Arthur's Pass** (p197)
🚆 Begins in Christchurch

Lake Pearson

Spend a day discovering local wineries in the **Waipara Valley** (p191)
🚗 45min from Christchurch

Korowai-Torlesse Tussocklands Park

Ashley River

Porters Pass

Waimakariri River

Pegasus Bay

Rakaia River

● **Christchurch**

● **Lyttelton**

Lake Ellesmere

Banks Peninsula

● **Akaroa**

Canterbury Bight

South Pacific Ocean

Explore bookable experiences in Central South Island

0 · 0 · 25 miles · 50 km

Practicalities

UWE ARANAS/SHUTTERSTOCK ©

ARRIVING

Christchurch International Airport The major transport hub for the region. Local buses connect the airport with the city centre on a regular basis. You can purchase a ticket from the driver for $8.50. Many travellers choose to pick up a rental car from the airport if they intend to travel to more remote areas on the South Island. The airport is approximately 15 minutes' drive from the city centre.

HOW MUCH FOR A

Coffee
$4.50

A pint of Monteiths beer
$11

Pub meal
$25

GETTING AROUND

Car Long distances with remote areas and mountainous terrain make cars the best way to get around. This is a region that lends itself to road trips, with many small towns to visit and spectacular scenery on the way. Cars are also widely used in Christchurch, although there is public transport available.

Train There are two scenic train routes, connecting Christchurch with Kaikōura on the east coast and Greymouth on the west coast.

Local buses The best public transport option in Christchurch city centre is taking a local bus. Buy a metro card for $5 for discounted bus fares. Cards available at the bus exchange and local libraries.

WHEN TO GO

DEC–FEB
Hot and dry. Best time for hiking, swimming and seeing the lupins bloom.

MAR–MAY
Cooler temperatures are perfect for hiking and outdoor activities.

JUN–AUG
Cold, slightly more rainfall. Best time for skiing and snow-capped-mountain photos.

SEP–NOV
Warm days. Waterfalls are at their best.

EATING & DRINKING

The central South Island is known for its seafood. Try crayfish (pictured right top) in Kaikōura, whitebait on the West Coast and salmon farmed in glacial rivers in Twizel. Some of the country's best salami and sausages come from Blackball, a small town on the West Coast. And, if you're after a drink, stop for a beer at Monteiths Brewery in Greymouth and try the local wine in North Canterbury, an upcoming wine region in New Zealand.

Best pie
(perhaps even in New Zealand)
Fairlie Bakehouse (p205)

Must-try whitebait fritters
Cray Pot, Jackson Bay (p205)

CONNECT & FIND YOUR WAY

Wi-fi Free wi-fi is available at cafes, libraries and hotels, however, it's easiest to buy a local SIM card when you arrive in the country. You may lose data connection (and phone signal) when driving on remote roads.

Navigation Signage is good on most major routes. There is also signage for major attractions and photo stops.

WHERE TO STAY

The central South Island region is relatively sparsely populated, with long distances between major towns. Consider basing yourself in one or more of the towns below, while you explore the surrounding area.

Town	Pro/Con
Christchurch	One of New Zealand's major cities. Food and accommodation options at all price points. Undergoing a post-earthquake regeneration.
Twizel	Good base for Tekapo and Mt Cook National Park. Good range of affordable accommodation options.
Kaikōura	Coastal town known for marine life and seafood. Accommodation available for all budgets.
Hokitika	Historic town on the West Coast with good food and accommodation options. Local greenstone (jade) can be purchased here.
Franz Josef	Small village near the glaciers. Very tourist-orientated and busy in summer.

PUBLIC HOLIDAYS

Many cafes and restaurants close on public holidays (especially on the West Coast), so buy groceries or book a table in advance if travelling around Christmas.

MONEY

Fill up your car in major towns as petrol can be expensive in small towns. Consider buying local wine and delicacies from the supermarket at lower prices, if you don't mind skipping the tourist experience.

38 Dark Skies & **STARS**

STARGAZING | NIGHT ACTIVITY | FAMILY-FRIENDLY

Discover stars and constellations unique to the southern hemisphere in one of the largest Dark Sky Reserves in the world. On the shores of Lake Tekapo, you can wonder at faraway planets and galaxies while learning about the local Māori connection to the night sky. The surrounding mountains and lakes also provide the perfect setting for trying your hand at astrophotography.

How to

Getting here Lake Tekapo is about three hours' drive from Christchurch and the same from Queenstown.

Expect to pay $170 for an observatory tour.

Weather Stars are visible all year round, however, winter is best for cloudless skies. Spend a few days in the region to increase your chances of a clear sky.

What to wear The wind can be cold on the summit so wear warm clothes, even in summer.

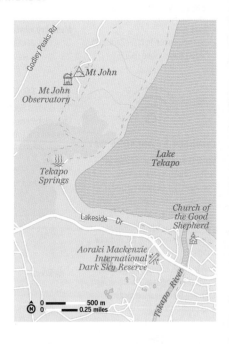

Dark skies for miles

Tekapo is situated in the heart of the **Aoraki Mackenzie International Dark Sky Reserve**, the largest dark sky reserve in the southern hemisphere. Stretching 4300km, there is minimal light pollution in the area, meaning that the stars look incredibly bright and you can easily see the Milky Way, Magellanic Clouds and Southern Cross on a clear night. On rare occasions you can even see the Aurora Australis (Southern Lights).

Reaching for the stars

To get as close as you can to the stars, head up the summit of **Mt John**. The hill rises above Lake Tekapo and is home to New Zealand's premier astro-nomical research centre, the Mt John Observatory. This is one of the few observatories located in a Dark Sky Reserve in the world, and the views through the telescopes are spectacular.

MATT MAKES PHOTOS/SHUTTERSTOCK ©

♨ Hot Springs & Stargazing

For an indulgent take on stargazing, marvel at the night sky from a hot spring. Bathe yourself in the hot waters at **Tekapo Springs**, while staring at the heavens and learning about the constellations overhead.

This is a particularly special experience in winter, when you'll be greeted with a hot chocolate at the dimly lit Tekapo Springs complex. Rather than shiver in the cold, submerge yourself in an underwater hammock, with the best of the night sky on display above you. It's a relaxing way to see the stars, in complete comfort, with next to no light pollution.

Soak and stars experiences are available at Tekapo Star Gazing (tekapostargazing.co.nz).

Through the telescope

Gaze through powerful telescopes and see the marvels of space up close. Depending on the time of year, you can see various planets and distant star systems including Alpha Centauri and the Globular Star Cluster.

Capturing the experience If

you want to learn more about astrophotography, there are several tours you can join – just remember to bring your camera and a tripod. A photo of the Church of the Good Shepherd with the Milky Way shimmering overhead is a particularly beautiful way to remember your trip.

Above Aoraki Mackenzie International Dark Sky Reserve

39 Taking the Mountains
TO THEIR LIMIT

HIKING | SKIING | MOUNTAINEERING

▬▬▬ Explore glaciers, turquoise lakes and sheer mountain peaks in some of New Zealand's most photogenic countryside. Make your way through tracks bordered by alpine forest and past fields of colourful wildflowers as you head into the heart of the Southern Alps.

How to

Getting here Aoraki/ Mt Cook National Park is approximately 3½ hours from Christchurch by car.

When to go November to May for hiking and July to October for skiing. Helicopter rides and day walks are accessible all year round. January and February is tourist season. Lupins are at their best from late December to January.

Getting around Hire a car. It's a beautiful road trip and not accessible by public transport.

Walks Beneath Soaring Peaks

Exploring **Aoraki/Mt Cook National Park** is possible for all ages, with trails of varying lengths and options suitable for different levels of ability. Take a flat trail past colourful lakes, or opt for a short yet strenuous climb up multiple stairs which culminate on the edge of the **Tasman Glacier Terminal Lake**. You can do a short walk to the Tasman Glacier and or try the half-day Hooker Valley Track, which meanders through alpine streams, past glaciers and over swing bridges.

For those after more of a challenge consider an overnight hike instead, staying in one of the DOC huts in the national park. The Mueller Track is a popular overnight hike, while the three- to four-day **Ball Pass Crossing** is a demanding alpine trail best suited to experienced hikers.

Flower Fields

For postcard-worthy photos of blue, pink and pastel flowers on the shores of blue lakes, time your visit for between late November and mid-January. At this time of year, lupins flower throughout Mackenzie Country. If you decide to drive from Christchurch to Aoraki/ Mt Cook National Park, prepare to stop frequently for colourful, Insta-worthy shots.

Above left Tasman Glacier Terminal Lake
Above Tourist helicopter, Aoraki/Mt Cook National Park
Left Hooker Valley Track

Those looking for more relaxing options should consider a lakeside walk at the foot of the mountain along the shores of **Lake Pukaki**. The **Pukaki Boulders** and **Lake Pukaki Track** are popular choices. Or, if you don't feel like walking, you can also do a 4WD adventure through theTasman Valley for incredible views of the region.

Ski from Great Heights

For a unique experience, try heliskiing in the Aoraki/Mt Cook ranges, home to New Zealand's highest peak and exciting skiing and snowboarding terrain. Helicopter up and ski among glaciers and alpine lakes with runs across six mountain ranges. Best for experienced skiers and snowboarders.

Fly over a Glacier

Take flight and see Aoraki/Mt Cook National Park from its best vantage point, with the glaciers and snowfields spread out below you. Fly between mountain peaks and along the length of the Tasman Glacier, before

❄ Why Are Glacial Lakes So Blue?

As you travel through Mackenzie Country, you'll quickly notice that the water in the lakes and rivers is a remarkable turquoise colour. When you see Lake Tekapo and Lake Pukaki, it can be hard to believe that the lakes are naturally this colour.

The turquoise hue is caused by fine silt particles (or glacial flour) in the water. The silt is so fine, it remains suspended in the water and when the particles catch the light, the water appears an intense blue-green colour. The turquoise lakes and rivers contain a large amount of water from melting glaciers.

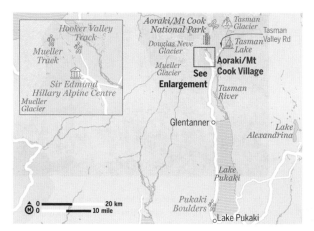

Left Lake Tekapo
Below Statue of Sir Edmund Hillary by Bryn Jones

seeing Mt Cook up close. Many flights include a snow landing and it's also possible to fly to the West Coast and Westland National Park to see the impressive Franz Josef and Fox Glaciers too.

Discover New Zealand's Greatest Explorer

Learn about Sir Edmund Hillary at the **Sir Edmund Hillary Alpine Centre**, at the Hermitage Hotel. The museum pays tribute to the great explorer and showcases the Aoraki/ Mt Cook National Park region. If you can't get out into the mountains, the 3D film is the next best thing to flying through the mountain range, hiking up the peaks or skiing between the glaciers. There is also a planetarium on-site.

Explore a Glacial Lake

Get out on the Tasman Glacier Terminal Lake to see the magnificent Tasman Glacier by boat and enjoy remarkable mountain views. The lake is growing as the glacier melts and there are frequently icebergs floating on the lake, which have torn from the glacier. As you go past, it's possible to touch and even taste the glacial crystals. If you have some kayaking experience, it's also possible to kayak on the lake and get even closer to the icebergs.

Maramataka: The Māori Lunar Calendar

MICHAL TESAR/SHUTTERSTOCK ©

THE TURNING OF THE MOON

Traditionally, the Maramataka was an integral part of Māori life, signalling the best times to go fishing, plant crops or gather food. Working with the rhythms of nature was vital to the survival of early Māori in New Zealand, and this ancient knowledge still has relevance today.

Like many seafaring societies, Māori have traditionally lived their lives by the cycle of the moon and its influence on the tides and land. The Māori lunar calendar is called the Maramataka, which literally means the turning of the moon.

In June, the Matariki star cluster (the Pleiades) first appears in the sky, signalling the New Year and the start of the Maramataka. Throughout the year, the Maramataka gives people guidance around the best time to gather food and whether the next season will be an abundant one. Included in the lunar calendar are the most appropriate and inappropriate times for gathering food, planting and harvesting crops, and catching seafood (*kai moana*).

Months of the Maramataka

Each month begins on the night of the new moon and has a star or constellation associated with it.

The months of the Maramataka:

Pipiri (May–June) All things on earth are contracted because of the cold; likewise man.

Hongonui (or Hōngongoi; June–July) Man is now extremely cold and kindles fires before which he basks.

Here-turi-kōkā (July–August) The scorching effect of fire is seen on the knees of man.

Mahuru (August–September) The earth has now acquired warmth, as have vegetation and trees.

Whiringa-ā-nuku (September–October) The earth has now become quite warm.

Left Fireworks to celebrate Matariki
Centre Full moon, Kaikoura
Right The Pleiades

Whiringa-ā-rangi (October–November) It has now become summer, and the sun has acquired strength.

Hakihea (November–December) Birds are now sitting in their nests.

Kohi-tātea (December–January) Fruits are now ripe, and man eats of the new food of the season.

Hui-tanguru (January–February) The foot of Rūhī (a summer star) now rests upon the earth.

Poutū-te-rangi (February–March) The crops are now harvested.

Paenga-whāwhā (March–April) All straw is now stacked at the borders of the plantations.

Haratua (April–May) Crops are now stored in pits. The tasks of man are finished.

Do People Still Use the Maramataka Today?

Fishing and planting food in accordance with the moon, the tides and the elements is still common today and so the Maramataka still plays an important part in many people's lifestyles.

> The Maramataka gives people guidance around the best time to gather food.

For example, eel fishing during a full moon often results in a smaller catch as eels generally avoid brighter light. Shellfish are also more common after a low tide. Some of the months also coincide with the seasons for planting or fishing.

There are still many different types of Maramataka in use across Aotearoa New Zealand.

☀ The Stars Marking the New Year

Matariki is a star cluster which appears in the sky in June (midwinter), marking the start of the Māori New Year.

The Matariki star cluster (the Pleiades) brings the old lunar year to an end and marks the beginning of the new Maramataka. Matariki takes place after the traditional harvest, which meant people had more time for family and festivities.

Traditionally, this was a time of renewal and new beginnings with festivities and celebrations including lighting ritual fires, making offerings to god and honouring ancestors while celebrating life.

Nowadays, Matariki is celebrated with community events often involving light shows and fireworks.

40 An Exciting FOOD SCENE

FOOD | VINEYARDS | BREWERIES

███████ Christchurch has re-emerged from the devastating earthquakes of 2011 with a burgeoning and exciting food scene. Changes in the city layout and a wealth of non-traditional spaces have created new dining destinations. Experience Christchurch's gastronomical revolution in new eateries around the city, sample local beer and venture just a little further afield for the best of North Canterbury wine.

TRAVELLIGHT/SHUTTERSTOCK ©

🗺 How to

Where to go Head to the city centre for the highest concentration of good restaurants and bars. You'll also find some cheap eats and international food options.

Expect to pay From $15 for a cheap lunch. Fine dining restaurants can charge up to $40 for a main.

Local favourites Try Christchurch's take on souvlaki – a cone-shaped pita overflowing with meat, salad and sauce.

TRABANTOS/SHUTTERSTOCK ©

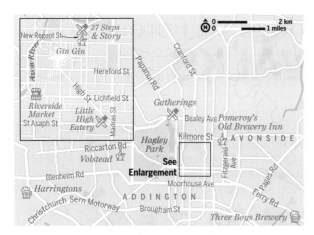

Left New Regent St
Below Riverside Market

Quick eats If you're after a quick eat or need to cater for a diverse group of eaters, head to either **Riverside Market** or **Little High Eatery** in the city centre. Riverside Market is situated near the river and is open all day, with indoor and outdoor seating. Along with some new dining options, many of the city's most popular eateries have a presence here. Further from the river, Little High Eatery offers a range of food and a fun atmosphere. It can get busy around the dinner rush but its urban setting provides for the perfect mix of tasty food and people-watching.

Cocktails and dinner Walk along **New Regent St** for a variety of delicious food options in a charming setting. Grab a pre-dinner cocktail at **Gin Gin** before heading to a nearby restaurant for dinner – both **Story** restaurant and **27 Steps** are excellent choices (see p204). If you have the time, venture slightly north of the CBD to try **Gatherings** restaurant (p204), a local favourite and one of Christchurch's top-rated restaurants.

Sample local craft beer Local breweries have been thriving in Christchurch in recent years and, if you like beer, visiting a local microbrewery is a must. There are several good bars in the city including **Harringtons** and **Three Boys Brewery**. On the city fringe, try **Pomeroy's**, the **Volstead** and **Darkroom Bar**, which are popular with locals.

Wine Country with Mountain Views

Take a drive out of Christchurch and explore the North Canterbury wine region. Waipara Valley, on the road to Lewis Pass, has excellent wine, locally grown food and relatively few visitors.

An up-and-coming wine region, North Canterbury is known for its aromatic whites, particularly pinot gris, riesling and gewurtz, and is building a reputation for its pinot noir too.

There are over 90 vineyards in the region, and **Waipara Springs Winery and Restaurant** makes an excellent destination to stop for lunch and taste some of the region's produce for yourself.

41 Bridges & Forest **WALKS**

WALKS | DAY TRIP | SWIMMING

■■■■ Pick your path to the Hokitika Gorge and marvel at the turquoise waters and thick native forest. Stop for a quick photo, head down to the river or take an easy 2km walk through the bush and over a swing bridge with wonderful views of the gorge. Stop for a swim at glacial LakeKaniere and waterfall on the way back to Hokitika.

RAIMUND LINKE/GETTY IMAGES ©

🗺 **How to**

Getting here Hokitika Gorge is about half an hour's drive from Hokitika.

When to go There are fewer visitors early in the day or late in the afternoon, although the colour of the water tends to be more intense around midday. Avoid visiting after heavy rain as the water looks grey rather than deep blue.

Top tip Take insect repellent as there are mosquitos and sandflies in the gorge.

SHAUN JEFFERS/SHUTTERSTOCK ©

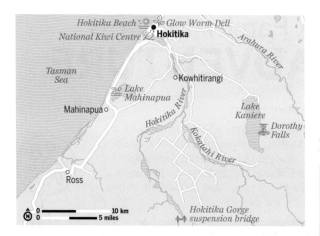

Hokitika Gorge suspension bridge

Left Hokitika Gorge suspension bridge
Below Dorothy Falls

Gaze at the turquoise water Sweeping views of the Hokitika Gorge are visible from a viewing platform just a five-minute stroll from the car park. This part of the track is accessible for wheelchairs and prams and the viewpoint looks out over the turquoise water and majestic swing bridge, making a great photo stop.

Relax on the river bank Continue through the forested track and cross the swing bridge to enjoy more spectacular views of the river. Take a detour through a small gate, to the rocks and a small beach at the river below. Take note of the warning signs, as swimming in the river can be dangerous. It's a peaceful spot, particularly at quiet times, with clear water flowing across the white rocks at your feet.

Cross the suspension bridge For those craving a longer walk, follow the trail past small waterfalls and native bush to the impressive upper Hokitika Gorge suspension bridge. Cross the bridge, then walk through the shady forest to the car park. The loop takes about an hour to complete and is suitable for children.

Take the scenic route back Head back to Hokitika via Lake Kaniere, a half-hour drive from the gorge. Take a picnic and relax by the water. Then head around the lake, back to Hokitika, stopping at Dorothy Falls, a cascading waterfall, on the way.

◎ **Things to do in Hokitika**

- Visit the **Glow Worm Dell** after dark to see the glowworms lighting up the trees and the forest.

- Watch the sunset on **Hokitika Beach**.

- Feed the eels and see kiwi at the **National Kiwi Centre**.

- Take a walk along **Lake Mahinapua**, just 10km south of Hokitika. This is particularly good for children, with safe swimming.

- Follow the **Hokitika Heritage Walk** for interesting insights into local history.

- Take a ride on the **West Coast Wilderness Trail** as a day trip or longer.

■ Recommended by Sharyn & Butch Symons
Hokitika locals and owners of Amberlea Cottages

42 A Family-Friendly ADVENTURE

FAMILY-FRIENDLY | HIKING | SWIMMING

━━━ Walk through the forest, alongside a blue, glacial river to a lake with mirror-like reflections of mountains and sky. Camp at the lakeside or stay in a modern hut and spend your time swimming, fishing or simply marvelling at the stars. The track to Lake Daniell is accessible for all ages – you can walk it, run it, stay overnight or just visit for the day.

STEVE TODD/SHUTTERSTOCK ©

🗺 How to

Getting here Lake Daniell is signposted off SH7 near Lewis Pass. It's a 2½- to three-hour drive from Christchurch, or just over an hour from Hanmer Springs.

When to go Go in summer if you want to swim. During winter, you'll have snow on all the peaks around you – just remember to check for avalanche risks.

What to bring Layers, a swimsuit, sunblock, insect repellent and a raincoat, just in case.

NICKSPLACE/GETTY IMAGES ©

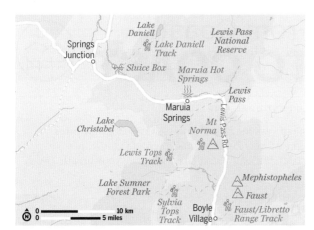

Left Lake Daniell Track
Below Tomtit

A hike for the whole family A great trail for beginners or families, the Lake Daniell Track is reasonably flat and takes around two to three hours one way. The route takes you through forests and over bridges with views of the surrounding mountains.

A highlight on the walk is the **Sluice Box**, a narrow channel cut into the rock by the Maruia River. The water is a deep blue and the bridge over the small gorge makes for gorgeous photos.

Relax at the lake The hike culminates at **Lake Daniell**, a clear, shallow lake tucked into mountains. On a still day, the reflections of the nearby peaks in the water make for remarkable photos. Stay overnight to give little legs a rest and make the most of the safe swimming and good fishing.

The DOC hut at the lake has double glazing and a fire, and is very spacious and modern. You do need to book in advance, but that guarantees your bed, which gives you peace of mind when travelling with little ones. There is also a cooking shelter for campers.

Feathered companions The track to Lake Daniell is part of a special biodiversity area, meaning the area is predator-free. As a result, you're likely to see some of New Zealand's favourite birds on the walk with tomtit, rifleman, tūī, fernbird, silvereye, grey warbler, bellbird, and even kākā living in the area.

 Looking for More of a Challenge?

Try one of the several tracks that take you up on one of the peaks, also known as the Tops. There are four to choose from: Sylvia Tops, Mt Faust/ Libretto Range, Lewis Tops and Mt Norma.

Go running or hiking, savour the forest, camp by tarns and enjoy the stars.

Then soak it all away at **Maruia Hot Springs**, natural hot pools overlooking rugged, mountainous landscapes. They are geothermally heated and all electricity is hydro generated. The pools are in a stunning location and they have a number of accommodation options.

 ■ **Recommended by Aaron & Mariska Penman** *Canterbury locals and outdoor enthusiasts*

43 From Coast **TO COAST**

MOUNTAINS | SCENIC TRAIN | NATIONAL PARK

▬▬▬ Make your way through sweeping mountain views, past alpine lakes and rivers, and through some of New Zealand's most remote landscapes. The route from the South Island's east to west coast will take your breath away, and fill your camera's memory card.

STEVE HEAP/SHUTTERSTOCK ©

🗺 How to

Getting When to go Visit all year round. The pass is especially beautiful between June and October, when the mountains are covered in snow. Use chains in June and July as there can be ice on the roads.

Stop for photos Take your camera and allow extra time for the trip. There are many beautiful viewpoints on the route which are well-signposted.

Top tip Stop in Arthur's Pass village to see the kea, a native mountain parrot.

🚆 An Alpine Railway

The TranzAlpine railway connects Christchurch and the West Coast via the Waimakariri River Gorge (pictured) and the spectacular Arthur's Pass. The journey takes just under five hours and meanders through some of New Zealand's most beautiful scenery, which can be fully appreciated through the train's viewing carriage.

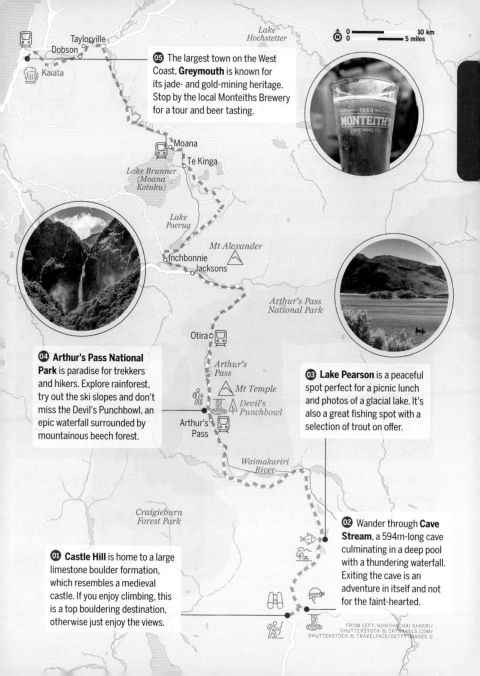

Taylorville

Dobson

Kaiata

05 The largest town on the West Coast, **Greymouth** is known for its jade- and gold-mining heritage. Stop by the local Monteiths Brewery for a tour and beer tasting.

Lake Hochstetter

0   10 km
0   5 miles

Moana

Te Kinga

Lake Brunner (Moana Kotuku)

Lake Poerua

Mt Alexander

Inchbonnie

Jacksons

Arthur's Pass National Park

Otira

Arthur's Pass

04 Arthur's Pass National Park is paradise for trekkers and hikers. Explore rainforest, try out the ski slopes and don't miss the Devil's Punchbowl, an epic waterfall surrounded by mountainous beech forest.

Mt Temple

Devil's Punchbowl

Arthur's Pass

03 Lake Pearson is a peaceful spot perfect for a picnic lunch and photos of a glacial lake. It's also a great fishing spot with a selection of trout on offer.

Waimakariri River

Craigieburn Forest Park

02 Wander through **Cave Stream**, a 594m-long cave culminating in a deep pool with a thundering waterfall. Exiting the cave is an adventure in itself and not for the faint-hearted.

01 Castle Hill is home to a large limestone boulder formation, which resembles a medieval castle. If you enjoy climbing, this is a top bouldering destination, otherwise just enjoy the views.

44 Whales in THE WILD

WILDLIFE | MARINE LIFE | NATURE

See the giant sperm whale up close in the waters of Kaikōura, on the east coast of the South Island. Search for whales by boat or in the air and take in your beautiful surroundings with dramatic mountain landscapes in the distance. If you're lucky, you'll also see a variety of other marine animals including orca, dolphins, humpback whales, seals and seabirds.

WINTAWATWINWIN/SHUTTERSTOCK ©

How to

Getting here Kaikōura is under 2½ hours' drive from Christchurch. You can also take a scenic train from Christchurch or Picton.

When to go Sperm whales are resident in Kaikōura all year round.

Expect to pay $150 to $200 per adult. Tours start at $60 for children.

What to wear Prepare for all weather conditions and bring rain jackets, hats, wind breakers, extra layers, sunblock, glasses etc.

NATALIA KHLAPAK/SHUTTERSTOCK ©

FELICITY MEADE/SHUTTERSTOCK ©

Far left Sperm whale
Below Yellow-eyed penguin
Left Dusky dolphin

Getting out on the ocean Spend a day in a boat searching the seas for whales. The giant sperm whale is visible all year round and watching one in the water is a magical experience. There is a high chance of seeing a whale on boat tours (there's even a partial refund if you don't) and on clear days, you can even catch a glimpse of these majestic creatures from shore.

Whale watching from the sky If you're after an extra special whale-watching experience, head to the skies. Take a helicopter ride over the ocean and mountains and spot the whales from the air. In winter, you can also land on a snowy mountaintop, and the scenery is breathtaking all year round.

Meet the other marine visitors There is more than sperm whales to see in Kaikōura. Visit in January, February or March to see the wide variety of species visible off the coast, including dolphins, orca, penguins, seals and albatross. From June to August there is also an opportunity to see other migrating whales, including humpback whales, pilot whales and even blue whales.

The ultimate memento If you are in search of the ultimate scenic photograph, go whale watching between May and August. The air is clear and the mountains are covered in snow, providing the ultimate backdrop.

🐋 Tips for Whale-Watching

The weather and sea conditions are very unpredictable – we suggest you prepare for all weather conditions.

Make sure you have plenty of space on your phones or cameras for footage and images. Both the scenery and the marine life you will encounter are worthy of capturing for lasting memories.

If your sea legs aren't great and you tend get a wee bit queasy on the sea, the local pharmacy has created a lifesaver for sea sickness. Just ask for the 'Kaikōura Cracker' at the pharmacy in town.

■ **Recommended by Abba Kahu**
Whale Watch Kaikoura
@whalewatchkaikoura

45 Cycle the Wild **WEST COAST**

CYCLING | FOREST | HISTORY

Cycle along historic bush tramlines past alpine lakes and through shady forests and wetlands to the rugged coast. Follow the tracks made by pioneering miners and discover historic gold-mining towns and old bridges, with views of the snowcapped Southern Alps in the distance.

ANDREW BAIN/ALAMY STOCK PHOTO ©

CENTRAL SOUTH ISLAND EXPERIENCES

🗺 Trip Notes

Getting around The West Coast Wilderness Trail (pictured above) takes four days to cycle; however, you can pick a section of the trail for a day trip. It's also possible to drive between the towns and explore your surroundings by foot.

Bike hire There are bike hire and repair shops in the nearby towns of Greymouth and Hokitika.

Luggage transfers You can do a cycle tour which includes shuttles and luggage transfers, or book as a single service.

A Day Ride: 🚲 Hokitika to the Tree Top Walk

This 15km route crosses the Hokitika River and continues through Mahinapua Forest. The trail winds through the dense bush, birds are singing and the sun peeps through the treetops. You will cycle through wetlands and over a boardwalk with old relics visible alongside the trail.

■ Recommended by **Donna Baird**
West Coast Cycle and Tours, Hokitika
@westcoast_cycle_tours

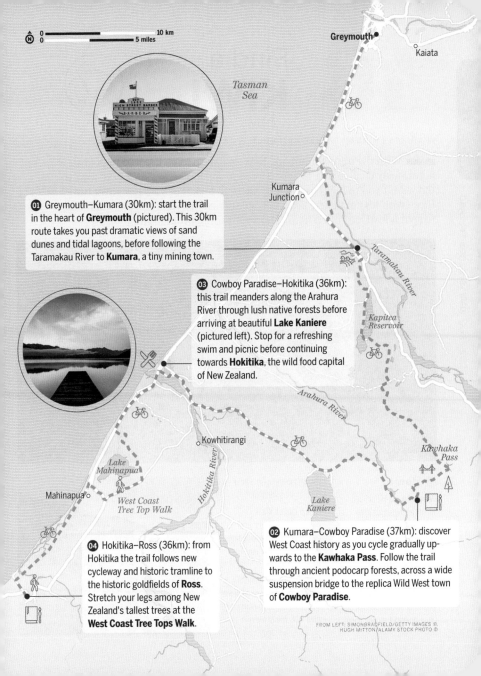

Greymouth
Kaiata

Tasman Sea

Kumara Junction

Taramakau River

Kapitea Reservoir

01 Greymouth–Kumara (30km): start the trail in the heart of **Greymouth** (pictured). This 30km route takes you past dramatic views of sand dunes and tidal lagoons, before following the Taramakau River to **Kumara**, a tiny mining town.

03 Cowboy Paradise–Hokitika (36km): this trail meanders along the Arahura River through lush native forests before arriving at beautiful **Lake Kaniere** (pictured left). Stop for a refreshing swim and picnic before continuing towards **Hokitika**, the wild food capital of New Zealand.

Arahura River

Kowhitirangi

Kawhaka Pass

Lake Mahinapua

Hokitika River

Mahinapua

West Coast Tree Top Walk

Lake Kaniere

02 Kumara–Cowboy Paradise (37km): discover West Coast history as you cycle gradually upwards to the **Kawhaka Pass**. Follow the trail through ancient podocarp forests, across a wide suspension bridge to the replica Wild West town of **Cowboy Paradise**.

04 Hokitika–Ross (36km): from Hokitika the trail follows new cycleway and historic tramline to the historic goldfields of **Ross**. Stretch your legs among New Zealand's tallest trees at the **West Coast Tree Tops Walk**.

10 km
5 miles

46 Find a KIWI

WILDLIFE | BIRDS | FAMILY-FRIENDLY

With dwindling numbers, New Zealand's icon, the flightless kiwi, is notoriously challenging to spot. Here are some places you can see kiwi in the wild if you're lucky and know where to look. For younger adventurers or those with less patience, head to a wildlife centre where you're guaranteed to spot a kiwi and often help support breeding programmes.

NATURE PICTURE LIBRARY/ALAMY STOCK PHOTO ©

🗺 How to

When to go Head out at night-time as kiwi are nocturnal. Try to keep things as dark as possible and consider covering your torch (flashlight) to dim the light.

What to wear Clothing that doesn't make too much noise when you move is essential.

Keep quiet Walk extremely slowly and quietly, looking into the bushes around you for movement.

Expect to pay Wildlife centre tickets are around $25 to $35 for adults and $15 for children.

VIKTOR HEJNA/SHUTTERSTOCK ©

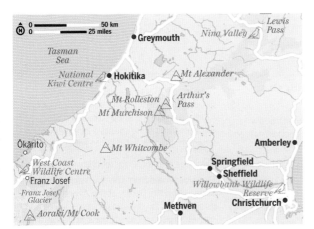

Left Rowi, Okarito Forest
Below Nina Valley, Lewis Pass

In the wild in a valley in North Canterbury A local high school has worked with DOC to repatriate 18 kiwi in the **Nina Valley**, near Lewis Pass in North Canterbury. Over the last decade, Hurunui College students have been managing the conservation of native roroa (great spotted kiwi) and whio (blue duck) here. It's a beautiful spot to stay overnight, camping by the river or sleeping in a DOC hut. While you are here, take a night-time walk and see if you can spot a kiwi in the wild.

Fully grown kiwi in the forest The thick forests of the secluded West Coast are the home of a kiwi conservation programme run by the charity Kiwis for Kiwis in partnership with DOC. The programme is called **Operation Nest Egg**, where kiwi eggs are taken to incubation sites, hatched and sent to predator-free islands to grow. When they are too large for stoats to kill, they are returned to the Ōkārito Forest in South Westland.

Visit a wildlife centre For guaranteed kiwi viewing head to the **National Kiwi Centre** in Hokitika, the **West Coast Wildlife Centre** in Franz Josef or the **Willowbank Wildlife Reserve** in Christchurch. All three have kiwi in residence and the centres in Franz Josef and Christchurch also have fascinating kiwi breeding programmes on-site. Younger visitors can also enjoy seeing a range of other animals or feeding eels in Hokitika.

South Island Kiwi

Haast tokoeka Found in the subalpine grasslands near Haast and identifiable by their brown and grey plumage with a reddish tinge.

Roroa (great spotted kiwi) Found from Arthur's Pass to the Paparoa Range and the northwestern top of the South Island. They are also known as the great grey kiwi.

Rowi (Ōkārito brown kiwi) Found in Ōkārito, this is New Zealand's most endangered kiwi. They are distinguished by their greyish colour and often have white patches on their face. The rowi can live up to 100 years of age – twice as long as the North Island brown kiwi.

Listings

BEST OF THE REST

Meals Worth Lingering Over

Blue Lake Eatery, Tekapo $$

Beautifully presented food in an attractive setting in the heart of Tekapo. Good variety to the menu, with good craft beers on offer.

Gatherings, Christchurch $$$

A small, intimate restaurant known for its delicious food. Locally sourced, high-quality ingredients are served in creative ways. The seafood is especially popular. Sample the impressive wine selection on offer. Bookings recommended.

Gatherer, Hokitika $$$

If you're vegetarian or vegan, look no further for a colourful, flavoursome meal. Mexican-inspired, plant-based food which everyone will love, accompanied by an extensive list of cocktails, craft beer and organic wine.

27 Steps, Christchurch $$$

A wonderful dining experience with great food and excellent service, right in the city centre. One of the most popular restaurants in Christchurch; bookings are essential.

Story, Christchurch $$$

Indian food, with a fine-dining twist, served in a cosy atmosphere. It's renowned for its set menus, so good when you're hungry. Be sure to book in advance.

Great Coffee, Better Food

Greedy Cow, Tekapo $$

Go for breakfast or lunch or get a pastry or sandwich on the go and enjoy arguably the best coffee in Tekapo. It's situated in the centre of town, so grab a snack and eat it by the lake.

Barker's Foodstore & Eatery, Geraldine $$

Stop in for brunch and coffee and enjoy good-sized portions and delicious, hearty food. Check in the shop to sample the chutneys and condiments. Accessible for wheelchairs and prams.

Riverside Market, Christchurch $$

Pick your meal from the Riverside Market, situated on the banks of the Avon River. A good choice for diverse groups – you'll find something to suit everyone's tastes at the market.

Sevenpenny, Greymouth $$

A local favourite serving good food throughout the day, with friendly staff in a great, central location. Head here for breakfast and you won't be disappointed!

Little High Eatery, Christchurch $$

An upmarket food court in central Christchurch. Take your pick from several eateries with a shared seating area. Good for catching up with friends, particularly if you have different tastes.

Pork Belly Apple Pie, Fairlie Bakehouse

Café Verde, Geraldine $$

Situated in a garden and perfect for those travelling with children. Enjoy good food and well-sized portions in a peaceful setting, with playground equipment on-site for the little ones.

Betsy Jane Eatery & Bar, Fox Glacier $$

The best burgers in glacier country. A great option for a filling meal after a long day exploring the national park. The steak and blue cod is also worth a try.

 Quick & Affordable Eats

Sheffield Pie Shop $

Stop for a quick bite with some of the most popular pies in New Zealand. Filling, simple fare that's sure to keep you going during your outdoor adventures.

Cray Pot, Jackson Bay $$

Widely regarded as the best fish and chip shop on the West Coast and renowned for its blue cod, whitebait fritters and crayfish salad. Fresh and perfectly prepared every time.

Hokitika Sandwich Shop $$

If the bottomless coffee isn't enough to attract you, the substantial sandwiches definitely will be: fresh baked bread piled with local ingredients. Order ahead if you're in a rush as there's often a queue.

Fairlie Bakehouse $

Serving award-winning pies that are a must-try if you're in the area. Pies are freshly baked daily, using local ingredients. The salmon pie is especially popular. Gluten-free options are available.

Nourish Nook, Westport $

Get your caffeine fix from a quaint food truck, with artisan sandwiches, breakfast bowls and pastries on the go. Great-tasting food and more-ish coffee. A must for coffee addicts.

Sir Edmund Hillary Alpine Centre

Cocktails, Wines & Beer

Terrace Edge, Waipara $$

Award-winning, organic winery offering aromatic white wine and a small selection of light reds. Opt for the food pairing with your wine tasting to sample carefully prepared local foods. Follow with a stroll through the expansive grounds.

Reefton Distilling Co $$

A gin-lover's paradise, perfect for long afternoons sipping gin flavoured with local botanicals. Sample a selection of gins and discover more about the gin-making process on a tour of the modern distillery.

Monteiths Brewery, Greymouth $$

The home of Monteiths beer. Stop by for lunch or a pint. The brewery tours and tastings are incredibly popular, offering a glimpse behind the scenes of a large-scale brewery.

Heritage, Nature & Hot Springs

Sir Edmund Hillary Alpine Centre

Learn about the life of Sir Edmund Hillary at this small museum. There's a range of memorabilia on display and documentaries to view. Situated in Aoraki/Mt Cook National Park.

Tekapo Springs

A perfect place for families to stop after a long drive, right in the middle of Tekapo. Relaxing hot pools, offering ice skating in winter and a fascinating stargazing night-time experience.

Dark Sky Project, Tekapo

Located in the Aoraki Mackenzie International Dark Sky Reserve, this is a wonderful place to see some of the brightest stars in the world. Learn about the southern skies and Māori astronomy or go on a guided tour to Mt John Observatory.

Maruia Hot Springs

A great place to relax tired muscles after a hike, especially in winter. Soak in quiet, peaceful surroundings with expansive bush views. Situated in the Lewis Pass National Park.

West Coast Tree Top Walk

Stroll above the rimu and kamahi trees and marvel at the views over Lake Mahinapua, the beautiful West Coast forest, and the majestic Southern Alps. Suitable for all ages.

Ross Goldfields

Explore the old goldfields near the tiny village of Ross. Discover the history of the site, wander past abandoned machinery and see an old mining cottage. You can even pan for gold in the river!

△ Glacier Adventures & Mountain Expeditions

Franz Josef Wilderness Tours

Go kayaking, fishing or take a cruise in lakes with a mirror-like reflection among the Southern Alps and glaciers. Or challenge yourself by exploring glaciers on foot, by helicopter or on a quad bike.

Mt Cook Ski Planes & Helicopters, Mt Cook

Fly through the Southern Alps, see the lakes and Hochstetter Icefall from the air and land on New Zealand's longest glacier, the Tasman Glacier. Walk along the glacier and explore ice caves if the weather allows.

Mt Cook Heliskiing

Head to the largest heliski area in New Zealand, with alpine guides taking you on the most exciting trails in Aoraki/Mt Cook National Park. Explore the incredible terrain through New Zealand's highest peaks.

Alpine Guides, Mt Cook

Your go-to for guided climbing, mountaineering and glacier hikes. New Zealand's longest established mountain-guiding company can take you on the hidden tracks to make the most of your South Island adventure.

Getting Close to Wildlife

Whale Watch Kaikoura

Gaze at sperm whales, dolphins and seals in their natural environment from an excellent vantage point on the water. A unique opportunity to learn about marine mammals and seabirds in an extraordinary setting.

South Pacific Helicopters NZ, Kaikōura

Head into the sky and see whales, dolphins and fur seals from above. Take a scenic flight over Kaikōura's dramatic landscape and look down on the stunning coast. An exhilarating experience.

Maruia Hot Springs

NARUEDOM YAEMPONGSA/SHUTTERSTOCK ©

Willowbank Wildlife Reserve

A must for learning about New Zealand birds and wildlife and a wonderful opportunity to see a kiwi up close. Wander through the trails and learn about Māori culture and native birds.

Franz Josef Wildlife Centre

See kiwi and tuatara up close and learn more about conservation efforts and kiwi breeding programmes. Take the backstage tour to see the incubation and kiwi-rearing facilities.

 **Scenic Journeys**

TranzAlpine Railway, Christchurch

Take one of the world's greatest scenic train journeys from Christchurch to the West Coast. Admire the remarkable scenery from the viewing carriage or stop along the way to explore the mountains and countryside.

West Coast Cycle & Tours, Hokitika

Get everything you need to cycle the West Coast Wilderness Trail, including bike hire, shuttle pick-up and great advice. Challenge yourself on the four-day ride, or opt for a day out in the stunning natural surroundings.

Underworld Adventures, Charleston

Explore caves adorned with glowworms, try underwater rafting or take a scenic train ride through peaceful rainforest with views of huge karsts. Good for families with older kids and outdoor enthusiasts of all ages.

Local Delicacies

Mt Cook Alpine Salmon, Pukaki

High-quality salmon, sustainably farmed in the glacial water in the Mackenzie region. Fresh and smoked options available at the shop, as well as sashimi, which can be eaten on-site with stunning lake views.

ALISHA NEWTON/SHUTTERSTOCK ©

Takahe, Willowbank Wildlife Reserve

Blackball Salami Co

Award-winning producers of excellent salami, black pudding, bacon and sausages. High-quality products with tastings available in store. A great option if you're self-catering during your trip.

 Carefully Crafted Treasures

IaNZ Art Copper Artisan, Hokitika

Intricate and fascinating copper artwork and a range of gemstones on display. Learn more about the pieces and copper-working and purchase a unique piece of art or jewellery to take home.

Hokitika Glass Studio

Beautiful, unique pieces of handblown glass in a variety of colours, including bowls, vases and tiny figurines. Watch the fascinating process of glassblowing and pick a treasure to keep.

Traditional Jade Hokitika

Handmade New Zealand *pounamu* (greenstone) perfect to give as gifts (traditionally greenstone is given, not bought). Learn the meanings behind the Māori symbols or choose a more contemporary piece.

 Scan to find more things to do in Central South Island online

THE DEEP SOUTH

ADVENTURE | SCENERY | WILDLIFE

Experience
the Deep
South online

Explore bookable experiences in the Deep South

Climb **Ben Lomand**, high above Queenstown, for views to die for (p214)
🚶 *5min from Queenstown*

Drive the spectacular **Milford Road** into Fiordland (p220)
🚗 *240km return from Te Anau*

Milford Sound

Paradise

Fiordland National Park

The Divide

Glenorchy

Te Anau Downs

Mavora Lakes

Lake Te Anau

Jane Peak

●**Te Anau**

Deep Cove

Lake Manapōuri

West Arm

●**Manapōuri**

Mossburn○

Takitimu Forest

Resolution Island

Lake Monowai

○**Ohai**

Lake Hauroko

○Clifden

Lake Poteriteri

●**Tuatapere**

Colac Bay

Riverton

Foveaux Strait

THE DEEP SOUTH
Trip Builder

▬▬▬ Think of the Deep South as being a tad like the Wild West. Almost anything goes here, with adventurous mountain resorts, remote fiords and islands, weird and wonderful wildlife, plus historic goldfields and world-famous wineries.

Oban

Stewart Island/ Rakiura

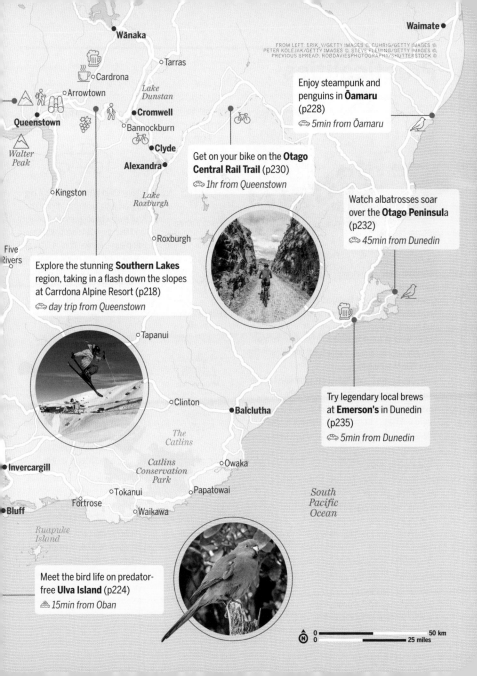

Waimate •

Wānaka

○ Tarras

Cardrona

○ Arrowtown

Cromwell

Queenstown

○ Bannockburn

Lake Dunstan

Clyde

Alexandra

Walter Peak

○ Kingston

Lake Roxburgh

Enjoy steampunk and penguins in **Ōamaru** (p228)
🚗 *5min from Ōamaru*

Get on your bike on the **Otago Central Rail Trail** (p230)
🚗 *1hr from Queenstown*

Watch albatrosses soar over the **Otago Peninsul**a (p232)
🚗 *45min from Dunedin*

○ Roxburgh

Five Rivers ○

Explore the stunning **Southern Lakes** region, taking in a flash down the slopes at Carrdona Alpine Resort (p218)
🚗 *day trip from Queenstown*

○ Tapanui

○ Clinton

Try legendary local brews at **Emerson's** in Dunedin (p235)
🚗 *5min from Dunedin*

Balclutha

• **Invercargill**

The Catlins

Catlins Conservation Park

○ Owaka

○ Tokanui

○ Papatowai

South Pacific Ocean

Fortrose

• **Bluff**

○ Waikawa

Ruapuke Island

Meet the bird life on predator-free **Ulva Island** (p224)
⛴ *15min from Oban*

0 ──── 50 km
0 ──── 25 miles

Practicalities

STOCKPHOTO MANIA/SHUTTERSTOCK ©

ARRIVING

Queenstown Airport Located 7km east of the town centre, this is the region's busiest airport and fourth busiest in the country. International flights wing in from Australia. Orbus Queenstown (orc.govt.nz) runs buses into town and around the Lake Wakatipu Basin.

Dunedin Airport Located 22km southwest of the CBD. Shuttles and taxis run into the city.

Invercargill Airport Located 2km west of the city. There are flights from here to Stewart Island/Rakiura (stewartislandflights.co.nz).

HOW MUCH FOR A

Bungy jump
$200

Daily lift pass
$130

Milford Sound cruise
$80

GETTING AROUND

Your Own Wheels This is a big region with far-flung attractions. Your own wheels provide flexibility and the chance to stop whenever you please. Rental cars, 4WDs and campervans are readily available at major airports and towns. Rental bicycles are all over.

Buses & Shuttles InterCity (intercity.co.nz) operates buses between the region's cities, while shuttle companies run to smaller towns and hiking trailheads. Buses depart daily to the ski areas from the resort towns in winter.

Ferry Hop on the ferry at Bluff for the one-hour crossing of Foveaux Strait to Stewart Island/Rakiura.

WHEN TO GO

DEC–JAN
The height of summer; expect crowds of Kiwi families.

MAR–APR
Golden autumn leaves; temperatures starting to cool.

JUN–OCT
Snow time at the Queenstown and Wānaka resort ski areas.

NOV–APR
Hiking season on tracks throughout the south.

EATING & DRINKING

For craft beer, try Altitude (p235) in Queenstown, Emerson's (p235) in Dunedin and Scotts Brewing (p235) in Ōamaru. Central Otago wineries are renowned for their pinot noir, while the Cardrona Distillery crafts fine spirits. Cafes abound, none better than Queenstown's Bespoke Kitchen (p215).

The resorts boast an abundance of eateries. Try venison at Redcliffs (p237) in Te Anau, legendary Bluff oysters (pictured bottom right; season March to August), and don't pass on seafood at the South Sea Hotel (p236) on Stewart Island/Rakiura.

Best bar
Blue Door (p235), Arrowtown

Must-try burgers
Fergburger (pictured top right; p236), Queenstown

CONNECT & FIND YOUR WAY

Mobile Networks & Wi-Fi There is good coverage in the cities and resort towns, but limited coverage in remote mountain areas.

DOC There are DOC visitor centres (doc.govt.nz) in Queenstown, Wānaka, Te Anau, Dunedin and in Oban on Stewart Island/Rakiura.

DRIVING ROUTES SOUTH

State Hwy 1 (SH1) runs down the east coast from Christchurch to Dunedin; SH8 goes through the middle to Central Otago; and SH6 runs between the west coast and Wānaka.

WHERE TO STAY

Visitor hotspots offer good accommodation options; most have places to suit all budgets. Book early for the summer season (November to March) and the winter sports season in the resorts (June to September).

City/Town	Pro/Con
Queenstown	Plenty of options but can get busy in Aotearoa's top resort town.
Wānaka	Popular mountain and lakeside resort with lots of places to stay and play.
Te Anau	Caters for all budgets as the gateway to Fiordland National Park.
Dunedin	The South Island's second-biggest city is a good base for exploring Otago Peninsula.
Ōamaru	Stay to see the penguins in the evening, but options are limited.
Oban	Book before you go as accommodation is limited on Stewart Island/Rakiura.

MONEY

Check out Queenstown start-up company **First Table** (firsttable.co.nz) for 50% off your food bill when you book the 'first table' for breakfast, lunch or dinner at participating restaurants (rapidly expanding throughout the country).

 Climbing Ben
LOMOND

HIKING | SCENERY | ADVENTURE

▬▬▬▬ Queenstown may be known
as 'the adventure capital of the
world', but you don't have to jump
in a jetboat or throw yourself off
a bridge with a rubber band tied
to your ankles to have an exciting
outdoor experience.

▢ How to

Getting here Walk up to the Skyline Gondola from central Queenstown.

When to go Best hiking is from November to April; visit Queenstown's DOC office (doc.govt.nz) for track conditions.

Best advice Shorten the day with a gondola ticket (skyline.co.nz), taking two hours and 500 vertical metres off the climb and descent; allow five to six hours for the return hike from Skyline.

Be prepared Ben Lomond's summit is nearly 1500 vertical metres above Queenstown; take warm clothing, sunscreen, and plenty of liquids and snacks.

THE DEEP SOUTH EXPERIENCES

Skyline Views

Named after Ben Lomond in the Scottish Highlands, Queenstown's Ben Lomond is the massive mountain that towers almost directly behind town. At 1748m, it provides a spectacular alpine backdrop for Lake Wakatipu and the country's best known resort.

Thanks to **Skyline Gondola**, however, the peak is surprisingly accessible. The gondola whisks visitors up from town to 800m above sea level at Skyline in five minutes – leaving less than 1000 vertical metres of climbing to the summit. You'll recognise the stunning vista from Skyline's viewing deck from all those iconic images that enticed you to come to Queenstown in the first place. While the township sits far below, **Lake Wakatipu** is a mesmerising deep blue and the rugged Remarkables mountain range dominates

☕ Bespoke Kitchen

Named NZ's Cafe of the Year only six months after opening, **Bespoke Kitchen** (bespokekitchen.nz) isn't far from the Skyline Gondola's bottom station. Either fuel up for the hike in the morning, or recover here later with tasty delicacies off the menu or from the enticing cabinet choices.

Above left Queenstown
Above Ben Lomond Saddle
Left Skyline Gondola

to the east. Taking endless photos is as far as most visitors get though.

Climbing to the Peak

Get mentally prepared to go higher. Head out the back of the Skyline building and follow signage for Ben Lomond, initially through and over Skyline's luge tracks, then into the dark Douglas fir forest. By this stage you'll have left the populated world behind. Within 10 minutes, your first views of the peak of Ben Lomond from the track unfold before you, dead ahead. It's a magnificent mountain, if a somewhat daunting looking climb.

After passing through a patch of native beech forest, you'll be above the treeline and climbing steadily towards Ben Lomond Saddle on a well-formed track, fringed with low-growing tussock. Views to the south and east out over glacial-carved Lake Wakatipu and its surrounding mountains just get better and better as you climb. Once you hit **Ben**

⚠ Ben Lomond Tips

Climbing Ben Lomond is a highlight of any trip to Queenstown, but shouldn't be taken lightly. It's a big climb, especially if you walk the whole way to the summit from the bottom of the gondola. I highly recommend using the gondola, at least on the way up, for a more enjoyable day. Don't forget to head out to the Skyline viewing deck for spectacular views before you start walking. The weather can change very quickly up in the mountains. Check forecasts before you go and be adequately prepared.

■ Recommended by **Henare Dewes**
mountain and fishing guide
@exploremaorisamurai

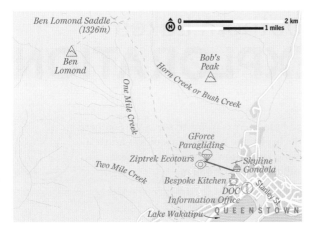

GForce
Paragliding

Ziptrek Ecotours

Skyline
Gondola

Bespoke Kitchen

DOC
Information Office

Lake Wakatipu

QUEENSTOWN

Left Hiking, Ben Lomond
Below Paragliding from Skyline

Lomond Saddle at 1326m, snowcapped distant peaks pop into view to the north, and it's time for a break.

There's still a 420m climb to the imposing peak though, high to the southwest. As you ascend up the ridgeline, the track you walked up from Skyline sits far below, then as the trail curls around near the peak, horseshoe-shaped Moke Lake appears below to the west. After a final push you'll be at the top, with a 360-degree panorama of mountains and lakes. It feels strange to be so high above and looking down on aircraft approaching to land at Queenstown Airport. It's kind of like sitting on top of the world. If you're lucky, kea (alpine parrots) will soar in to see what they can steal from your picnic lunch. They've done this before and work in teams, so don't fall for any of their tricks!

A Quick Descent from Skyline

From the peak, you'll be walking back down to Skyline on the same track you climbed on. Should you be looking for more excitement, a couple of gravity-fuelled opportunities await for the final descent into Queenstown: tandem paragliding (nzgforce.com) down to land on Queenstown School's sports ground, or zipping down through the forest on one of the world's steepest ziplines (ziptrek.co.nz).

48 Southern Lakes
EXPLORATION

CULTURE | WINE | HISTORY

With Queenstown as a base, there is plenty to see in the Southern Lakes region. Head out on the big loop to Arrowtown, quirky Cardrona, Wānaka, Cromwell, then back to Queenstown through the rugged Kawarau Gorge and vineyard-filled Gibbston Valley.

JOHN A DAVIS/SHUTTERSTOCK ©

🗺️ **Trip notes**

Getting around Make the most of the day with your own wheels (but you'll need a designated driver).

When to go Year-round. The golden leaves of autumn are gorgeous; the Crown Range Rd can get icy in winter.

Best advice Leave the wineries until later in the day. Do the loop clockwise, heading to Arrowtown first, then over the Crown Range Rd to Cardrona.

Don't miss The Cardrona Bra Fence, opposite the Cardrona Alpine Resort entrance.

🍇 **My Favourite Wineries**

Rippon Vineyard (pictured above; rippon.co.nz) Stunning Lake Wānaka scenery.

Mt Difficulty Wines (mtdifficulty.nz) Winery restaurant in Bannockburn.

Te Kano Estate (tekanoestate.com) Wine, architecture and art.

Mt Rosa Wines (mtrosa.co.nz) Rustic cellar door in the vineyards.

■ **Recommended by Heidi Farren**
co-founder of Altitude Tours
@altitudetoursnz

03 Wander the waterfront and town centre of popular lakeside resort town **Wānaka**. It's hard to beat the backdrop, especially at Rippon Vineyard and Glendhu Bay.

02 At the alpine village of **Cardrona**, drop into the rustic 1863 Cardrona Hotel (cardronahotel.co.nz) for a coffee or Cardrona Ale, visit the Cardrona Distillery, and make a donation to the attention-grabbing Bra Fence.

01 In picturesque **Arrowtown**, walk historical Buckingham St, visit the Lakes District Museum and stroll by the Arrow River in this 1860s gold-rush town. April's Autumn Festival is a highlight.

04 The orchards and vineyards around **Cromwell** beckon with seasonal stone fruits and world-renowned pinot noir. Stroll the historic precinct, pick your own cherries in summer and revel in the countless wineries.

05 **Gibbston Valley** is home to wineries galore and the infamous bungy bridge (if wine has fortified your courage!). The drive to Chard Farm winery is an adventure in itself.

Lake Hāwea

Lake Wānaka

Rippon Vineyard

Albert Town

Roys Peak

Luggate

Tarras

Mt Cardrona

Bra Fence

Arrow River

Crown Peak

Mt Pisa

Bendigo

Arrow Junction

Kawarau Bridge

Gibbston

Chard Farm

Mt Rosa Wines

Kawarau Gorge

Lowburn

Lake Dunstan

Te Kano Estate

Bannockburn

Mt Difficulty Wines

0   10 km
0   5 miles

49 DRIVE TO
Milford Sound

SCENERY | WILDLIFE | ADVENTURE

With rugged snowcapped mountains, steep-sided, glacial-carved valleys and few roads, Ata Whenua/Fiordland is not the easiest to explore. But, the Milford Rd is, without doubt, one of the most spectacular drives in the world. While many race on through to meet a cruise departure point, it is woth taking your time for fascinating scenic stops and short walks along the way.

How to

Getting here Te Anau is the gateway to Fiordland National Park.

When to go Year-round, though winter driving conditions can be hazardous; occasionally closed due to avalanche danger in winter.

Recommendation Visit Fiordland National Park Visitor Centre and check weather forecasts in Te Anau before you go.

Important There are no petrol stations after Te Anau and no mobile-phone coverage after Te Anau Downs (28km from Te Anau).

Map showing: Tasman Sea, Milford, Milford Sound, Milford Foreshore Walk, The Chasm, Mt Talbot, Homer Tunnel, Hollyford, Gertrude Valley, Kaka Creek Lookout, Mt Anau (1956m), Fiordland National Park, Lake Gunn Nature Walk, David Peak, Knobs Flat, Eglinton Valley, Te Anau Downs, Lake Te Anau, Mavora Lakes, Mt Lyall, Fiordland National Park Visitor Centre, Te Anau. Scale: 0–20 km / 0–10 miles.

Engineering marvel
Before the Milford Rd was completed, the only way to get to Milford Sound/Piopiotahi was to walk on the Milford Track or to sail into the fiord from the Tasman Sea. But since the completion of the **Homer Tunnel**, visitors can drive the 120km to Milford from Te Anau. The 1.2km tunnel is an engineering marvel, a civil works project started in Depression-era 1935, but not completed until 1953.

The high point Jumping out of your car at the tunnel's eastern portal: the road's highest point, 945m above sea level and 99km from Te Anau, is an experience in itself. Sheer granite walls tower above, topped by ice and snow. Mangled steel and concrete by the tunnel entrance and melting piles of ice beside the road pay testimony to violent avalanches that have crashed down the precipitous walls. There's also a boulder-strewn valley,

Best Stops on the Milford Road

Eglinton Valley (53km from Te Anau) Mind-blowing views of this massive glacial-carved valley.

Lake Gunn Nature Walk (75km) A 45-minute loop walk through ancient beech forest; a top spot to see native birds.

Kaka Creek Lookout (88km) Glorious views into the Darran Mountains and of the Routeburn Track traverse.

Gertrude Valley (97km) A short walk into the valley to a proliferation of native flowering plants in summer.

The Chasm (110km) Short walk through beech forest to dramatic waterfalls.

Milford Foreshore Walk (119km) An enjoyable 20-minute walk with magnificent views out to Milford Sound.

 ■ **Recommended by Steve Norris**
owner of Trips & Tramps, Te Anau
@tripsandtramps

Above Approaching the Homer Tunnel, Milford Rd

and a thunderous waterfall that drops off the side of 2105m Mt Talbot. Below Talbot's eastern face is aptly named **Psychopath Wall**. The sheer steepness of the valley walls is breathtaking.

Don't be fooled! Adding to the alpine atmosphere, cheeky kea – super-intelligent, mountain parrots – emit raucous 'kiyaaaa' calls as they glide in to land on car roofs to see what they can steal or cadge from gullible visitors. This unbelievably rugged setting is Fiordland at its best. Savour it before driving through the tunnel and dropping down into Milford Sound.

SOUTHERN LIGHTSCAPES AUSTRALIA/
GETTY IMAGES ©

What's in a Name?

**IS IT TIME FOR A
FEW CHANGES?**

There are some weird and wonderful names in New Zealand. Milford Sound is actually a fiord and the Mt Cook lily is really the world's largest buttercup. Nobody knows who bestowed the name New Zealand on these islands and there's increasing interest in the use of te reo Māori as a language of public life.

As you drive out to magnificent Milford Sound/ Piopiotahi, consider this: Milford Sound is not actually a sound, but a fiord. A sound is a river valley flooded by the sea, while a fiord is carved by glacial action. The fiords of Fiordland were misnamed by early European explorers. In 1952, the new national park, highlighting the inconsistencies, became Fiordland National Park, but the individual fiords kept their names as sounds. Confused? Should such historical inconsistencies be corrected?

Who Named New Zealand?

Ask Kiwis who named New Zealand and you'll be surprised at the variety of answers. Many think that it was Dutchman Abel Tasman, the first European to turn up in 1642, but Tasman mistakenly named his discovery Staten Landt, thinking it was part of a land already called that by other Dutch explorers. When Dutch map-makers recognised Tasman's mistake, they needed a new name for his discovery. It's thought that as they already had a New Holland (later to become Australia) on the western side of what is now the Tasman Sea on their map, they labelled their name-needing landmass Nova Zeelandia after the Dutch maritime state of Zeeland.

It took 126 years for the next Europeans to show up. Captain James Cook dropped by in 1769, using a Dutch map, and as the land was labelled Nova Zeelandia on his map, he anglicised that to New Zealand. While New Holland became Australia in 1824, New Zealand didn't have any form of government at that time to consider such a change.

Left Milford Sound/Piopiotahi
Centre James Cook
Right Prime Minister Jacinda Ardern

Despite few Kiwis knowing where *old* Zealand is, and *new* Zealand having no relationship whatsoever with *old* Zealand,

Is it time for New Zealand to become Aotearoa New Zealand?

the name has stuck. Between 1840 and 1852, the North Island, South Island and Stewart Island were known as New Ulster, New Munster and New Leinster. Most breathe a sigh of relief on hearing that these names were scrapped.

These days, the North Island is also officially named Te Ika-a-Māui (the Fish of Māui), the South Island is Te Waipounamu (the Waters of Greenstone) and Stewart Island is Rakiura (Glowing Skies).

Time for a Rethink?

It's nearly 200 years since New Holland became Australia in 1824. Is it time for New Zealand to become Aotearoa? Or Aotearoa New Zealand? There are growing calls for recognition of Māori place names throughout the country, names that fit with an island nation in the South Pacific. Auckland is increasingly becoming known as Tāmaki Makaurau/Auckland – Tāmaki Makaurau meaning 'Tāmaki desired by many', in reference to its abundance of natural resources. Mt Cook has officially been known as Aoraki/Mt Cook since 1998, and the volcano that Captain Cook called Mt Egmont in 1770 is now known as Mt Taranaki.

Polls suggest that Kiwis like the name Aotearoa New Zealand. The practice of performing the national anthem in Māori, then in English, has been in place since the 1990s and in a similar fashion, it may not be long before the country's name becomes Aotearoa New Zealand.

 Road to a Republic?

The British monarch is head of state of New Zealand, presenting an interesting set of conundrums for a modern, egalitarian, immigrant country. A New Zealander cannot become head of state of New Zealand, as the head of state is chosen by birth, and as the British monarch is also the head of the Church of England, New Zealand's head of state can only be of one religion.

A number of former prime ministers, including David Lange, Jim Bolger and Helen Clark have expressed support for a republic, while present prime minister Jacinda Ardern believes the country will become a republic 'in her lifetime'. In early 2022, the Māori party called for a 'divorce' from Britain's royal family.

50

Bird Life on
ULVA ISLAND

ADVENTURE | WALKING | WILDLIFE

Discover wonderful bird life on the predator-free sanctuary of Ulva Island/Te Wharawhara, a short boat ride from the township of Oban on Stewart Island/Rakiura. Ulva is bristling with birds, including the flightless kiwi and weka, plus species such as the tīeke (saddleback) and mōhua (yellowhead), reintroduced to the island as part of conservation efforts to ensure their survival.

CHRISTIAN HANDL/GETTY IMAGES ©

🗺 How to

Getting here You'll need to get to Stewart Island/ Rakiura first. For Ulva Island, take a guided tour, or for a self-guided visit, take a water taxi from Golden Bay Wharf, just over the hill from Oban.

When to go Best between October and April.

How much? Ulva's Guided Walks (ulva. co.nz) $145; **Rakiura Charters & Water Taxi** (rakiuracharters.co.nz) $35 return.

What to take Sturdy footwear, refreshments, wet-weather gear, warm clothing.

DAVID C TOMLINSON/GETTY IMAGES ©

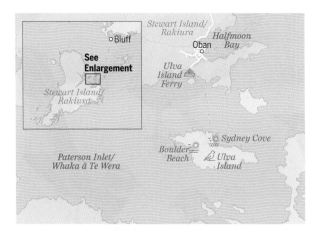

Left West End Beach
Below Toutouwai

Ulva history This half-day adventure starts with a 10-minute boat ride across Paterson Inlet from Golden Bay Wharf to Post Office Bay on Ulva Island. The post office was a focal point for locals living around the inlet from 1872 to 1923, when the postmaster would raise a flag to alert them that the mail boat had been by. In the 1880s the Tourist Department provided funding for the island's walking tracks, and in 1922 Ulva Island became the first scenic reserve in the country.

Boulder Beach walk Pick up an *Ulva: Self-guided Tour* pamphlet at the jetty and start by walking the track to Boulder Beach (45 minutes). The tracks are in great shape, well signposted and easy to follow. You'll hear myriad calls, similar to the choruses that enthralled early European settlers before the introduction of predators such as rats, stoats and possums that have decimated the country's native bird life. Never milled, Ulva Island has been pest-free since 1997. If you hear scratching in bushes by the track it's likely to be a flightless weka.

The west end From Boulder Beach, take the track to West End Beach (45 minutes). The stunning native podocarp forest is dominated by rimu, southern rātā and kāmahi, with stands of tōtara and miro. Allow an hour to walk back across to Sydney Cove, then 20 minutes to get back to Post Office Bay to meet your boat.

🐦 Ulva's Top Tips

If you want to see lots of birds on Ulva Island, the key is to take your time. Don't rush along the trails. Make as little noise as possible and when you come across a bench to sit on by the track, take a seat, watch and listen. If birds come close by, avoid making fast movements. Stay as still as possible. A toutouwai (robin) may even come and stand on your shoe.

You'll be walking under the native forest canopy most of the time, so an umbrella isn't a bad option in rain.

To learn more about Aotearoa's birds and the country's conservation efforts, take a guided tour.

■ **Recommended by Ulva Goodwillie** *author of Ulva Island: A Visitor's Guide*
@ulvasguidedwalks

BIRDS
of Aotearoa

01 Tīeke (saddleback)

A conservation success story, the tīeke takes its name from its call (ti-e-ke-ke-ke-ke) and is better at hopping than flying.

02 Takahē

Thought extinct for 50 years, the flightless takahē has made a comeback after being rediscovered in remote Fiordland in 1948.

03 Pīwakawaka (fantail)

The much-loved fantail flits through the forest catching flying insects, enthralling hikers with its incessant chattering.

04 Weka

With a reputation as being curious, cheeky and feisty, the flightless weka is considered a vulnerable species.

05 Kererū

This plump native pigeon was once a major food source in Māori culture, but protection now ensures its survival.

06 Korimako (bellbird)

Surviving well, the korimako's distinctive calls featured in the dawn chorus of birdsong noted by early European settlers.

07 Kea

The world's only alpine parrot, the

endangered kea is intelligent, curious and cheeky, much loved by international visitors.

08 Kākā
The lowland cousin of the kea, the kākā is a large parrot found in native forests and even in urban areas such as Wellington.

09 Kiwi
The flightless kiwi has become so iconic that its name is used worldwide as a colloquial term for New Zealanders.

10 Kōkako
While the blue-wattled North Island kōkako struggles to survive, the orange-wattled South Island kōkako is believed extinct.

11 Ruru (morepork)
A small, mainly nocturnal owl, the ruru gets its more common name from its two-tone call: 'more-pork'.

12 Kākāpō
This large, flightless, nocturnal parrot, rescued from the brink of extinction, survives only on predator-free islands.

13 Tūī
The boisterous tūī, with its distinctive white throat tuft, boasts a noisy, complex song and is flourishing, even in urban areas.

51 Town of
CONTRASTS

STEAMPUNK | PENGUINS | CULTURE

███ The largest town in North Otago, Ōamaru has a couple of fascinating, if contrasting attractions. It's hard to go past its Victorian precinct, highlighted by Steampunk HQ and the town's claim to be the 'steampunk capital of the world', but it's a totally different ballgame along the waterfront with the nightly return of the penguins at the Ōamaru Blue Penguin Colony.

LUPENGYU/GETTY IMAGES ©

🗺 How to

Getting here Ōamaru (pop 14,000) is 247km south of Christchurch and 113km north of Dunedin. You'll want your own wheels to make the most of the place.

When to go September to February is the best viewing season for penguins; winter numbers may drop to below 20.

Enjoy the penguins Plan your day around the estimated daily returning time of the blue penguins (penguins.co.nz). Take warm clothing; no cameras. Adult/child from $40/25; it's all over in 60 to 90 minutes.

MARTIN PELANEK/SHUTTERSTOCK ©

RUSLANKALN/GETTY IMAGES ©

Far left Ōamaru
Left Steampunk HQ
Below Blue penguin

Quacking penguins This surprisingly interesting town deserves at least one night on your journey so you can watch the return of the blue penguins (korora) around dusk. Almost right in town, at the end of Waterfront Rd, the tiny penguins turn up in groups of 30 to 50 (safety in numbers!), after a day of fishing out at sea. Announcing their impending arrival by quacking like ducks, they make alarmingly inelegant beach landings, waddle tentatively up the rocky beach, avoiding pesky basking seals, then lean forward and start running for home when they hit flat land.

Noisy socialising As they've been feeding all day and have big bellies, there are inevitable balance issues, including the occasional face-plant. When the penguins have found a safe spot, they dry off and preen while socialising, before disappearing into their nests to feed chicks or chatter noisily with their mate. If you want to see what they get up to in their nests, check out the online Nest Cam. Up to 400 penguins return each evening, depending on the season.

The scenic route If you've got kids in tow, the tiny penguins, the world's smallest, are a source of great excitement, especially if they take the scenic route home by jumping some tiny steps and waddling right through the middle of your viewing grandstand, so close that you're bound to get a whiff of their somewhat fishy body odour. It's all part of the fun.

◎ Steampunk Capital

Ōamaru claims to be the steampunk capital of the world.

Steampunk is a quirky genre of science fiction that features steam-powered technology. It's set in an alternate, futuristic version of 19th-century Victorian England – the 'world gone mad' as Victorian people may have imagined it.

Steampunk HQ (steampunkoamaru.co.nz) features an intriguing collection of retro-futuristic, sci-fi art, movies, sculpture and sound in the 'Grain Elevator', an 1883 building at the entrance of the Victorian precinct. Upstairs in the Woolstore Complex, the **Gadgetorium** is a science fiction inventors' emporium showcasing alternate gadgetry, props, curios and collectables of merchant time travellers.

 ■ Recommended by **Merchant Lucretia** *owner, Gadgetorium* @merchantlucretia

THE DEEP SOUTH EXPERIENCES

52 Ride the Central
RAIL TRAIL

BIKING | ADVENTURE | HISTORY

▬▬▬ Take three days to ride the 152km gravel trail linking Clyde with Middlemarch, the route of the former Central Otago Railway (1892–1990). The rails and sleepers have been pulled up to produce a popular, family-friendly 'rail trail' for cyclists and walkers.

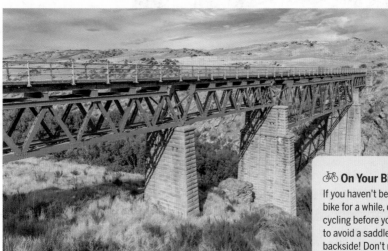

TRABANTOS/SHUTTERSTOCK ©

🗺 How to

Getting here Clyde is a one-hour drive east of Queenstown; drive yourself or hop on a Trail Journeys shuttle (trailjourneys.co.nz).

When to go October to April.

Practicalities Rent a bike or e-bike, and arrange luggage transfers, vehicle relocation or transport back to Clyde or on to Dunedin with Trail Journeys.

Best direction Allow three days to ride from Clyde to Middlemarch, with prevailing winds behind you.

Accommodation See otagocentralrailtrail.co.nz for options along the trail.

🚲 On Your Bike!

If you haven't been on a bike for a while, do a bit of cycling before you come to avoid a saddle-weary backside! Don't rush.

Take plenty of time to see the quaint little towns, meet friendly locals and enjoy the unique Central Otago scenery along the way, including the Poolburn Viaduct (pictured above).

■ Recommended by Stu Duncan
owner, Wedderburn Cottages
wedderburncottages.co.nz

02 From **Omakau**, you'll pass old station sites, cross rail bridges and pass through dark tunnels on the 30km ride to Oturehua; after a break, there's still 25km to ride to Ranfurly.

03 It's a long last day of 60km from **Ranfurly** to Middlemarch, but the gentle 1:50 gradient required by the steam trains of old is ideal for recreational cyclists and walkers.

Becks

Oturehua

Naseby

Lauder

Wedderburn

Kyeburn

Chatto Creek

Ophir

Waipiata

Kokonga

Daisybank

Tiroiti

04 Thirty-three kilometres into the last day you'll hit **Hyde**; check out the refurbished old railway station and a stone cairn memorial to 21 people who died in a tragic train crash in 1943.

Alexandra

01 Get organised at Trail Journeys at the **Clyde** trailhead. It's 25km to the welcoming Chatto Creek pub (chattocreektavern.co.nz), then 12km to Omakau, target for your first day.

Rock & Pillar

05 Expect to be weary at the end of the trail at **Middlemarch**; from the old Middlemarch Station transport options can take you back to Clyde or on to Dunedin.

Sutton

0   10 km
0   5 miles
N

53 MEETING
the Albatross

WILDLIFE | CRUISE | HISTORY

▬▬▬ The world's only mainland breeding colony of the northern royal albatross is only 30km away from Dunedin. Visit Taiaroa Head/Pukekura, first by sea on a Monarch Wildlife Cruise, then on land at the Royal Albatross Centre. Viewing the giant albatrosses with their massive wingspans soaring overhead and nesting at the tip of the rugged Otago Peninsula is positively breathtaking.

HLOW/ULLSTEIN BILD VIA GETTY IMAGES ©

 How to

Getting around You'll want your own wheels to fully explore the peninsula.

When to go Albatrosses are here year-round, but the best viewing is from December to March.

Best advice Head out along waterfront Portobello Rd to Portobello; make the return trip to Dunedin via Highcliff Rd.

Bookings Book the Double Albatross Combo at albatross.org.nz. Adult/child $98/34; self-drive with 60-minute cruise and 60-minute colony tour included.

SANKA VIDANAGAMA/
NURPHOTO VIA GETTY IMAGES ©

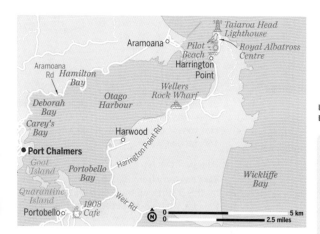

Out at sea Drive out to Wellers Rock Wharf for the cruise part of your combo, with scenic waterfront views over Dunedin, Port Chalmers and the protected inner harbour along the way. The Monarch Wildlife Cruise's sturdy little boat then putters out to Taiaroa Head and the open Pacific Ocean, searching out marine mammals such as blue penguins, dusky and Hector's dolphins, and seals, and keeping an eye out for soaring albatrosses and other seabirds. Over 10,000 seabirds live at Taiaroa Head, many nesting in large numbers on cliff ledges, so spotting birds won't be a problem. The historic 1865 **Taiaroa Head Lighthouse** is high above and it's easy to understand why it was needed to keep approaching ships off the rugged rocks below.

Back on land Back at Wellers Rock Wharf, it's an action-packed short drive to the **Royal Albatross Centre**. Keep your eye out for sea lions (rāpoka) lazing away on **Harrington Point Beach**, while fur seals (kekeno) are regulars at **Pilots Beach**, just below Taiaroa Head. At the centre, the 60-minute guided tour part of the combo includes a fascinating film on the albatross breeding cycle, then a walk to a glassed observatory to view the albatrosses soaring and nesting. Royal Cam is a 24-hour live stream of an albatross nest in breeding season, while a tracking map follows the incredible routes taken around the southern hemisphere by albatrosses hatched at Taiaroa Head.

Left Taiaroa Head Lighthouse
Below Northern Royal Albatross

THE DEEP SOUTH EXPERIENCES

◎ The Giants at Taiaroa Head

At the tip of the Otago Peninsula lies Taiaroa Head, home to a rather famous seabird with a 3m wingspan: the northern royal albatross.

Guided tours offer an exclusive look into this unique breeding colony. These large seabirds have a long breeding cycle of 11 months, which is great for visitors as there is nearly always something to see.

These giants are a sight to behold when flying by on the breeze over Taiaroa Head, best seen on windy days, with the wind often picking up in the afternoon. Allow plenty of time to enjoy all the centre has to offer.

■ **Recommended by Hoani Langsbury**
Ecotourism Manager,
Royal Albatross Centre
@albatrosscentre

Listings

BEST OF THE REST

∿ White-Knuckle Adventures

AJ Hackett Bungy

What could be more Queenstown than jumping off the original, the 43m-high Kawarau Bridge, with a thick rubber band tied to your ankles?

NZone Skydive

Tandem skydiving with up to 45 seconds of free fall with the Remarkables and Lake Wakatipu as the backdrop. As NZone says, 'embrace the fear!'

Ziptrek Ecotours

Zip down through the forest from Queenstown's Skyline on one of the world's steepest ziplines (they just keep getting steeper!).

Hydro Attack

No sharks in a lake, right? Wrong! Queenstown Hydro Attack's unique submersible 'sharks' dive into and leap from the water at blood-curdling speeds.

🏃 Epic MultiDay Hikes

Milford Track

This 54km classic, labelled 'the finest walk in the world' by the *London Spectator* in 1908, leads from the northern end of Lake Te Anau out to Milford Sound.

Routeburn Track

Thirty-three kilometre alpine adventure over the South Island's water divide in Fiordland and Mt Aspiring National Parks, that can be walked in either direction.

Kepler Track

Sixty-kilometre alpine loop starting and finishing in Te Anau. Walk the beech-forested shorelines of Lakes Te Anau and Manapōuri, plus tussock-covered ridgelines with spectacular views.

Rakiura Track

Take the ferry from Bluff over Foveaux Strait for this 32km loop track on Stewart Island/Rakiura, where 85% of the island makes up Rakiura National Park.

🍺 Historic Pubs & Bars

Danseys Pass Hotel $$

It's tough to get more remote than here in the Kakanui Hills between Central Otago and Ōamaru. Drop in for lunch or stay while driving over legendary Danseys Pass.

Chatto Creek Tavern $$

This 1886 classic is a sight for sore eyes and saddle-weary bottoms on day one for those riding the Otago Central Rail Trail. It's 10km to Omakau after a cold beer here!

Skydiving over Queenstown

The Church Manapōuri $$

This Presbyterian church built in the 1880s is now a rollicking restaurant and bar in Manapōuri, 21km south of Te Anau. The fireplace is always blazing in winter.

Blue Door $$

Arrowtown's classic venue for 'tiny room concerts' is loved by everyone. Wander down the side alley to find...a blue door with peeling paint in an ancient stone building.

Vulcan Hotel $$

You can stay at the iconic 1882 Vulcan in St Bathans, Central Otago, but it's rumoured to be haunted. Better to just drop in for a drink!

Best Craft Breweries

Emerson's $$

Born and bred in Dunedin (established in 1992), Emerson's has shiny new premises with brewery, taproom and restaurant on Anzac Ave. The Bookbinder Session Ale is legendary.

Scotts Brewing $$

Down in an old railway building near the waterfront in Ōamaru, Scotts is a popular locals' hang-out, brewing classics like the Harbourmaster IPA and Smokey Joe Smoked Red Ale.

Canyon Brewing $$

Popular Queenstown microbrewery and restaurant based in the Shotover Canyon at Arthur's Point. Innovative stuff going on here, including the Zenkuro Dry, a yuzu rice lager.

Altitude Brewing $$

Award-winning Queenstown craft brewery with changing visiting food trucks at Frankton Marina. Get its brews, including the Mischievous Kea IPA, all over the south.

Chatto Creek Tavern

Cafes & Cheap Eats

Bespoke Kitchen $

Queenstown's top spot to prepare for or recover from some major adventuring, with huge choices in enticing cabinet food.

Kai Whakapai $

'Kai corner' in Wānaka is the place to go for the town's best coffee by day. It's a relaxed bar by night; act fast to get a seat outside on sunny evenings.

Sandfly Cafe $

This is one Fiordland sandfly you'll be keen to lay eyes on in Te Anau; jump in here to fuel up before heading out into the wilds.

Just Cafe $

Stewart Island's tiny cafe, with Rakiura's best coffees, light fluffy scones, giant bliss balls and sandwiches to take away on your island adventures.

Remote Places to Stay

Kinloch Lodge

At the northwest corner of Lake Wakatipu, fully 70km from Queenstown, this is a remote, historic lakeside beauty, operating since 1868. Enjoy the peace, nature and exquisite cuisine.

Cardrona Hotel

Between Queenstown and Wānaka on the Crown Range Rd, the Cardrona Hotel is an ageless, iconic spot operating since 1863. Rumoured to be the most photographed building in the country.

South Sea Hotel

Remote in that it's on Stewart Island/ Rakiura. This is Oban's one-stop shop with rooms, restaurant, public bar and a legendary pub quiz on Sunday nights that's not to be missed.

Larnach Castle

Built in the 1870s high on Otago Peninsula, this mock castle may be the biggest surprise of your visit to the Deep South. Unique accommodation and dining.

Winter Ski Areas

Coronet Peak

As the closest ski area to Queenstown, just a 25-minute drive from the resort, Coronet is the busiest, with wide open pistes, well-groomed trails and unbelievable views.

The Remarkables

A 45-minute drive from Queenstown, high up in the Remarkables range, this family-orientated ski resort has a good range of runs and an excellent terrain park.

Cardrona Alpine Resort

High above the Cardrona Valley, an hour from Queenstown and 30 minutes from Wānaka, Cardrona has it all, from family-friendly runs to extreme snowboard terrain.

Treble Cone

A 30-minute drive west of Wānaka, this is the highest and largest ski area in the region, with long, uncrowded, groomed runs and gorgeous views out over Lake Wānaka.

Iconic Southern Foods

Jimmy's Pies

A Central Otago classic with its tiny shop in Roxburgh and an unchanged family recipe for five decades. Munch on a Jimmy's all around the south.

Fergburger

You can gauge how busy Queenstown is by the length of the line outside Fergburger, snaking up Shotover St. Known as the best burgers in the world.

Bluff Oysters

Hauled out of the Foveaux Strait each year between March and August, these fleshy delicacies have put the Aotearoa mainland's most southern town on world maps.

Mutton Bird

The sooty shearwater (tītī, aka the mutton bird) was said by one early commentator to taste remarkably like sheep meat. We think more like anchovies... A Deep South delicacy.

Cheese Rolls

A real local experience, sometimes cheekily known as 'southern sushi', these are a slice of bread smothered in grated cheese, rolled into a tube, then toasted.

HIZOR/SHUTTERSTOCK ©

Fergburger

Galleries & Museums

Lakes District Museum

Built around three historic buildings in Arrowtown's main street, here you'll find Lakes District history, including the gold rushes, plus a top art gallery.

Toitū Otago Settlers Museum

This regional history museum in Dunedin covers the territory of old Otago Province, though its main focus is on the very Scottish city of Dunedin.

Rakiura Museum Te Puka O Te Waka

Home to an extensive collection of historic items, artefacts and photographs, this is the story of Stewart Island/Rakiura; established and run by local volunteers.

Steampunk HQ

Intriguing stuff going on in Ōamaru's Victorian precinct with this fascinating collection of retro-futuristic, sci-fi art, movies, sculpture and sound in the 'Grain Elevator'.

Quality Dining Experiences

Botswana Butchery $$$

On Queenstown's waterfront in historic Archer's cottage, award-winning Botswana's menu has an extensive range of premium meat and seafood options.

Redcliff Restaurant & Bar $$

Te Anau's top restaurant, Redcliff has a reputation for great food, wine and friendly service. Try local hare and venison, straight from the hills.

Church Hill Restaurant $$

This boutique restaurant on Stewart Island/Rakiura focuses on island and Southland produce. Expect crayfish, paua (a shellfish), whitebait and mutton bird on the menu, along with Southland lamb and beef.

Curio Bay Petrified Forest

Bacchus Wine Bar & Restaurant $$

Award-winning Bacchus, on the lively Octagon in central Dunedin, offers a popular three-course menu, plus extensive cocktail, wine and whisky options.

Weird Geographic Phenoms

Moeraki Boulders

While some believe that these unusually spherical boulders on the beach south of Ōamaru are just balls of mudstone, others think they are alien eggs ready to hatch.

Elephant Rocks

These large weathered limestone rocks in a farm paddock inland from Ōamaru come in a fascinating range of shapes and sizes and are featured in the *Chronicles of Narnia*.

Curio Bay Petrified Forest

Wander out on the fossilised remains of an ancient Jurassic (yes...Jurassic!) forest that is exposed at Curio Bay in the Catlins on the south coast during low tide.

Tunnel Beach

South of Dunedin, take a walk to check out the amazing sea-carved sandstone cliffs, rock arches and caves – and even a man-made tunnel to the beach.

 Scan to find more things to do in the Deep South online

Practicalities

ARRIVING

240

GETTING AROUND

242

SAFE TRAVEL

244

MONEY

245

RESPONSIBLE TRAVEL

246

ACCOMMODATION

248

ESSENTIALS

250

Right Hiking the Mueller Track (p185), Aoraki/Mt Cook National Park

EASY STEPS FROM THE AIRPORT TO THE CITY CENTRE

Auckland is the primary point of entry for most visitors to New Zealand. Combining adjacent international and domestic terminals, the airport is 21km south of the city centre. Facilities include cafes, restaurants, ATMs and car rental desks. Christchurch, Queenstown and Wellington also receive occasional international flights (mainly from Australia). Cruise ships were regular visitors prior to 2020, but have largely stopped visiting following the Covid-19 pandemic.

AT THE AIRPORT

PHOTOS: BRIANSCANTLEBURY/
SHUTTERSTOCK ©

SIM CARDS
Buy SIM cards for unlocked phones (and NZ Travel Plans) from Vodafone or Spark. Both have stores in the international arrivals area, and other branches in central Auckland and the city's main shopping malls. Costs range from $29 (one month) to $59 (two months).

TRAVELEX
There is an exchange booth near the baggage claim area of international arrivals (6am to 6.30pm), and another outlet in the upstairs landside international departures area (12.30pm to 5.30pm). It also has booths on Queen St, central Auckland's main thoroughfare.

WI-FI Free and unlimited in the international and domestic terminals. Select the Auckland Airport network. Coverage reaches the pick-up point for ride-share services.

ATMS Machines linked to global networks are available in the arrivals hall of the international terminal, and also in the domestic terminal.

CHARGING STATIONS Upstairs, landside near the international departure gate, there are a few seats with adjacent wall sockets using NZ's three-point plugs.

COVID-19

At the time of writing, entry to New Zealand was limited to fully vaccinated travellers. Official proof of vaccination in either a digital or paper form must be provided. Travellers from all countries must also undertake self-isolation for a period of seven days upon arrival in New Zealand, and have completed a negative PCR test within 48 hours of the scheduled departure of their first international flight. Regulations can change, so check current rules carefully at covid19.govt.nz/international-travel/travel-to-new-zealand.

GETTING TO THE CITY CENTRE

SkyBus links the airport to the CBD and inner suburbs. Buy tickets online at skybus.co.nz or from the driver.

Super Shuttle (supershuttle.co.nz) provides a convenient minibus service from the airport to city hotels. Book online ($15 to $25 per person depending on group size).

Ride-share services operating from Auckland Airport include Uber, Ola and Zoomy. From the international terminal, cars depart from outside door 11 adjacent to the arrivals hall. The departure point for ride-share services from the domestic terminal is a walk, partially uncovered, of around 250m. See aucklandairport. co.nz/transport/rideshare.

Taxis depart from outside front entry/ exit doors of both the international and domestic terminals. Depending on traffic, the journey to central Auckland can take up to one hour.

HOW MUCH FOR A

SkyBus
$17
45–60min

Ride-share
$50
30–60min

Taxi
$60–80
30–60min

AT HOP Card
Available at Take Home Convenience in the international terminal, this card ($10) can also be used for bus and ferry transport around Auckland. Search AT HOP on at.govt.nz.

i-SITE
Source transport information and maps at this visitor information centre in the arrivals hall of the international terminal.

Bus & Train The AirportLink bus travels to the Puhinui train station every 10 minutes from 4.30am to 12.40am. From Puhinui, trains travel on the Eastern or Southern lines to the Britomart station in central Auckland. Total cost is $5.40 with an AT HOP card and travel time is approximately one hour.

NEW ZEALAND ARRIVING

OTHER POINTS OF ENTRY

Wellington airport is located 6km southeast of the city centre. As New Zealand's capital city, it's an important domestic hub, and has direct flights to Australian cities including Sydney, Melbourne and Brisbane. Taxis to the CBD cost around $45 and take from 15 to 25 minutes. Ride-share services are around $40 and transfers with SuperShuttle from $15.

Christchurch airport is the South Island's main gateway, located 12km northwest of the city. International destinations include major Australian cities, and pre Covid-19 also included China, Dubai, the USA and Singapore. Taxis to the central city take about 25 minutes and cost around $60. Ride-share services are around $35 to $40. For bus transport, take the Purple line or bus 29 to the Christchurch Bus Interchange (30 minutes).

Queenstown airport is 7km east of the town centre. Taxis charge around $50 to the lakefront and ride-share services around $30 (around 20 minutes). By bus, catch number 1 ($10, around 30 minutes). Flights to Queenstown from Australian cities increase in frequency during winter.

TRANSPORT TIPS TO HELP YOU GET AROUND

New Zealand is ideal for road trips, and many visitors enjoy the independence and flexibility of having their own rental car or campervan. Crossing Cook Strait by ferry is a classic Kiwi travel experience, while a trio of tourism-oriented train services showcase some of NZ's finest coastal and mountain scenery.

FERRY Interislander and Bluebridge offer competing services linking the North and South Islands across Cook Strait. Sailings can be booked a few days in advance, but school holidays and Easter may require more lead time. A daytime crossing taking in the Marlborough Sounds is recommended.

FLYING Air New Zealand's domestic network of 20 destinations provides the opportunity to fast-track your trip with fast and frequent internal flights. Airfares linking main cities are good value, but can become more expensive for secondary regional cities. Check online with **Grabaseat** (grabaseat.co.nz) for last-minute discounts.

CAR RENTAL PER DAY

from $90

Petrol approx $2.70/litre

City parking $2.50

CAR & CAMPER-VAN HIRE

Both can be hired from main cities, airports and tourist towns. Locally owned companies usually offer better rates; vehicles may be slightly older but still in good condition. Unlimited kilometre contracts are recommended and the minimum age to rent is usually 25.

ON-THE-ROAD INFORMATION

The New Zealand Automobile Association (aa.co.nz/travel) offers destination information and accommodation listings. Regional visitor information centres – known as i-SITES – are always helpful locations to source maps and local recommendations.

DRIVING ESSENTIALS

 Drive on the left: NZ steering wheels are on the right.

.05 Blood alcohol limit is 0.05% (0% for drivers under 20).

 One-way bridges are common in NZ. Give way if the smaller red arrow is pointing in the direction of your travel.

 Roads in NZ are often narrow and winding.

 Fuel prices are cheaper in bigger cities than regional areas.

Some rental companies are OK with travellers taking their cars with them on the Cook Strait ferry, while others prefer to have renters pick up/drop off different vehicles in either Wellington and Picton. Check specific conditions when you book, including the opportunity to take advantage of special deals the rental car companies often have with the ferry operators, Interislander and Bluebridge. Campervan rentals almost always allow for taking the same vehicle on the ferry.

JAMES HARRISON/SHUTTERSTOCK ©

ROAD CONDITIONS New Zealand's weather, particularly in alpine regions, can change from sunny to stormy in a matter of minutes, and washouts and road closures are not uncommon. Check road conditions at journeys.nzta.govt.nz. In rural areas, a common road hazard is farmers moving cows or sheep. Slow to a crawl, or stop your vehicle altogether, and let the animals move unrestricted. It's a classic Kiwi photo opportunity.

BUSES & SHUTTLES Intercity buses are a reliable and relatively frequent option for linking major cities; in regional areas, locally owned shuttles providing transport for hikers often offer a similar service. Without your own transport, you'll need to join tours to experience nearby attractions and destinations.

TRAINS Great Journeys of New Zealand (greatjourneysofnz.co.nz) has traditionally offered three scenic train services and the Interislander ferry service. During Covid-19, the spectacular TranzAlpine through the Southern Alps from Christchurch to Greymouth continued to run, but the Northern Explorer linking Auckland and Wellington, and the Coastal Pacific from Picton to Christchurch were on hold. Check the website for the latest information about their planned relaunch.

NEW ZEALAND GETTING AROUND

ROAD DISTANCE CHART (KMS)

	Auckland	Christchurch	Dunedin	Invercargill	Napier	Nelson	Queenstown	Wellington
Christchurch	980							
Dunedin	1427	360						
Invercargill	1631	570	210					
Napier	420	760	1104	1307				
Nelson	875	425	775	990	551			
Queenstown	1455	480	285	190	1235	820		
Wellington	640	340	791	995	320	238	815	
Whangārei	160	1230	1584	1788	580	1032	1707	790

KNOW YOUR CARBON FOOTPRINT
Flying from Auckland to Wellington would emit around 120kg of carbon dioxide per passenger. For road journeys, the corresponding emittance per person is 23kg in a bus and 127kg when travelling by car. By train would emit around 18kg per person. Calculate New Zealand–specific examples online with **Toitū Envirocare** (toitu.co.nz/calculators).

New Zealand's scenery includes beaches, forests and mountains, and it's important to follow guidelines to safely enjoy getting active in the outdoors. Violent crime is unlikely to impact visitors, but theft from vehicles is an ongoing issue.

SWIMMING SAFETY As an island nation, NZ unfortunately records around 40 deaths by drowning each year. At surf beaches, beware of rips and undertows, which can drag swimmers out to sea, and always swim between the flags where surf lifeguards are on patrol. Extra care should also be taken around lakes, rivers and waterfalls.

ROAD SAFETY NZ's roads are often winding and narrow, and driving is on a different side of the road for visitors from many countries. Take extra care when driving, and if you've arrived after a long-haul flight from North America or Europe, spend a night in your city of arrival and recharge before getting behind the wheel. See drivesafe.org.nz.

OPPORTUNISTIC THEFT Unfortunately it's not unknown for rental cars and campervans to be targeted by opportunistic thieves, especially at unattended car parks at beaches, remote trailhead locations and also some popular tourist areas. It's worth considering taking passports, money and any valuable items with you when you leave your vehicle.

Hiking safety in NZ's great outdoors includes the following guidelines: log your walk intentions online with **Adventure Smart** (adventuresmart. org.nz) and hire a PLB (personal locator beacon) from local DOC offices for more challenging experiences. See mountainsafety.org.nz.

Krazy Kea Expect the attention of kea, NZ's alpine parrots, in Arthur's Pass or outside the Homer Tunnel. They'll probably have a go at your windscreen wipers, and it's essential not to feed the inquisitive birds.

DRESS FOR SAFETY New Zealand's weather is very changeable, especially in mountain areas. Being equipped for 'four seasons in one day' is always a wise idea. Carry waterproof gear and dress in layers to reduce the chance of getting exposure.

RĀHUI Sometimes a beach or other swimming place will have a *rāhui* (temporary ban) placed on it by local Māori for conservation or cultural reasons. It's important to respect these directives.

QUICK TIPS TO HELP YOU MANAGE YOUR MONEY

CREDIT CARDS (Visa and MasterCard) are widely accepted for accommodation, activities, restaurants and bars, and are also essential when renting a car. Contactless payment is increasingly the norm, and Apple Pay and Google Pay are also be-coming more accepted. Credit cards can be used for cash advances at ATMs and banks, but transaction charges apply. Diners Club and American Express are not widely accepted in NZ.

CURRENCY

NZ dollar

HOW MUCH FOR A

Flat white coffee
$5

Pint of craft beer
$12

Brunch for 2
$55

PAYING THE BILL
While cafes and restaurants may have table service, it's often normal to pay your bill at the counter when you leave.

BARGAINING
Haggling isn't part of NZ's commer-cial culture. One exception could be buying fresh pro-duce at a farmers market at the end of the day.

TAXES & REFUNDS NZ's Goods & Services Tax (GST) is a flat 15% tax on purchases of all domestic goods and services. No GST refund is available to travellers when they leave the country.

ATMS & EFTPOS
ATMs are widespread around the country, inclu-ding in smaller rural and regional towns. Eftpos terminals – increasingly offering contactless transactions – are ubiquitous for retailers and hospitality venues.

MONEY CHANGERS
Foreign currency can be changed at most NZ banks and licensed money changers like Travelex, but the exchange rate for cash withdrawals at an ATM from your own bank will always be superior.

Tipping is completely optional in NZ and restaurants do not usually add a service charge.

Restaurants The total on the bill is all you need to pay. For excellent service, an additional tip of 5% to 10% can be added. Cafes often have cash tip jars at the counter.

Taxis It's common practice to round fares up to the nearest dollar.

Guides Kayaking and adventure sports guides are happy to accept tips. Ten dollars per person would be appropriate.

DISCOUNTS & SAVINGS

Most sights, activities and public transport services offer reduced rates for children and senior travellers. Family deals are also commonplace. When booking adventure activities, check websites for combo deals and online booking discounts. **New Zealand Card** (newzealandcard.com) enables discounts on accommodation, sights, activities and tours. Browse participating businesses before buying. Cost $40.

RESPONSIBLE TRAVEL

Tips to leave a lighter footprint, support local and have a positive impact on local communities.

ON THE ROAD

Calculate your carbon emissions while travelling with **Toitū Enviro-care** (toitu.co.nz/calculators).

Consider renting an electric vehicle. **Britz** (britz.com) rents electric campervans with inbuilt navigation to fast-charging stations; the campervans can also be recharged overnight in holiday parks. **Snap Rentals** (snaprentals.co.nz) has hybrid and fully electric cars.

Reduce fuel consumption by regularly emptying your grey-water tanks if you're travelling in a campervan.

Take the Tiaki Promise. Based around the Māori ethos of *kaitia-kitanga* (guardianship/protection), Tourism NZ's Tiaki Promise outlines ways for trav-ellers to care for the country's natural landscapes and respect NZ's cultural diversity. See tiakinewzealand.com for videos and information.

Kauri dieback disease is a significant threat to NZ's iconic kauri forests. Adhere to shoe-cleaning protocols at trailheads, and see kauriprotection.co.nz for more guidelines and advice on track closures.

BIRD AND SKY/SHUTTERSTOCK ©

GIVE BACK

Eat out for a good cause Active in both Auckland and Wellington, **Everybody Eats** (everybodyeats.nz) is a not-for-profit community-focused organisation providing meals to both drop-in diners and socially disadvantaged people. Shared-table meals are made from produce and ingredients that would normally go to waste.

Contribute to a greener Aotearoa Opportunities to facilitate tree planting, clean up waterways and inspire NZ's drive to offset climate change include the **Million Metres Project** (millionmetres.org.nz) and **Trees That Count** (treesthatcount.co.nz).

Clean up the coastline Join a regular volunteer event with **Sustainable Coastlines** (sustainablecoastlines.org).

Support wildlife biodiversity by visiting sanctuaries and protected reserves Excellent projects across Aotearoa include Sanctuary Mountain Maungatautari (pictured) and Zealandia.

DOS & DONTS

Do learn a few phrases in NZ's indigenous language, te reo Māori. Download the interactive Kupu app (kupu.co.nz) to get started.

Do experience a Māori perspective by seeking out Māori-owned tours and cultural experiences.

Don't enter a Māori *marae* (traditional meeting house) before being invited, and respect the *pōwhiri* (welcoming ceremony).

LEAVE A SMALL FOOTPRINT

Go bush Explore the best of NZ's national parks, Great Walks, campsites and nature reserves with comprehensive and authoritative information from the **Department of Conservation** (doc.govt.nz).

Two-wheeled adventures Set out on NZ's network of scenic cycle trails (nzcycletrail. com). Standout experiences include the Hauraki Rail Trail, the Otago Central Rail Trail and the West Coast Wilderness Trail.

Organic and sustainable Browse **Organic Explorer** (organicexplorer.co.nz) for organic food and wine producers, sustainably focused accommodation options, and ecotourism operators around the country.

HAM PHITCHAYA/SHUTTERSTOCK ©

SUPPORT LOCAL

Eat locally Buy fresh ingredients, artisan gourmet products and good-value food truck surprises at farmers markets around NZ. See farmersmarkets.org.nz.

Make a big impact on small towns Buy locally and support regional economies. See shoplocally.co.nz.

Support tangata whenua Literally 'people of the land', and the name given to Māori. See maoritourism.co.nz for listings of Māori-owned tourism experiences.

NEW ZEALAND POSITIVE-IMPACT TRAVEL

CLIMATE CHANGE & TRAVEL

It's impossible to ignore the impact we have when travelling, and the importance of making changes where we can. Lonely Planet urges all travellers to engage with their travel carbon footprint. There are many carbon calculators online that allow travellers to estimate the carbon emissions generated by their journey; try resurgence.org/resources/carbon-calculator.html. Many airlines and booking sites offer travellers the option of offsetting the impact of greenhouse gas emissions by contributing to climate-friendly initiatives around the world. We continue to offset the carbon footprint of all Lonely Planet staff travel, while recognising this is a mitigation more than a solution.

RESOURCES

doc.govt.nz
nzcycletrail.com
sustainabletourism.nz
qualmark.co.nz
maoritourism.co.nz

UNIQUE & LOCAL WAYS TO STAY

New Zealand's accommodation ranges from simple hostel dormitory rooms through to self-contained motels and hip design hotels in the main cities. The country's luxury lodges are among the world's best, while good-value and flexible campervans are a great way to experience NZ's stellar scenery. Beachside cottages – known as 'baches' – are a popular self-catering option for NZ families.

HOW MUCH FOR A

DOC campsite
$20–23/night

Beachside bach
$150–200/night

Luxury lodge
from $300/night

MAXSON_DESIGN/GETTY IMAGES ©

DOC CAMPSITES

Campsites run by NZ's **Department of Conservation** (DOC; doc.govt.nz) are usually located in tranquil, secluded and scenic spots, often in national parks.

Facilities can include kitchens, showers and toilets. Booking ahead online is recommended for the most popular locations. Note: some more basic sites cannot be pre-booked and only operate on an informal first-come, first-served basis. It's around $23 per adult/night for a powered site. Spectacular locations include White Horse Hill (pictured) in Aoraki/Mt Cook National Park and Fletcher Bay on the Coromandel Peninsula.

HOLIDAY PARKS

A convenient option for visitors, NZ's holiday parks offer unpowered and powered sites for tenters and campervan travellers, as well as cabins and self-contained units. Well-equipped shared kitchens, playgrounds and games rooms provide for travelling families. In regional NZ, holiday parks are often located near lakes, beaches or rivers.

LUXURY LODGES

Combining mountain, lake or coastal scenery with excellent food and outdoor adventure, New Zealand's luxury lodges rate among the world's best. Even if you're staying in motels most nights, splurge-worthy luxury options worth considering include the following:

Te Arai Lodge Mangawhai (tearailodge.co.nz)

Hapuku Lodge + Tree Houses Kaikōura (pictured; hapukulodge.com)

Lakestone Lodge Lake Pukaki (lakestonelodge.co.nz)

NIGELSPIERS/SHUTTERSTOCK ©

CAMPERVAN CAPERS

Hiring a campervan is a popular way for visitors to explore NZ. There are holiday parks around the country, most with family-friendly facilities. The Department of Conservation also offers many places to park up overnight in remote and scenic locations.

Okay2Stay (okay2stay.co.nz) has 100-plus locations where programme members can park overnight (free for one night) if they buy local products from their hosts. Popular locations include vineyards, craft breweries, dairy farms and fruit orchards.

Members of some overseas travel clubs can also apply to become interim members of the New Zealand Motor Caravan Association, providing the opportunity to stay at their own parks. Search for 'Overseas Clubs' at nzmca.org.nz.

FREEDOM CAMPING Don't assume it's OK to park and stay overnight anywhere. It's a significant area of discussion in NZ, and freedom camping regulations vary by region, with some local councils providing secure parking spaces. See freedomcamping. org for pre-trip planning and on-the-road information, and download the CamperMate and Camping NZ apps listing council-approved campsites around the country. Nationwide freedom camping legislation introduced in 2022 limited freedom camping strictly to vehicles with onboard toilet facilities.

BOOKING

Local visitor information centres (i-SITES) are an excellent destination when researching local accommodation options, and can usually make bookings on behalf of travellers. Booking accommodation in advance is recommended, especially for beach destinations during summer, school holidays and long weekends. Easter is also busy, and booking ahead is recommended during winter in snow sports hubs including Queenstown, Wānaka, Methven and Tongariro National Park.

Lonely Planet (lonelyplanet.com/new-zealand/hotels) Find independent reviews and recommendations on the best places to stay, and book them online.

Airbnb (airbnb.com) Wide range of options including city apartments.

Automobile Association (aa.co.nz/travel) Online bookings with a good selection of motels, B&Bs and holiday parks.

Bach Care (bachcare.co.nz) Listings for rentals with many beachfront options.

Book a Bach (bookabach.co.nz) Holiday home rentals.

Holiday Houses (holidayhouses.co.nz) Self-contained holiday rentals.

Luxury Lodges (luxurylodgesofnz.co.nz) High-end accommodation.

New Zealand Bed & Breakfast (bnb.co.nz) B&B and hosted accommodation.

Rural Holidays NZ (ruralholidays.co.nz) Farmstay and homestay options in rural NZ.

CHOOSE THE BACH LIFE

Renting a bach near the beach is a favourite summertime escape for Kiwi families. Places usually include a barbecue, and maybe bikes, kayaks and fishing gear to make the most of a stay.

ESSENTIAL NUTS & BOLTS

WAITANGI DAY
Commemorating the signing of 1840's Treaty of Waitangi between the British Crown and Māori tribal chiefs, 6 February is NZ's national day.

CHRISTMAS CLOSE-DOWN
Many businesses, including inner-city restaurants, close from just before Christmas to a week after New Year's Eve.

KEEPING FLEXIBLE
Changeable weather can see outdoor activities postponed at the last moment. Build flexibility into your schedule.

FAST FACTS

Time Zone
GMT+12 hrs

Country Code
64

Electricity
230V/50Hz

GOOD TO KNOW

The legal drinking age is 18. Drinking is not allowed near some beaches and in some parks.

Duty-free shopping is available at airports on arrival and departure and at selected retailers.

If you're invited for a barbecue or dinner at someone's house, it's customary to bring along wine, beer or a nonalcoholic beverage.

'Bring a plate' means bring along a dish to be shared with everyone at a dinner party or barbecue.

ACCESSIBLE TRAVEL

NZ accommodation caters for travellers with mobility issues, and most hostels, hotels and motels have ramps and a couple wheelchair-accessible rooms. B&Bs aren't required to have accessible rooms, though some do.

Wheelchair access is becoming more common. For advice on attractions, cafes, etc with good accessibility, ask at the local i-SITE visitor centre.

Tour operators with accessible vehicles operate in most major destinations, and key cities offer 'kneeling buses' and wheelchair-accessible taxis. Rental car companies usually

offer vehicles with hand controls, but booking well ahead is necessary.

For active travellers, the DOC has improved wheelchair access to a range of shorter walks; they are categorised as 'easy access short walks' on the DOC website. For accessible winter activity, check the 'Adaptive' section of snowsports.co.nz.

Firstport (firstport.co.nz) offers guidance on transport for mobility-restricted travellers; **Ability Adventures** (abilityadventures.co.nz) arranges bespoke NZ tours.

ONLINE AT THE LIBRARY
Public libraries almost always have free wi-fi hotspots, usually also available outside of opening hours.

SMOKING
Smoking is banned in restaurants, cafes and all retailers. Bars may have an outside area where it's allowed.

KEEP CUPS
Most cafes will fill customers' keep cups for takeaway coffee to reduce the use of packaging.

FAMILY TRAVEL
Family discounts Many attractions offer reduced rates for family groups.

Children's menus Midrange cafes, restaurants and pubs often offer a children's menu.

Seat belts Mandatory in all vehicles, including appropriately secured capsules and booster seats for the youngest travellers.

Changing rooms Many shopping malls and some cafes have dedicated rooms for changing nappies.

LetsGoKids (letsgokids.co.nz) Plenty of ideas for family adventures throughout New Zealand.

Kidspot (kidspot.co.nz) Check out the 'Family Fun' section.

MĀORI LANGUAGE
The use of te reo Māori, NZ's indigenous language, is fast becoming more accepted. On road signs, Māori place names are spelled correctly with macrons – indicating an elongated vowel – and don't be surprised if you're greeted with a cheery *kia ora* (hello).

CHRISTMAS AT THE BEACH
It may seem obvious, but some travellers overlook the fact that southern hemisphere seasons are opposite to the north. Look forward to a beach picnic or barbecue if you're visiting for Christmas, and wrap warmly in July and August.

LGBTIQ+ TRAVELLERS
New Zealanders are generally accepting of same-sex relations and gender fluidity, and laws protecting marriage, adoption and other human rights for same-sex couples were adopted in 2013, ahead of anywhere else in the Asia-Pacific region.

Auckland and Wellington have the most prominent LGBTIQ+ communities, and you're unlikely to experience overt homophobia and transphobia anywhere in an increasingly liberal and tolerant country.

See Gay Stay NZ (gaystaynewzealand.com) for links to many LGBTIQ+-oriented businesses and activities.

Winter Pride (winterpride.co.nz) makes Queenstown party central in August/September.

NEW ZEALAND ESSENTIALS

Index

000 Map pages

000 Map pages

"My favourite experience is climbing Ben Lomond from the top of the Skyline gondola in Queenstown. The alpine views are unbelievable, and I like to earn my beer!"

CRAIG MCLACHLAN

"As I was exploring the Pukeiti Gardens a sudden deluge of rain meant I had to shelter in the tunnel leading to the Misty Knoll for over 10 minutes."

NICOLE MUDGWAY

"Relaxing in the thermal springs in Waikite Valley with only three other people at the pools. Bliss."

ROXANNE DE BRUYN

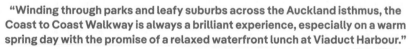

"I was driving through the evening in late autumn from Nelson to a resort deep within Kenepuru Sound for a weekend break. I was determined to arrive before dark because the thought of driving unsealed tracks with steep cliff drop-offs in the dark filled me with dread. Even though the sunset views along Kenepuru Drive were incredible, I drove through and, just as the last light faded from the sky, I reached the waterside resort in time for a buffet dinner. And the road wasn't that bad after all."

ELEN TURNER

"Winding through parks and leafy suburbs across the Auckland isthmus, the Coast to Coast Walkway is always a brilliant experience, especially on a warm spring day with the promise of a relaxed waterfront lunch at Viaduct Harbour."

BRETT ATKINSON

THIS BOOK

Design development
Lauren Egan, Tina García, Fergal Condon

Content development
Anne Mason

Cartography development
Wayne Murphy, Katerina Pavkova

Production development
Mario D'Arco, Dan Moore, Sandie Kestell, Virginia Moreno, Juan Winata

Series development leadership
Liz Heynes, Darren O'Connell, Piers Pickard, Chris Zeiher

Commissioning editor
Amy Lynch

Product editor
Claire Rourke

Cartographer
Rachel Imeson

Book designer
Ania Bartoszek

Assisting editors
Michelle Bennett, Andrea Dobbin, Gabrielle Stefanos

Cover researcher
Kat Marsh

Thanks Ronan Abayawickrema, Gwen Cotter, John Taufa